THE UNICORN

THE

UNICORN

Lise Gotfredsen

Translated from the Danish by Anne Born

THE HARVILL PRESS

LONDON

First published in 1999 by
The Harvill Press
2 Aztec Row
Berners Road
London N1 0PW

www.harvill.com

First impression

Text copyright © Lise Gotfredsen, 1999
English translation copyright
© The Harvill Press, 1999

Lise Gotfredsen asserts her moral right
to be identified as the author of this
work

A CIP catalogue record for this title
is available from the British Library

ISBN 1 86046 267 7

Designed by Isambard Thomas

Originated, printed and bound in
China by Toppan Printing Co. Ltd

Preface

Frontispiece
Ladies and Unicorns (detail)
Gustave Moreau, c. 1890
Musée Gustave Moreau, Paris

There is great interest in the medieval period at the present time. All the media reflect it: films, novels, scholarly treatises and the more serious strip cartoons. We are discovering, it seems, that the pre-Renaissance era – despite being described sometimes as a "dark" age – held certain qualities that we have need of today, and to which we have been blind for too long. This interest also includes the myths so popular in the Middle Ages, notably that of the Unicorn.

In fact the image of the Unicorn is far older; but it did not acquire its particular significance until the Christian Middle Ages. In a remarkable way it was linked both to the Virgin Mary and to the love lyric, and had a place in the coats of arms of the nobility as well as on the apothecary's sign and in countless works of art. It became a part of European culture, was familiar to all and for centuries has trotted through our dreams. An obvious example of its influence in modern times is Carl Gustav Jung's interest in the animal.

I have tried to write a "cultural history of the Unicorn", with pictorial art running as the scarlet thread through the profusion – a book that will interpret the complex medieval images and help the reader to trace the unfolding, growth and transformations of a myth, and to wonder at its wealth. At the same time, we shall follow the development of European thought from myth to scientific analysis, that is to say, from ambiguity combined with lively imagination, to a clarity that may have cost us our imagination . . .

I hope the book will provide pleasure for readers interested in the Middle Ages, or who have encountered the Unicorn in literature, paintings or drama, and grown curious about this remarkable animal. For those who wish to consult the sources, I have provided a bibliography.

I wish to thank the Queen Margrethe and Prince Henrik Foundation, and Judge V. Giese's Trust for support in the project. Thanks are also due to Museum Director Birgitte Wistoft for her kindness and helpfulness during my work on the book.

Lise Gotfredsen

In Colmar there is an altarpiece by the German painter Martin Schongauer of about 1450, entitled *The Sacred Hunt*. A young woman sits on a lawn enclosed by a rose-red wall. Her blue robe, long golden hair and halo show that she is the Virgin Mary. On her left kneels an angel greeting the Virgin with the well known words: "Ave – gratia plena" on a scroll. Between them grows a white lily. Everything indicates that the picture depicts the Annunciation, when Gabriel hails Mary.

The picture shows much more, however: Gabriel is equipped with a hunting horn and spear, and has four hounds on a leash, each with its name on a ribbon held in its mouth: Misericordia (Mercy), Justicia (Justice), Pax (Peace) and Veritas (Truth). On her lap Mary guards a white animal, resembling a little horse, but it has hoofs, a goat's beard and a long twisted horn in the centre of its forehead, with which it touches the Virgin's breast.

Around them the garden is full of strange objects: on the ground at Mary's side is spread a lambskin, there is a bucket filled with large balls and, above her head, God himself hovers in a burning bush. In the centre of the garden beside an octagonal well is an altar with twelve tall candles, and behind the angel is a locked gate. The whole scene is bathed in a gentle light which illuminates all the objects with quiet solemnity.

The little creature with the twisted horn is the Monoceros or Unicornus. But what is it doing there – and what does the whole scene mean? Let us begin at the beginning!

Overleaf
The Sacred Hunt
Martin Schongauer, *c.* 1450,
Musée d'Unterlinden, Colmar

THE UNICORN

uma · avria

vellus · gediouus

CHAPTER I
The Unicorn and the Orient

Ch'i-Lin
Chinese, c. 200 BC,
private coll.

This jade carving is possibly
the earliest known example of
a Chinese Unicorn

The beginning of this story lies in the remote past. We must go back to a time long before the birth of Christ, when agriculture replaced hunting around the great rivers in China, India and Mesopotamia; to the time when our shared myths evolved.

I mean myths in the proper sense of the word and not in the vulgarized and meaningless sense in which it is used today. We hear the word constantly in everyday speech. It is a "myth" that potatoes are fattening – it is a "myth" that girls are not interested in physics. In short, if something does not fit with our view of the world, it is immediately termed a "myth", which is thus synonymous with foolish superstition, old prejudice, lies or tall stories. The real myth is not a prejudice, and it is not invented. It is of the nature of dream and describes the common psychological structure and experience of human beings in the form of images and fables. Far from being a tall story, the myth is actually important truth, but on a different plane from small everyday truths.

In the various cultures, myths are transformed into legends and songs and religious ideas, or they materialize as fabulous creatures, expressing human instincts and powerful interacting forces that are hard to describe directly. Farming communities have myths concentrated on fertility and growth. They are about rain and drought, trees and animals – bad as well as good. People are so closely bound up with their four-legged confrères that kings consider it an honour to have a stag, a bull or a gazelle in the family. The heavenly bodies are mighty divinities, and sexuality is the essential core of existence. For this reason, horned animals are highly regarded. Two horns are good; one horn may be better. That was the view in India.

This was the milieu in which the legend developed of the hermit Gazelle Horn, which appears in the Indian saga, the *Mahabharata*.[1] The hermit Risyasringa (Gazelle Horn or the Wise Horned One) is the son of Vibhandaka the ascetic and the daughter of a god transformed into a gazelle. He lives with his father in the depths of the forest, in human form but with a horn in the middle of his forehead. Being halfway to the son of a god, he is protected by the god Indra and has power over the rain.

Now it happened that a great drought plagued the land of Anga. It was a punishment inflicted upon King Lomapada because he had driven away a Brahmin. His soothsayer told him that no rain would fall before he captured Risyasringa. The king

was at a loss; but then his daughter Nalini came to him and offered to help. With feminine inventiveness she built a leaf hut that would float on the river and sailed through the forest to the place where Gazelle Horn lived. When she arrived at his dwelling she attired herself in her finest clothes, let down her long hair and went ashore to seek him out.

Suddenly he stood before her, staring at her with big eyes, for he had never seen such a lovely creature before. They spoke to each other and he showed her his hut, thinking she was a young recluse like himself. Eventually she returned to her boat.

That evening his father noticed that something had affected his son, and warned him against the evil spirits that could destroy his innocence. Next day Nalini came again and hardly had Gazelle Horn caught sight of her than he forgot everything and, without realizing what he was doing, went on board the boat with her. Here she served him with wine, which always seems to have been dangerous for children of nature, for she sailed off with him to the king's palace, and he made no resistance. When Gazelle Horn stepped over the threshold, the rain began to fall. This story has a happy ending. Gazelle Horn's father is brought to the castle and the young couple are married and establish a great family. The story does not tell us whether their children ran around with little fleshy horns between their ears. But in Indian reliefs Gazelle Horn himself is generally shown with a phallic horn on his forehead.

The legend is found in five variants, of which the one in the *Mahabharata* is the most detailed. It is also found in Sanskrit, Pali, Tibetan and Chinese, and is related to the Babylonian epic. The myth was probably suited to communities which still remembered their hunting past, but were developing into an organized state with a farming class. In the legend we see the horned animal-human who can unite himself with a woman without difficulty and enter the race, as in the Greek legend of Europa and the Bull. We see his power over rain and plant-life, and how he must be captured with cunning and taken to the ruler who is responsible for his people's welfare, but who has no direct control over nature. Nature can be outwitted, because the potent but naive creature can be seduced by a woman so that the ruler may have a share in his power. Such a taming of wisdom is familiar from many other stories: Samson and Delilah, Aristotle who crawls on all fours with Phyllis riding on his neck, and the story of Merlin the magician's defeat and death. Later we shall see how this legend, with many others, arrives in Europe and finds a place in medieval culture.

When the story appeared in China, the stag with one horn had already been long known there, first mentioned in the second millennium BC. By the time it was defined in detail, in a dictionary published shortly before the birth of Christ, it was well integrated into Chinese cultural tradition, adorning the red wedding chair of the bride in the form of small statuettes. It was then one of the four animals which symbolized the elements: the turtle represented water, the phoenix, which burned itself up, fire, the flying dragon, air, while the Unicorn stood for the fertile earth. It was called *Ch'i* (he) and *Lin* (she), and was thus characterized as androgynous. The Ch'i-Lin resembles a stag but is larger and has an ox's tail and horse's hoofs. Its forehead is furnished with a twelve-foot-long horn with a soft tip. Its five sacred colours are black, white, red, blue and yellow. That is, it carries the three primary colours, together with black and white. It also radiates light and has a voice like a monastery bell. As a sacred animal, it lives in solitude and is seldom seen; it does not tread on living plants and

Ch'i-Lin
Chinese, Kang Hsi period, 1662–1722, private coll.

Porcelain dish painted in underglaze blue with design of a Ch'i-Lin, mouth agape, seated with its front right hoof raised amidst a palm tree, rocks and bamboo

eats no living creature. But it grazes with the gazelle, drinks with cattle, and its heart rejoices with the concourse of the waters and possesses all the holy virtues, including goodness, righteousness, faith, wisdom, asceticism, harmony and a long life. This animal has no connection with the rhinoceros, but is a little "heavenly horse", a noble animal. Although seldom seen, it can make an appearance when good rulers are in power and, if it is wounded, this is a bad omen. This belief in the animal's prophetic gifts is seen in the following legend. In the year 481 BC a gifted prophetic Ch'i-Lin appeared to the wife of a Governor Tsou:

"Before Kungfutse was even born a Ch'i-Lin entered Governor Tsou's house and disgorged a jade prophecy. Its inscription ran thus: the son of the mountain crystal (water-essence) will perpetuate Chou's decaying kingdom and rule as king without any royal insignia. Mother Yen wondered at this and tied an embroidered ribbon around Ch'i-Lin's horn. It stayed there for two nights and then went away."[2]

This account is the most beautiful prelude imaginable to the European Unicorn Hunt which would become a favourite theme 1,500 years later. The heavenly creature prophecies the birth of a king without outward splendour to the wondering woman who ties a ribbon around its magical horn — remarkably like the Virgin who puts a collar on the Unicorn or caresses its magical horn. But here the animal plays the role

Above
The Life of Kungfutse
Chinese, Ch'ing dynasty, 18th century, Dekker coll., Meilen

These drawings are from Sheng-tsi-tu, an illustrated life of Kungfutse. Ch'i-Lin announces the birth of Kungfutse, the governor's wife receives the message; Ch'i-Lin foretells the death of Kungfutse, the master expresses horror at seeing the slain animal on the ground

Left
Ch'i-Lin
Chinese, Ming dynasty, 14th–16th century, private coll.

This silk embroidered insignia of a first-class military rank — here cut from an official coat and inserted in the frame of a Tibetan tanka — is one of the best examles of the Ch'i-Lin in Chinese textile art

Ch'i-Lin
Japanese, Momoyama period,
late 16th or early 17th century,
private coll.

Rare example of a Japanese
Ch'i-Lin on a cloud-scroll
pattern, in silk interwoven
with gold foil

of messenger; why there should have been this change in the Christian version will become clear later.

Ch'i-Lin also prophesies the death of Kungfutse. In the fourteenth year of the reign of Duke Ais a Ch'i-Lin was caught and killed during a winter hunt in the west. Kungfutse was disconcerted at this and stopped writing. In the legend, Shu-sun's family burned down a thicket and caught a Ch'i-Lin, but no one recognized it. They threw it on the crossroads near Wu-Fu. The disciple Jan-Yu reported this and said: "A stag's body with a fleshy horn, is not this a portent of misfortune from heaven?" When Kungfutse went and looked at it, he wept and said: "This is a Ch'i-Lin. Ch'i-Lin, the good animal, appears and dies. My tao is finished."

Japan too has an ancient myth, later used in Noh plays and opera. It tells of a one-horned demon in human form, the son of a hind. His name is Ikakkakky. In contrast to Gazelle Horn, he is wicked and imprisons animals and good spirits in a grotto, and stops the rain from falling. On the king's orders he is seduced by the Princess Senda, who rides him home to the castle and robs him of his power. She frees the rain dragons and the other animals so that the rain can fall again. Although good and evil are differently distributed, the relationship with the Indian legend is unmistakable.

The peoples inhabiting the river areas of the Middle East also cultivated the Unicorn idea. As early as 1000 BC it is mentioned in *Enuma Elish*, the Babylonian Creation myth, among the monsters created by the goddess Tiamath when she was preparing to battle with the hero Marduk. She produced eleven monsters who were all evil spewers of poison and hostile to Marduk:

"She conjured up sea serpents, fiery glowing sea serpents, giant lions, howling wolves and scorpion men, gusty winds, fish men and Unicorn . . ."[3]

In this company the one-horned creature represents evil and destruction. Marduk entered his battle chariot and conquered Tiamath and her monsters; he split her in two and from these two parts made heaven and earth — and created human beings.

The Sumerian legendary cycle *Gilgamesh* was also known to the Babylonians. It is an epic in twelve songs, about a third the size of the *Odyssey*, and its subjects are Prince Gilgamesh and Enkidu. Enkidu lives like a child of nature in the forest and gathers the animals around him at a watering place to ensure they can drink in peace. Gilgamesh wants to capture him and tells his huntsman:

"Go, my huntsman, take a harlot with you. When he leads his flock to the water, allow them to meet. She will bare her breast, and he will lie with her — and the animals will flee from him . . ."[4]

The harlot from Ishtar's temple "tames" him and leads him to the king's castle, where he is humanized by bread and wine. Here on the king's orders he fights with lions, wolves and a heavenly bull, and becomes the king's friend.

Although Enkidu has no horn, so many elements in his story are reminiscent of the Indian Gazelle Horn legend that the two stories are considered either to have in-fluenced each other or to have had a common source. We see again the hermit who can be lured by a woman, thereby losing his innocent relationship with nature, and whose powers will benefit the ruling monarch.

Most fascinating of all is the story of the Great Ass. The Persian religion takes a dualistic view of life, considering that the world is divided between good and evil. In the collection of writings known as the *Avesta*, ancient mythic material becomes part of later moral teaching and literature linked with the name of Zarathustra, founder of religion. The section dealing with the Creation and the battle between good and evil — known as the Bundahish Myth — relates how the good god

Marduk, detail from the Ishtar procession
Enamelled bricks, Babylonia, *c.* 570 BC, St Louis Art Museum, Missouri

Ahura Mazda (or Ormudz) creates his good animals – horse, ass and bull – to fight the wicked Ahriman, who strikes back with lion, snake and the fearful manticore, with its needle-sharp teeth. The evil animals pollute Vourukasha, the world sea, which covers a third of the earth's surface, so no animal can drink of it. Then the shining god Tishtrya descends – he is actually Sirius, the dog star – in the form of a white horse, to fight against the evil, assisted by a remarkable and sacred animal, described thus:

"It is said of the three-legged ass that it stands in the middle of the wild sea [Vourukasha], and it has three feet, six eyes, nine mouths, two ears and one horn. Its body is white, it eats spiritual food and is virtuous. And two of its six eyes are in the eyes' place, two on top of its head and two on its rear; with these six sharp eyes it sees all who do evil and destroy.

Of the nine mouths, three are in the head, three on the back and three on the inner side of the flanks, and each mouth is the size of a house. The animal itself is as big as the mountain called Alvand. Each of its three feet take up as much ground as a herd of a thousand sheep when they are gathered together, and each rear part is of such extent that a thousand men with a thousand horses can be placed within it . . . The single horn is of gold and hollow, and a thousand branches grow out of it, some like those of a camel, some like those of a horse, some like those of an ox, some like those of a god, both small and large. With that horn it can strike and shatter all corruption that comes from harmful animals.

When that ass submerges its neck in the ocean its ears will terrify, and all the water in the wild sea will tremble with agitation, and the side of Ganavad shall shake. When it utters a roar, all the she creatures of the sea and Ahura Mazda's animals will teem with young, and all the venomous water creatures will drop their young at that scream. When it makes water in the sea all the water in the seven regions of the earth will be cleansed; – this is why every ass which goes into the water, makes water in it . . . And the words say: If thou, O three-legged ass, had not been created for the water, all the water in the sea would be corrupted by the infection which the Evil Spirit brought down into its waters on the death of Ahura Mazda's creatures."[5]

This text seems to take us back to the dawn of time, when the world is dewy with vapour and burgeoning vegetation and there is no sign of a human being. Mythical creatures, as huge as mountains, are generated from the elements. And out of the fog rises an animal – a male animal – ruled by the number three, with a golden horn which like a common denominator contains within itself the horns of every other animal. It is a good and vigilant animal, which fights against evil and is closely connected with the life-giving water; for the first time we experience the cleansing with water which simultaneously generates. Above all, the animal is a sexual creature, the very principle of masculinity, which impregnates the female element, water, and the animals that live in it. At its side is another female symbol: Gokard, the Tree of Life, which grows from the primeval mud on the bed of the world ocean. The association in this myth of tree, water and horned animal persists throughout the history of the Unicorn and seems to be an essential requirement.

There is something primeval about this tripartite animal and its actions, and no one knows when the story first passed from mouth to mouth. It was not recorded in writing until after the birth of Christ, in the Pahlavi language, as part of Zara-thustra's teaching, and it was unknown in the West before then.

About 600 BC, Ahura Mazda's good bull was portrayed in Persian art in the hall of the forty pillars in Persepolis, the capital city of the great king. In the reliefs there, lions fight with bulls which have hoofs and apparently only one striped horn. For a long time this "unihornity" led scholars to think that the European Unicorn had come into being as a misinterpretation of these pictures. But Persian sculptures of

A king fights with a one-horned demon, on a relief from Persepolis, *c.* 500 BC

The Satyrical Papyrus, detail
1305–1170 BC, British Museum,
London

A lion plays the senet game
with an ibex or a horned ass.
It is questionable whether the
animal is meant to represent a
true Unicorn or whether the
creature appears to have only
one because it is seen in
profile. If it is a Unicorn, this
would be one of the earliest
known representations of it

bulls, both free-standing and in relief, show animals with two horns, and the flat pictures are merely an expression of the stylization common to much early art. However, certain ancient non-spatial images do pose serious problems. For example, how are we to interpret the "chess-playing" antelope in the Egyptian papyrus in the British Museum?

The Great Ass from Vourukasha was probably never represented in Persian art, but there is a Persian example of a true Unicorn. A relief from the palace in Persepolis shows the great king defeating the "Dragon of Chaos", that is, the good organizing principle defeats the evil one. The mighty king clad in his ritual costume struggles with a demon composed of all the most aggressive elements of the animal kingdom: vulture's claws, hawk's wings, lion's head and scorpion's tail. With one hand the king plunges his sword into the animal's stomach, while with the other he grips a twisted horn in the centre of its forehead; in other words, he seizes the very root of vitality and at the same time pierces the animal with his own phallic symbol, the sword. The significance attached to this royal act can be seen in the multiple replication of the theme uppermost on the wall, visible to all.

Two other Oriental representations demonstrate the same idea. A drinking horn made from an elephant tusk – it is known as an "Oliphant" – bears reliefs of Islamic origin, in which we see a fight between a bull and a lion (see fig. on p.18). The lion clutches in one paw the single horn in the centre of the bull's forehead and thus reproduces the king's gesture. This image still recalls the ancient myths and the clash of powerful forces. Whether there is one horn or two, the juxtaposition of horned animal and tree again reveals that the central meaning of the horn is sexual: we are shown the divine power of the horn and a procreation, a meeting of horn and tree – he and she – or between horned animal and an opponent who desires a share of the power. If the king can seize the horn his desire will be fulfilled.

It is a common feature of the legends that the horned creature lives alone in nature and shares in its reproductive power. It allows itself to be enticed and tamed by a woman – maiden or courtesan – and the king needs its gifts. It can forewarn and, if desired, protect against poison and sickness. Above all, though, the horn-power is an expression of fruitfulness, which is the real and sacred mission of all horned male animals.

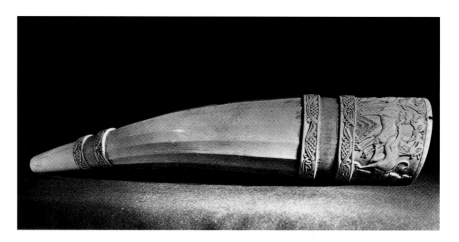

Oliphant
Ivory, 11th century,
Kunsthistorisches Museum,
Vienna

This Oliphant, which
belonged to the Habsburg
Count Albrecht III, depicts a
lion fighting a one-horned
bull, possibly a Unicorn

This is sufficient reason for the birth of the myth. We need not search for visual explanations. It is of minor importance to know how far the rhinoceros influenced the appearance of the Unicorn, whether a flat painting of a bull in Persia was misunderstood, or whether someone saw an oryx silhouetted against the evening sky and thought that it had only one horn. All this is marginal. The Unicorn has a far deeper origin. In one nation after another it sprang up as a brilliantly imaginative sexual symbol, carried by the common logical idea that one horn concentrates power better than two. As we move from Asia to Europe we shall discover that this idea accompanies us.

CHAPTER 2

The Classical Inheritance

The earliest description of the Unicorn on European ground is from Greece. It was written by a doctor, Ctesias, who left the island of Knidos about 416 BC to become court physician to Darius II, king of the Persians, and his queen Parysatis. He later accompanied Prince Ataxerxes to the battlefield of Cunaxa to fight Darius's younger son, Kyros. The king was wounded in the battle and Ctesias treated his wounds.

The gods alone know what he saw and heard in Persia, and whether he really went to India; but when he returned to the Peloponnese in the year 398 he wrote twenty-three "books" on Persia entitled *Persica*, and also a work called *Indica*. The young Alexander the Great had to learn them in his preparatory studies. Twenty-five fragments of *Indica* are extant, some of which were revised by the Byzantine patriarch Photius in ninth-century Constantinople. Ctesias describes numerous remarkable animals from India, among them pygmies, dogs' heads and the dangerous manticores, which later appear in medieval travel books and art. In Book 25 we read:

"Ctesias says that in India there are certain wild asses as big as horses. Their bodies are white, their heads purple, their eyes a dark blue colour. They have one horn in their foreheads, about a cubit in length. The lowest part of the horn is white, two handsbreadths up it is flaming crimson, but in the centre of this quite black. The Indians drink from these multicoloured horns. They say that whoever drinks from this horn is free of incurable illness, for he will not contract cramps or the holy sickness (epilepsy) or succumb to poisoning, and even if he had previously drunk something harmful he will vomit it up and be saved.

Other asses – both tame and wild – and all animals with solid hoofs have no ankle bones and no gall in their liver; but these have both ankle bones and gall. This bone – the most beautiful I have seen – is like that of an ox in appearance and size, but it is as heavy as lead, and its colour is like vermilion all through. The animal is swifter and stronger than any other, so no animal, neither the horse nor any other, can keep pace with it. When it starts to run it goes slowly but it gradually increases its speed wonderfully, and the further it goes, the swifter.

This is the only possible way to capture them: when they take their young to pasture you must surround them with many men and horses. They will not desert their offspring and fight with horn, teeth and tail and can only be brought down with arrows. You cannot catch them alive. The flesh of this animal is so bitter that it is inedible; it is hunted for its horn and ankle bone."[1]

This remarkable passage, reproduced here in its entirety, is one of the most important sources for the Unicorn, and acquired great significance. It describes a number of the characteristics we shall later find attributed to the animal. It has the body of a white horse, with hoofs. Its colours are white, black and vermilion, with blue eyes, and these are precisely the sacred colours of mythical animals which we saw in the Ch'i-Lin. It is swift and wild, and will not allow itself to be captured. The pictures seen in the margins of many early manuscripts, depicting hunters attacking the Unicorn with bows and arrows, may possibly have been influenced by Ctesias's hunting scene.

As a doctor, Ctesias is naturally interested in the pharmaceutical qualities of the animal, and he finds that its strength is lodged in its horn, and it protects against both sickness and poison. The remarkable ankle bone, which Ctesias describes so exactly, as if he had held it in his hand, is slightly puzzling. Had he perhaps seen a coloured die from the well known "astragal" game, a kind of fivestones, made of ox or sheep bones?

It is tempting to analyse the component parts of Ctesias's animal. Presumably the natural sources are the wild swift ass of Persia – the so-called "onager" – known from royal hunts, and perhaps the rhinoceros with its accelerating gait. He may also have taken the idea of the horn functioning as a drinking horn and its healing power from this source. But the varied colouring of the animal indicates mythical features. Do its colours originate from Indian legends that he had heard? Or are they visual impressions from many-coloured Oriental silks with animals and trees? We cannot know. The bull reliefs from Persepolis would scarcely have affected Ctesias. Presumably he understood the imagery of his own time, and he speaks expressly of *asses*.

His book circulated widely and was cited for over a thousand years. This was primarily due to the fact that it was acknowledged by Aristotle, who later assembled all the facts then known about nature by Greek authors. Contemporary writers had little faith in Ctesias and accused him of tall tales, so Aristotle's approval was crucial, since he was of course the scientific authority for the whole medieval period. Any doubt on his part would have been a catastrophe for the future of the Unicorn! Although Aristotle is somewhat sceptical, in his *Historia Animalium* he ends up in favour of "the one-horn idea".

In this, the first natural history to have been preserved, he attempts a first classification of animals according to their characteristics and thus brings order out of chaos. Although to our eyes the book is extremely unsystematic and comes to some strange conclusions, its incipient division of the fauna is still an achievement.

The author divides mammals into various groups, including hoofed and cloven-footed animals – and also into horned and non-horned. He says that most horned animals are cloven-hoofed – for example, oxen, deer and goats – and that there are no hoofed animals with horns, with one exception: for it is stated that the Indian ass bears a single horn in the centre of its head. This statement, of course, comes from Ctesias, who is thus given definite credence. In a chapter on horns, Aristotle offers an explanation as to why hoofed animals have no horns, or only one: they use so much horn material for their hoofs that there is none left over.

The only cloven-hoofed animal which has one horn, says the author, is the oryx. This deer, often mentioned in connection with the Unicorn, was perhaps classified with the single-horned beast because it is so frequently seen in silhouette and thus assumed to have only one.[2]

So Aristotle acknowledged the one-horned ass — to the pleasure of his pupil, Alexander the Great, and then of Pliny and the later Aristotelians, who were more than delighted to be able to refer to him every time they were in doubt. The Unicorn had arrived in Europe in the form of an ass, and the Oriental bull or dragon of chaos never played any part here. The animal had been channelled into a definite form.

Megasthenes was an eminent official who was sent, about 300 BC, to the most remote country of the Macedonian empire, India. He wrote four books about the remarkable land, *Indica*, of which extracts are extant. He records an Indian Unicorn called "Cartazon", of which the Indians had told him. It is as large as a horse, with broad hoofs resembling elephant's feet; its tail is curly like that of a wild boar, and between its brows it has an extremely sharp, strong and black horn. Megasthenes is worth remembering because he is the first to mention that this horn bears spirals or rings. He is also the first to describe the animal's fearsome roar, and he emphasizes that "it is wild and belligerent and even fights with its own species."[3]

These three authors form the core of the otherwise sparse ancient natural history before the Romans. The Greeks were not specially interested in the Unicorn, although they had a liking for "compound" animals. Their fables are full of accounts of human beings turned into animals and of amalgamated species; but although they described centaurs, sphinxes, griffins and sirens, they never depicted a Unicorn.

Nor did the Romans do much about the Unicorn, although they were fond enough of telling stories about the strange animals they met on their campaigns around the world. In his famous notes on the Gallic Wars, Caesar tells us that in the Hyrcanian forests there lived an ox shaped like a stag, which bore a single horn between its ears, divided in the middle like a hand. This description best fits an elk that has lost one of its horns, and no myths grew up around it.[4]

The great natural historian Pliny the Elder (AD 23–79) mentions the Unicorn. He is a link in a scientific tradition and must surely have read Megasthenes, for he writes in his *Naturalis Historia*:

"The Orsaeyan Indians hunt apes, which are white — but the wildest animal is the Monoceros, whose body is like a horse but which has the head of a stag, elephant's feet and a wild boar's tail. It utters a deep, growling sound, and a black horn, two cubits long, protrudes from the centre of its forehead. It is said that this animal cannot be captured alive."[5]

Pliny uses the name Monoceros, and it must be emphasized that in no way does he confuse the animal with the rhinoceros. As a Roman citizen he was familiar with the rhinoceros, which was exhibited on the occasion of Pompey's triumphal procession, and he particularly describes it as the animal that battles with the elephant in the arena. When he later recounts how the Unicorn and the elephant fight as enemies, and that the Unicorn spears the elephant on its horn, it is likely that the recollection of fights between rhinoceros and elephant is active in his subconscious.

The next important witness was Julius Solinus, another natural historian, who wrote a *Polyhistoria* about 218 AD. He naturally based his account on Pliny; but we find a significant improvement on the story when he lengthens the black horn to four feet:

"But the cruellest is the Unicorne, a Monster that belloweth horrible, bodyed like a horse, footed like an Oliphant, tayled like a Swyne, and headed like a Stagge. His horn sticketh out of the midds of his forehead, of a wonderfull brightnesse about four foote long, so sharp, that whatsoever he pusheth at, he sticketh it through easily. Hee is never caught alive: kylled he may be, but taken he cannot bee."[6]

Now the animal stands before us as large as a horse at the edge of the forest, on four clumsy elephant's feet, swinging its pig's tail and uttering terrifying roars. This creature cannot possibly be confused with a rhinoceros for it has no resemblance to any other animal in the world.

The most important source from later antiquity, however, is Claudius Aelianus. About AD 220 he wrote *On the Nature of the Animals* in Greek. In Books 3 and 4 he added the most detailed description yet of the Unicorn to ancient natural history. By his time the source material had become so profuse that the author was bewildered: what is this animal, described so variously, really like? Can there be two, or even more, types? To be on the safe side Aelianus describes three varieties. The first two are almost identical and very similar to those of Ctesias: the animal has a white body, red head and three-coloured horn. He also mentions the drinking horn with the golden rings and bitter flesh; but in his version the ankle bone is black. This is how he describes the third variation:

"In certain regions of India . . . they say that there are impassable mountains full of wild life, and that they contain just as many animals as our own country produces, only wild. For they say that even the sheep there are wild, the dogs too and the goats and the cattle, and that they roam of their own sweet will in freedom and uncontrolled by any herdsman. Indian historians assert that their numbers are past counting and among the historians we must reckon the Brahmins, for they also agree in telling the same story.

And in these same regions there is said to exist a one-horned beast which they call *Cartazonus*. It is the size of a full-grown horse, has the mane of a horse, reddish hair, and is very swift of foot. Its feet are like those of the elephant, not articulated and it has the tail of a pig. Between its eyebrows it has a horn growing out; it is not smooth but has spirals of quite natural growth, and is black in colour. This horn is also said to be exceedingly sharp. And I am told that the creature has the most discordant and powerful voice of all animals. When other animals approach, it does not object but is gentle; with its own kind however it is inclined to be quarrelsome. And they say that not only do the males instinctively butt and fight one another, but that they display the same temper towards the females, and carry their contentiousness to such a length that it ends only in the death of their defeated rival. The fact is that strength resides in every part of the animal's body, and the power of its horn is invincible. It likes lonely grazing-grounds where it roams in solitude, but at the mating season, when it associates with the female, it becomes gentle and the two even graze side by side. Later when the season has passed and the female is pregnant, the male Cartazonus of India reverts to its savage and solitary state. They say that the foals when quite young are taken to the King of the Parsii and exhibit their strength one against another in the public shows, but nobody remembers a full-grown animal having been captured."[7]

The "Cartazon", also described by Megasthenes, as we saw, is Sanskrit for the "King of the Wilderness". It is found also in Arabian literature, for instance in the story of Sinbad the Sailor, where it is called the "Carcadan" and has a horn six metres long.

Ctesias, Megasthenes and Pliny are obviously important sources for Aelian. The detail of the horn's "natural rings" is possibly taken from Megasthenes; but if Aelian really means spiralling twists this may also signify that the narwhal tusk, already a trading commodity by Hadrian's time, is beginning to make its appearance in the story (see Chapter 18). Still more interesting is the fact that here for the first time we are told that the Unicorn is "brought to the king". This may be a manifestation of the Indian myth – for Aelian lives in the period of the Alexandrian libraries – but many other sources may have been lost.

Finally one more author must be mentioned, the Alexandrian Greek Cosmas Indicopleustos (The India-farer), who stayed at a monastery on Sinai from AD 545 to

Unicorn
Bronze, Luristan, 9th century BC, coll. Foroughi, Teheran

This statuette is Iranian, but the "Ethiopian" figures seen by Cosmas may have been of a similar character

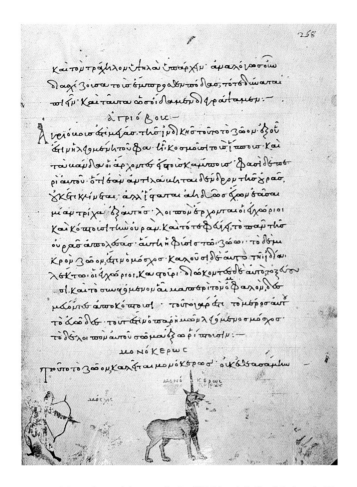

547, writing about his travels in "Ethiopia" for his book *Topographia Christiana*. In Book 11 he writes that the Ethiopians cultivate the Unicorn and, although he has not seen it himself, he has seen four bronze figures of it on the Emperor's palace with the four towers, and he adds these salient words: "From those figures did I draw him, as you see . . ."[8] And he really did! Cosmas illustrated his work with a drawing and, into the bargain, it was preserved in copies of later centuries. The drawing shows a statuesque type of antelope or horse with a tall erect horn as long as the animal's legs, and with a ribbon around its neck. It is the colour of polished bronze. This sketch – the first one we know of a Unicorn in Europe – is the real prototype of the version which came to dominate in art.

Where had Cosmas been? This is not as easy to determine as it seems. For we must not think of Africa when we hear the word Ethiopia. Many sources describe the country as "that Ethiopia which lies close to India". This is stated by the great traveller, Mandeville and also "Prester John", to be discussed later, and much indicates that this "country" was situated in the great, little known area of Ararat, traditionally the region of Paradise. It is even more interesting when we compare Cosmas's Unicorn with some small, Iranian bronze figures in the museum in Teheran. Did Cosmas see figures of this kind? If so, the Iranian bronzes are the true ancestors of the proud Unicorn which was to be tamed by the Virgin in medieval Europe. In other respects Cosmas's description follows that of Ctesias, and the name he uses is the Greek Monoceros. He adds an amusing detail:

"People say he is completely invincible and that his whole strength lies in his horn. When he knows he is being pursued by many hunters and about to be captured, he leaps up to a clifftop and throws himself down from it, and as he falls he turns himself in such a way that his horn completely cushions the shock and he escapes unharmed."

Next follow references to Psalm 22 and other Bible texts, for Cosmas lives in the Christian era. The story of the horn's saving power is also told of the goat-like "Ibex", of which the natural historians say:

"There is an animal that is called the Ibex Chamois, which has two horns. And such is their strength that if it is hurled from a high mountain top into the abyss its entire body will remain unharmed with the aid of these two."[9]

It can be seen that the ancient Unicorn was created out of words. It was constructed by storytellers and literary scholars, who cribbed from each other and made small improvements, which begin by enriching the accounts, but end by rendering them absurd. No one thought of checking the traditions by personal investigation, and as a rule they started off with: "It is said that . . ." or "I have heard that . . ." In that respect the Unicorn is of course not unique; manticores, dragons and many other fabulous animals evolved in the same way through the ages.

The Unicorn stands somewhere between myth and natural history. It is large and wild, and is composed of horse, stag, wild boar, goat, rhinoceros, ass and, into the bargain, elephant. But its chief substance seems to have been horse/ass. It has hoofs or elephant feet but is not cloven-footed. The horn is black and its length grows in the best fishing-story manner, from about half a metre to almost two, and can pierce through an enemy or save the animal from a fall. Two of the authors mention that in some way or other the horn is striped or has spirals. It has a dreadful roar and, as a whole, is not particularly amiable. There are a few allusions to pharmaceutical qualities; but it is worth noting that the greatest physicians of antiquity, Galen, Hippocrates and Dioscurides, make *no* mention of them.

The animal has no moral attributes and is certainly not divine. It is treated on a level with griffins, rhinoceroses and other animals appealing to the imagination, and it wanders with them from book to book. In the matter-of-fact reasoning system of antiquity it is described as a possible natural phenomenon created out of rumours from distant lands – especially Persia, India and "Ethiopia". It is not confused with the rhinoceros. In its travels it does not meet with a virgin!

All the same, the records add up to a wealth of material weighted with unwavering authority: did Ctesias himself perhaps take the flaming red ankle bone in his hand? And did not Aristotle acknowledge the four-footed creature with one horn in the middle of its forehead? So then there are no grounds for doubt.

The Gundestrup silver cauldron, detail
Celtic, 2nd or 1st century BC, Nationalmuseet, Copenhagen

Probably from Hungary, but found in North Jutland, here is clearly an early representation of the Unicorn, horse-like and with hoofs

CHAPTER 3

Biblical Texts

When Alexander the Great founded the city of Alexandria, where the Nile runs into the Mediterranean sea, it was with forethought. In a short time a wealthy centre of commerce had grown up, which also became a cultural hub for the whole Mediterranean area. People from every nation in the world met here to exchange knowledge: myths, religions, art and scientific findings were debated. From the north the city was dominated by Greek culture, as the residence of the Ptolemaic dynasty, and from neighbouring countries came Persians, Phoenicians, Indians and a large strain of Jews, and later on the Romans. The city was a melting pot whose smouldering heart engendered a rich literature which was stored away in two great libraries. The largest of these – the renowned Museion – was reputed to be stacked with about 500,000 papyrus rolls containing the assembled knowledge of the age. Rotulus lay beside rotulus on the shelves and could be used by interested individuals, wishing to study Plato, Aristotle or Pythagoras, Jewish mysticism and Oriental legend, in the reading room. They might be lucky enough to encounter Archimedes or Euclid in the flesh. When the library went up in flames in Julius Caesar's time, it was an irreplaceable loss to European culture.

Despite the disaster, literature continued to flourish. After the victory of Christianity the Christian sects met here – Desert Fathers, Copts and combative theologians of many persuasions – and various Christian dogmas took shape in the later flowering of the city between the birth of Christ and AD 400, in a silver age of late antiquity. It was not by chance that the story of one of the most beloved female saints – Catherine of Alexandria – and her battle with the scholars, took place in Alexandria, city of philosophers.

It is not surprising, therefore, to discover that many tracks of the Unicorn's hoofs lead back to Alexandria and lose themselves there. If the great library still existed today, we should undoubtedly find one document after another on its shelves which would throw light on the history of the animal. We might, for example, have found the Alexander Romance and the earliest natural histories – the so-called Physiologi (see Chapter 5) – in which the animal is described, as well as alchemistic writings and perhaps the Indian story of the Virgin. We would certainly have found the translation of the Old Testament which brought the Unicorn into the Bible and so into European consciousness.

In Alexander's time the Old Testament was still available only in Hebrew; but tradition has it that about 250 BC one of Alexander's successors on the throne of Egypt, Ptolemy II, ordered a translation into Greek. It was completed in seventy-two days by seventy-two Jewish scholars from Alexandria, working on the island of Pharos, which lies close to the city. Legend is not truth; it condenses an occurrence and emphasizes points according to the convention of legend. But it is true that a translation was carried out at that time and given the name of Septuagint, perhaps after the seventy Jewish scribes who executed the work under the direction of the two eldest.

Thanks to the Septuagint, the Unicorn made its entrance into the Bible, with incalculable consequences. Indeed, we owe it thanks for bringing into being the medieval Unicorn tradition. For the translators came on the Assyrian word *remu* (Hebrew: *re'em*), meaning a large wild animal, today considered to be the wild buffalo of Asia Minor — *Bos primigenius* — which was already extinct in the translators' time. However that may be, they were not sure what the word covered and perhaps they searched the "natural historians" and hit on the Greek Monoceros, which we know from traditional antiquity to have been large and wild. This translation appeared in eight places in the Septuagint and when, 600 years later, Jerome, one of the Fathers of the Church, used this book as the basis of his Latin translation, he carried the misunderstanding further. Perfectly logically, he translated *monoceros* with Latin *unicornis* or *unicornus* — or in one or two instances with *rhinoceros*.

From that moment on, the Unicorn paced steadily and calmly through all the Bible translations in Europe. We find the Unicorn in Luther's German version, in a Danish one of 1825 and in that of King James I right up to the Oxford edition of 1897. Not until our own century does the wild ox take its place.

It is true that the animal does not appear unambiguously as one-horned except in the Book of Daniel; but the misunderstanding in itself carried the idea. Let us look at the passages that were so decisive for the continuing life of the Unicorn.[1] The first two are in Numbers and Deuteronomy; they describe the strength of the Lord and His faithfulness to Israel when he led the people out of Egypt and through the desert: "God brought him forth out of Egypt; he hath as it were the strength of an unicorn" (Numbers 24, 8); " . . . his horns are like the horns of unicorns: with them he shall push the people together to the ends of the earth" (Deuteronomy 33, 17).[2] Originally there seems to have been reference here to a two-horned animal — the great bull who leads his herd and paces at the head with the crescent of his horns aloft, ready to gore anything that threatens his flock. These two citations were very significant to the earliest theologians, who laid weight on describing God's mightiness.

The next extract is from the Book of Job 39, 9–12, a passage which contributed significantly to the interpretation of the Unicorn. God has smitten Job with great misfortune. His children are dead, his flocks wiped out, now he sits sick and miserable among the ashes and scrapes his boils with a potsherd. He finally loses patience and takes God to task, but then Jahweh himself comes and reads Job a text. In one of the grandest passages in the Old Testament, God demonstrates his might to the puny human being in the ashes. He reminds Job who it was that laid the measurements of the earth and showed the stars their places. He sets forth the wonders of the animal kingdom, which man has no power over — and says:

"Will the unicorn be willing to serve thee, or abide by thy crib?
Canst thou bind the unicorn with his band in the furrow? or will he harrow the valleys after thee?
Wilt thou trust him, because his strength is great? or wilt thou leave thy labour to him?
Wilt thou believe him, that he will bring home thy seed, and gather it into thy barn?"[3]

This passage, for which medieval scholars showed a particular predilection, was of great importance for art. Gregory the Great makes use of it in his commentaries on Job, which were very widely known.

Three of the Psalms also borrowed the horn as an image of the power that emanates from both good and evil. One of the most quoted and discussed verses is from Psalm 22, which begins with Jesus's last words from the cross: "My God, my God, why hast thou forsaken me? why art thou so far from helping me, and from the words of my roaring . . ." A litany of agonized lament and beseeching is followed by these words in verse 21: "Save me from the lion's mouth: for thou hast heard me from the horns of the unicorns."[4] This psalm was read at the beginning of the mass for Palm Sunday, so it was natural for the illustrators to paint Christ on the cross surrounded by all his enemies, among whom were the lion and the unicorn.

In Psalm 29, 5–6, David praises and honours the Lord: "The voice of the Lord breaketh the cedars; yea, the Lord breaketh the cedars of Lebanon. He maketh them also to skip like a calf; Lebanon and Sirion like a young unicorn."[5] And Psalm 92, 10 runs: "But my horn shalt thou exalt like the horn of an unicorn."[6] In the first quotation it seems almost to be the joyful people who are likened to playful calves and young creatures. In the second, the Lord is praised for his promises to David. Luke links this "exalted horn" to the city of David, and this was quickly taken by attentive scholars as one of the surest proofs that the Unicorn was David's successor, Christ.

Among the prophets who predicted the destiny of the Jews we find one single mention, in Isaiah, where he announces that the Lord will punish his enemies. The destructive powers of heaven shall come down upon the people: "And the unicorns shall come down with them, and the bullocks with the bulls; and their land shall be soaked with blood, and their dust made fat with fatness" (Isaiah 34, 7).[7] Here too the original image must have emerged among cattle breeders; the Unicorn ran with the oxen in massive herds that trampled everything down, and their behaviour most resembles that of wild oxen. But these small discrepancies did not worry the readers. The Unicorn stayed where it was.

In 560 BC, the third year of the reign of Nebuchadnezzar, Daniel the prophet had a vision in Shushan. He sees a ram with two horns, one larger than the other, which butted to every side so that nothing could get near it, and it became great. The prophet continues:

"And as I was considering, behold, an he goat came from the west on the face of the whole earth, and touched not the ground; and the goat had a notable horn between his eyes.
And he came to the ram that had two horns, which I had seen standing before the river, and ran unto him in the fury of his power.
And I saw him close unto the ram, and he was moved with choler against him, and smote the ram, and brake his two horns: and there was no power in the ram to stand before him, but he cast him down to the ground, and stamped upon him: and there was none that could deliver the ram out of his hand". (Daniel 8, 5–7).[8]

THE UNICORN

Daniel interprets the two-horned ram as the kings of Media and Persia, Darius and Cyrus. They are overpowered by "the rough goat", the Greek king Alexander of Macedonia. After this the goat's great horn is split into four smaller ones, which signify the four so-called Diadochi (princes) who divided the kingdom among themselves after Alexander's death. The number four thus stands for four kings or kingdoms; but the idea that one horn is stronger than two is not disputed. The fact that the animal was in fact a he goat did not worry writers or artists.

Finally, the horn receives one mention in the New Testament, in Luke 1, 68–69: "Blessed be the Lord God of Israel; for he hath visited and redeemed his people. And hath raised up an horn of salvation for us in the house of his servant David."[9] As I mentioned above, it was no doubt the reference in Psalm 92 which had inspired the Evangelist.

In the Latin Vulgate the identity of the Unicorn is not really clear. It is sometimes referred to as "unicornus", sometimes as "rhinoceros", and the number of horns is not defined except in the account of Daniel's vision and the Horn of Salvation. Later interpreters were not in doubt, however. When they speak of the Unicorn, they do mean a one-horned animal. Both the bible texts and ancient literature carry on the notion of something large and wild, which does not willingly allow itself to be tamed. But because of the error in translation and the confusion with the wild ox, the development of the mythical animal goes off on a wrong track. It was driven into a context in which it did not properly belong, and this led in the course of time to many absurdities and psychological problems.

During the same period, about the year AD 300 and the time of Constantine the Great, Jewish religious tradition was collected and written down in the Talmud.[10] This contains many references to the one-horned animal, for the Jews were particularly engrossed with horn power. Adam's first sacrifice was a one-horned ox and the Unicorn was the symbol of Ephraim's tribe. The beast is most vigorously elaborated in various accounts of the Flood. The best known recounts that the Unicorn, which was as big as the mountain of Tabor, had to make do with staying outside the Ark, as it could not possibly get inside. Some said that it was tied to the Ark by its nostrils or its horn, others that it tried to keep afloat by swimming, but that the multitude of exhausted birds which sat on its horn finally dragged it under the water, so that it drowned. Later the rarity of the Unicorn was explained in this fashion.

Stuttgart Psalter
Illustration to Psalm 22, c. 820, Württembergische Landesbibliothek, Stuttgart, cod. bibl. 2°23, fol. 27

Christ is surrounded by enemies: two soldiers, and the roaring lion and the Unicorn about to pierce Him. The chalice is ready to receive His blood. The conversing soldiers may be the centurion who acknowledges Christ and Longinus, who waits with his spear. Christ is between the earthly plane of human life and the cosmic, whose symbolic monsters come from the deep

Another story is linked to Psalm 22, "Save me from the lion's mouth ..." A *medrasch* (commentary) on the psalm explains that, as a young shepherd, David once mounted a huge Unicorn that was lying down, which he took for a hill where he could pasture his sheep. When the monster moved, David grew frightened and prayed to God for help and promised to build a temple. Then God sent a lion, which forced the Unicorn to its knees so that David could crawl down. But then he took fright at the lion's jaws, and so the passage runs: "Save me from the lion's jaws, as thou hast liberated me from the horn of the Unicorn."

These religious writings show us that the Unicorn preserves its status as a cosmic creature in contact with the elements and as of ritual significance. It is so huge that it touches the clouds and is compared with mountains as in the Bundahish Myth, mentioned in Chapter 1. Until then it had actually adopted a fairly low profile, as a cross between myth and natural history. It was a speciality. The animal possessed enormous power, but in the era of antiquity there was no particular use for it. With the coming of Christianity, the Unicorn fell into the hands of the Church Fathers and Christian theologians — and things began to change.

Daniel's Vision
Valladolid Beatus manuscript,
c. 1000, Gerona Cathedral

Daniel is sitting in the "Sousa
civitas", watching the battle
of two animals. The ram on
the left has lost both horns;
the Unicorn has struck them
both off with its red horn.
Four smaller horns grow out
of its neck

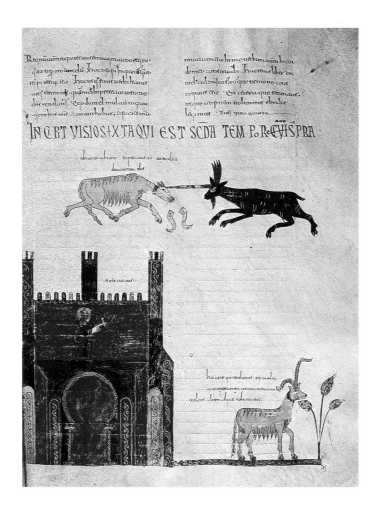

THE UNICORN

CHAPTER 4

Industrious Theologians

On the shelves of many university libraries can be found formidable rows of thick black volumes arranged in two series, entitled respectively *Patrologia Graeca* and *Patrologia Latina.* They contain the writings of the Greek – later Byzantine – and Latin "Fathers" of the Church. These books are a literary treasure not widely known, but a *sine qua non* for the student of medieval Christian thought, or of the Unicorn's journeying through theology. The books hold the biblical exegesis of the four Church Fathers and many other theologians, their biographies of saints, their sermons and ideas about nature, art, poetry, mathematics and music, and as the work ranges from the third to the thirteenth century, it covers the historical development of Christianity from the days of the primitive Church to the Gothic period.

A vast edifice of thought was built up. Every little stone in the text of the Bible was turned over and over, thousands of verses considered and annotated. Comparisons and explanations passed from hand to hand; they were expanded, ratified or changed in accord with the belief and taste of changing times, and in due course the whole of the Bible had been subjected to microscopic examination so that each animal or plant, each person and action had been allotted its irrefutable place. God's great work of creation was explicated as completely as human intelligence and emotion could make it. Here too the nine verses citing the Unicorn were adapted and fused into the whole faith in a logical process that seemed completely natural to medieval eyes.

Among the authors of interest to us are the lawyer Tertullian of Carthage, Augustine, Ambrose and Gregory the Great the Church Fathers, the Spanish bishop Isidore of Seville and finally Honorius of Autun, who lived in the period of the Crusades. All of these theologians form a vital link between the culture of antiquity and the middle ages. If they had not meticulously studied the old translation of the Septuagint, and its errors, it is unlikely that we should have had a Unicorn at all to take interest in today. But as soon as they included it in interpretation and moral teaching it became a reality which even Luther did not dare to argue against.

To begin with, they simply followed the word of Scripture, which in fact provided material enough for many treatises; but to obtain more detailed description of the animal's appearance and characteristics they searched the ancient writers and later the Physiologus (see Chapter 5). Thus the animal took shape in the writers' imagination, and pictures and comparisons soon proliferated.

the Physiologus (see Chapter 5). Thus the animal took shape in the writers' imagination, and pictures and comparisons soon proliferated.

One of the earliest writers was Tertullian of Carthage (c. 160–220), who, long before the Vulgate appeared, maintained that the Unicorn was Christ. In his work *Adversus Judaeos* (Against the Jews), he interpreted the quotation from Deuteronomy 33, 17, which describes the god with strong horns, and here the wild ox still seems to have a place in the scene: "His glory is like the firstling of his bullock, and his horns are like the horns of unicorns: with them he shall push the people together to the ends of the earth . . ." Then follows the commentary:

"It is not the rhinoceros that is designated as a Unicorn and the Minotaur as two-horned, but Christ is designated thereby: as a bull on account of two characteristics: For some He is cruel as a judge, for others mild as a Saviour. These its horns [the bull's] were the furthest ends of the cross. For on the yard of a ship also, which is part of a cross, the outermost ends are called horns. But the pole [or mast] in the centre is called one-horn. Finally, it is by virtue [strength] of this cross that, according to the custom of horned animals, He pierces every race with faith, lifting them from earth to heaven, and subsequently at the Day of Judgement He will cast them from heaven to earth."[1]

Holy cross between two monsters
Marble slab, c. 800, Museo Nazionale, Lucca

The monsters seem tame and are licking the foot of the cross. Their "headgear" may perhaps show the merging of their horns described by Tertullian

THE UNICORN

This must be one of the earliest biblical commentaries to link the Unicorn with Christ. And it is based on the Septuagint. Here we see the beginnings of medieval typology. The passage is typical of early writers who try to explicate difficult texts for the first time, and they write commentaries almost more obscure than the text itself. The meaning must be that Christ is like a two-horned bull in his might, and the bull's two horns are compared to the two ends of the two horizontal arms of the cross. But He is also one-horned, and this "Unicorn" is the vertical middle post of the cross, which is the "sharp horn of Faith" with which He — according to Moses — is to pierce the nations. Finally, the cross is compared to a ship's mast with its cross-yard.

The passage is hard to interpret precisely because the early writers are frequently more rhetorical than visual in their exegesis. One feels that they are overwhelmed by the power of their own words and pile up image on image without reaching a clear synthesis. This kind of passage is almost impossible to illustrate, but has to be perceived as a magnificent piece of rhetoric.

St Eustace of Antioch, known as Basileus (*c.* 330–379), is the next writer. In his great essay on the Creation, the *Hexameron* (The Six Days of Work), he mentions the Unicorn as an Indian animal, but this time as a dangerous demon: it is "ingenious in wickedness" and can pierce a man with its horn. As in Psalm 28 Basileus regards the horn as a threat, and we can begin to glimpse the duality in the biblical use of the great animal. In a sermon on Psalm 28, Basileus says that the Unicorn is so overmastering in its brute power that man could never subdue it. Christ is this divine strength and this is why He is called the Unicorn, and His single horn signifies that His power is as mighty as that of the Father.[2]

Here the strength is the strength of the good God, personified in Christ, and the horn expresses the unity between them. This author may also have paid a visit to the library, for he is the first to suggest that the animal can be captured with the aid of a virgin; perhaps he found this story in the Greek *Physiologus* (see Chapter 5). But he still does not draw any conclusion from his new material.

Bishop Ambrose of Milan, one of the four Latin Fathers of the Church (340–397), agrees in his commentaries with the statement about the god who will gore the nations, but he also says something important about the genesis of the Unicorn:

"Who is this Unicorn but God's only son? The only word of God who has been close to God from the beginning! The word, whose horn shall cast down and raise up the nations?"[3]

With these words he enables image and poetry to depict the Unicorn at God's side in the Garden of Eden even before the creation of Adam, and it was not long before artists took up the theme, particularly in manuscripts and fresco painting.

"Bona cornua!" exclaims Ambrose. "Good horn, that runs through the lion, that great opponent." For Satan too bears horns, as spoken of by Daniel. He too saw that horn fighting a holy fight. Man himself has no horn with which to defend himself and accordingly: "Cornu nostrum es tu, Domine Jesus!" (Thou art our horn, Lord Jesus).[4] A chorus of voices greets us from zealous theologians stating with burning conviction what the Unicorn *must* signify when the Scriptures are read with attention. He is Christ. He is the horn-power which protects us. His horn signifies unity with the Father and is the centre post of the cross. It can protect but also pierce with the Father and is the centre post of the cross. It can protect but also pierce through, and at the Day of Judgement it will punish and gore the godless.

Many other theologians – not least the Byzantine – energetically wrote commentaries on the Unicorn. One of the most frequently cited is the great Greek Church Father, the Patriarch John Chrysostom, who lived in Constantinople from 398 to 403. His words on the Unicorn who is Christ were not only quoted in psalters and in natural histories, but also accompanied pictures of Chrysostom himself, standing in the attitude of prayer with outspread hands beside his verses.

About AD 600 the decisive step was taken towards the pictorial art of the medieval period. Two great writers were responsible: Gregory I, the Great, Pope from 590 to 604, and the Spanish bishop Isidore of Seville (560–636). In almost identical descriptions the Jewish and Hellenistic traditions unite, and they had far richer source material to make use of than their predecessors. Gregory is one of the first really to make use of the Physiologus. He is very interested in the Book of Job and gave a commentary on it in his so-called *Moralia in Job*. Here he takes God's words to Job, "Numquid volet rhinoceros servire te?" (Will the rhinoceros serve you?) and writes:

"Rhinoceros in Greek is called Monoceros. He is said to be so strong that the strongest hunter is unable to capture him. So, as they tell us, who study the nature of animals with assiduity [namely, the natural historians], a pure maiden is set before him, who, when he approaches, opens her lap to him, and he lays his head in her lap, thereby relinquishing all his wildness, so that he can be seized by those who seek to catch him."[5]

Floreffe Bible, detail
1165, British Museum, London,
see p.49

Gregory also says that he is the colour of the box tree and that sometimes he makes an attack on the elephant, being said to rip open its stomach with the horn that protrudes so uniquely from his nose, so that after wounding the softer parts he easily slays his enemies. He goes on:

"The Unicorn, as well as the rhinoceros, a chaste creature which will only allow itself to be coaxed by a pure virgin, signifies Christ, who only consented to be born of a virgin, and as newborn was laid in a crib."[6]

Here the Unicorn is clearly linked to Mary and the crib, and thus with the Incarnation itself. Gregory's *Moralia* was widely known and published in illustrated editions right up to 1400; it was part of the cultural heritage. In moralized Bibles of the Gothic period two medallions were juxtaposed, one with Job in his misery on the dung heap, with a Unicorn at his side drawing a harrow or plough; the other with the baby Jesus in a crib, with Mary. As a result of Gregory's somewhat uncertain attitude towards the rhinoceros, she sometimes sits with a little rhinoceros on her lap (see fig. on p.49). Gregory is especially interested in the ambivalence of the animal, for in the same passage he likens it to Saul, when he was "savage" and persecuted the Christians. God led this savage animal to the crib, fed him with Holy Scripture and harnessed him to his plough! This savage Saul became Paul. For God himself in his wisdom is able to tame the wild creature and turn it into a useful animal in his service, "Sapientia Dei".

A contemporary of Gregory, the venerable Spanish bishop Isidore of Seville, was quite a different sort of writer. It is not as an independent commentator, whose poetic or powerful interpretations would decide the development of symbols for centuries to come, that he is important to us, but rather as a preserver of tradition.

Isidore wrote a *Liber Etymologiae*, a "glossary" or dictionary , which is one of the first in the series of *summae* or surveys, containing the learned ballast of the time, that would later be so common. Obviously an encyclopedia like this from the seventh century is a goldmine, and Isidore never fails to supply an explanation for problems. These books were used in the monasteries as textbooks and reference books and held the authorized answer to everything, because they were always based on writers from antiquity and the early Church Fathers. So one can be almost certain that what is to be found in them had been regarded as general knowledge in monastic circles for centuries – and was consciously made use of by artists as a guide.

As Isidore is first and foremost a compiler, that is, a collector of earlier knowledge, he happily jumbles up Pliny with the Bible – and unfortunately also the Unicorn with Pliny's description of the rhinoceros in the arena, and uncritically continues Gregory's error. This affects the art of the following period:

"Rynoceron in grewe [Greek] is to meanynge an Horne in the nose. A Monoceros is an Unycorne: and is a ryght cruell beast. And hath that name for he hath in the mydull of the forehed an horne of foure fote long. And that horne is so sharpe and so strong that he throwyth downe al or thyrleth al that he resyth on . . . And this beest fyghtyth ofte wyth the Elyphaunt and woundyth and stycketh hym in the wombe, and throwyth hym downe to the grounde: And the Unycorn is so strong that he is not take with myghte of hunters. But men that wryte of kynde of thinges meane that a mayde is sette there he shall come: And she openythe her lappe and the Unycorne layeth theron his heed, and levyth all his fyerinesse and slepyth in that wyse: And is taken as a beest wythout wepen and slayne wyth dartys of hunters."[7]

In his notes Isidore refers to Pliny, Solinus, Aelian and Ctesias, and we can see that besides these he knows the current natural histories of Oriental origin. From then on, the story of the virgin becomes an integral element and starts to exercise its quiet influence.

All of these authors describe a large wild animal, which makes God's words to Job seem plausible. It can conquer the elephant and its strength symbolizes God as invincible. Emphasis is laid on the "Oneness", and again and again we see the expression "Unigenitus Unicornus" (the Only-begotten Unicorn), whose single horn is raised up for our salvation. The image of the mighty animal corresponds exactly to the weight laid by the period on Christ as hero and conqueror, when He descends to the Kingdom of the Dead and puts Satan in chains. It is possible, however, to tame the Unicorn and make it draw God's plough, and taming opens the way to a milder image which gained significance in the long run. The myth of the maiden, occasionally touched upon by the theologians, still remains as an undeveloped embryo in their writings, its far-reaching import as yet unrealized.

Like the lion and the dragon, the Unicorn continues to be ambivalent in interpretation and may be demonic: arrogant, lifting high its horn, the Jews who have only one testament, Death and even the Devil himself. Here the basis is Psalm 22, and the Unicorn is the "Princeps Terrenus" (Prince of the Earth), who attacks Christ on the cross as in the Stuttgart Psalter (see fig. on p.29). Accordingly, like so many symbols, the Unicorn can be interpreted only with certainty in a context, and it is very important to understand this. In practice this means that every single object included in a picture of the Unicorn affects its interpretation. Everywhere we come across the medieval urge to fill the world with similes pointing to the divine mysteries. Each

used in the service of the symbol: its size and behaviour, its horn and colour and its complex nature, and we meet bewildering variants in which the animal's goodness and ferocity clash in strange patterns.

The names, used at random – the Greek Monoceros and Rhinoceros and the Latin Unicornus – do nothing to lessen the confusion. It is true to say that, as usual, the medieval statements are colourful, poetic and profound – yet anything but unambiguous. There is no question, however, that the animal's most important function is to symbolize Christ. The Bible says so, the authorities say so; so there is no ground for doubt.

About 1100 we arrive at the Crusades, when Europeans first came into close contact with Arab culture, which had retained more lasting links with antiquity than the West. Interest was reawakened in classical literature, this time to be received more willingly by an established Church. We find abbots, abbesses and even worldly authors adopting the Unicorn, all of them enthroned on the treasures handed down to their libraries. As this Romanesque period was also the era of the great pilgrimages, when tales of adventure on long journeys, and the inhabitants and creatures of remote lands flourished, it was not strange that the world picture was considerably enlarged. Europe received and developed new literary forms, for instance, the Arthurian Legends, troubadour poetry, the Romance of Alexander and amplification of the repertoire of the natural historians.

Two of the most influential writers of this period are Honorius of Autun and Albertus Magnus. Honorius of Autun – called "Augustodunensis" after his town, founded by the Emperor Augustus – was active as a writer between 1106 and 1135. Like Isidore he is a medieval "compiler", the Christian scholar who knows his classics and conscientiously gathers in centuries of experience, in order that nothing shall be lost of all that man knows about God and the signs of His presence in all things. Honorius's *Speculum de Mysteriis Ecclesiae* (The Mirror of the Church's Mysteries), 1120, is as rich a source for us today as it was for the art of its own day, not least the passage on the birth of Christ, *De Nativitate Domini*:

"The extremely wild animal with a single horn is called the Unicorn. In order to capture it a Maiden is made to sit on the ground, the animal approaches her, and as it rests in her lap it is captured. By this animal is Christ represented, and by its horn His invincible strength. He, who laid himself in the body of the Virgin, has been captured by the huntsmen, that is: He was found in human form by those who love Him."[8]

Two important things are happening here. Because the Unicorn is identified with Christ, the story of the Virgin is associated with His conception, something which had been gradually approaching, and divine potency was linked with the horn. Besides this, the persecutors of the animal are now described as "those who love Him", that is, the Christian congregation in search of salvation, and thus the malice of the apparently hostile pursuers is underplayed. These significant sentences were included in the sermons given by Honorius and his monks on Lady Day, 25 March, and this linked the Annunciation and the Unicorn more and more closely in the listeners' consciousness. That is to say, we may perhaps give Honorius the credit for connecting definitively the Unicorn and the Annunciation. This might have occurred anyway; but he popularized the idea through his sermons, and his new interpretation of the huntsmen was certainly of considerable import.

In *De Imagine Mundi* (On the World Picture), which was a geography, the Unicorn appears as part of the Indian fauna, with the manticore, humans with dogs' heads and some of the other fabulous creatures that flocked through contemporary travel writing, and could actually be seen in Autun, carved on the great tympanum of the cathedral. In Honorius's description the Unicorn once again takes the form given it by Megasthenes, with elephant's feet, a loud roar and a horn 1.2 metres long. We have to acknowledge a dichotomy, however, between the large, savage creature from antiquity, which remained alive in travel literature particularly, because travellers relied on the ancient natural historians in their descriptions, and a smaller, gentler animal which could jump on to the Virgin's lap. Many reasons combined to make the time ripe for this adaptation of the Christ-animal.

One of the greatest authors of the thirteenth century is Albertus Magnus (1200–1280). He regards the Unicorn as a fundamental cosmic power imbuing the entire theological scene, but as he is a disciple of Aristotle he also seeks to make it "scientific", in the sense of this word in the Gothic period. This meant that although one consulted the Bible and the authorities for every sentence one wrote, one's own intelligence was called upon in dealing with the information. Both in his *Bestiarium* and in the *Summa de Creaturis* (also a natural history) Albertus mentions the Unicorn.

After acknowledging the Unicorn as Christ, with the overwhelming horn-power, he goes on to describe the ungovernable animal which raged through the Old Testament:

"This Unicorn revealed itself to be savage and excitable when, at the mere thought of the pride of Lucifer, it drove Adam out of the Garden of Eden because he ate of the apple and destroyed the primordial world with the Flood. So too He destroyed the Sodomites with the fire of Hell and brimstone. Thus the Unicorn raged in heaven and earth until our radiant Lady took Him in her lap when He penetrated her citadel – that is to say, into the lap of her chaste body, so that she could nurse Him at her breast and dress Him in humble flesh, and where – according to divine purpose – the unseizable animal might be captured by His pursuers, namely by Jews and Gentiles (the converted heathens) and voluntarily submit to death on the cross. As it runs in Job [39, 9–24]: Will the Unicorn be willing to serve thee! He will die of fury when he sees that He is captured. He swalloweth the ground with fierceness and rage. Thus did Christ die of the wrath He felt towards sinners."[9]

To Albertus the Unicorn is again Job's violent animal, suited so well to the scenes on the great church portals. He is the motivating power of cosmic events, has existed since the creation of the world and has a part in everything. He it is who drives Adam out, causes the Flood and the fall of Sodom and is so uncontrollable that his taming becomes a necessity and a heroic deed. The hero is to be Mary, who opens her gates to him like a castle. And then he gives himself up willingly to those who search him out – to Jews as well as heathens. The voluntary sacrificial death and humility of Christ are becoming newly important aspects of medieval thought and led similarly towards the creation of new motifs in the history of the Unicorn. The animal sensitively follows the fluctuations in thinking, now under the influence of a neo-Franciscan view of Christ, which slowly shifts the weight from the victorious hero traversing the Kingdom of Death to a humanized Saviour, who renounces his kingship for a while to share in the fortunes of humanity.

Albertus is also one of the great writers on alchemy, and with him ideas take their own winding paths, coloured by the secrets of the alembic. This accounts for his concentration on the womb, which to the alchemists was the alembic in which the Philosophers' Stone would form. Neither is Albertus blind to the sexual aspect: he emphasizes the perforating power of the horn, so that the subject approaches incest between mother and son, which would also come as no surprise to an alchemist.

In the writings of these theologians we can still see the shadow of the great animal of antiquity, kicking and striking. But something new is happening in Germany. Along the Rhine and in the Black Forest, in Thuringia and Saxony, the Unicorn begins to develop in quite a different manner.

The Unicorn is old in German culture. Germany's apostle, the holy Boniface, who lived at Fulda in the seventh century, had a kneeling Unicorn on the crooked head of his crosier, and the monks saw this as a symbol of meditative solitude in the wilderness and retained it on their monastery seal. Later, in the ninth century, a prelate of

RATGARII ABBATIS SCHEMA.

a sterner cast of mind ruled at Fulda, the abbot and architect Ratgar. During his time the monastery was rebuilt, under such tyranny that Ratgar was dubbed by his monks "Rampagenus Unicornus" (Raging Unicorn) and depicted standing in the vestibule of his church, crook in hand, while a Unicorn storms through the flock of sheep. An engraving in Antwerp dated 1612 reproduces an original illustration.

Something new is also happening in the nunneries. The nuns are taming the Unicorn. One of the most respected women of the time was Abbess Hildegard of Bingen (1098–1179), who became known as the "Sibyl of the Rhine". She was a contemporary of Honorius and Bernard of Clairvaux, and one of the quite numerous women who presided over convents and castles, and who left theological works behind them. Her book *Physica*, above all a natural history, following the trend of the time, also describes the Unicorn.

Hildegard tells us that the Unicorn is a very strong animal that lives in the forests. Once a year it goes to the rivers of Paradise and scrapes up the finest plants with its hoof and eats them. It cannot be caught in the usual manner; but the "natural historian", who for long searched in vain for a Unicorn, has seen how it can be done. Several maidens of good family – they must on no account be of country or farming stock – are to go for a walk in the forest. They must not be too old, nor children, but of a suitable age. When the Unicorn sees the girls gathering flowers, it stops short at once and looks at them; they look at it – and then it approaches very slowly, and sits down on its rump looking at them for a long time from a distance. It is surprised by the fact that although on the whole the girls look like human beings they have no beards, and it loves them because it sees they are mild and friendly, and while it stares at them and its wild and innocent heart is drawn to them in admiration, the huntsmen sneak up from behind, slay it and cut off its horn.[10]

Here we see a charm and an observation of small things that is unfamiliar in the male theologians. Despite the tragic climax of the story, everything takes place in a refined atmosphere among people of breeding. Hildegard emphasizes the social standing of the girls – one must take care where one selects one's novices! There is almost a touch of troubadour lyricism in the description, heightened by an addition: she mentions that beneath the animal's horn there is a little piece of metal or glass in which a man can see his own face. We shall meet this remarkable idea later in other contexts. It is the "carbuncle", described in the Arthurian legends of chivalry.

Strangely, Hildegard makes no mention of the usual Virgin story, but lays great weight on the healing properties of the animal. She writes:

"Take some Unicorn liver, crush it and blend it with egg yolk to an unguent. All kinds of leprosy can be healed if treated frequently with this salve, unless the patient is determined to die and God will not help him. For this animal's liver possesses a good, pure heat, and the yolk is the most valuable part of the egg and like an ointment. Leprosy is often caused by black bile and by phlegmatic black blood. Take some Unicorn leather and cut a belt of it and put it round the body. It wards off attacks of plague or fever. Make shoes of Unicorn leather as well and wear them. This ensures healthy feet, thighs and joints, nor will the plague ever attack these limbs. Aside from these parts, nothing of the Unicorn can be used medicinally."[11]

This passage is typical of the medieval style of medical book and the remedies available to the convents for their nursing. The last sentence is rather odd, for it shows that Hildegard apparently did not know about – or discounted – the healing properties of the horn itself, which was just then becoming dominant in medieval pharmacy. Otherwise this passage may be the first Unicorn prescription known, possibly acquired from Arab sources.

A different hand later made an addition to the manuscript:

"Those who fear poisoning should place the hoof of a Unicorn under the plate containing his food, or the beaker that holds his drink. If hot food and drink are poisoned the hoof will make them 'sweat'; if they are cold it will make them steam. Thus one can discover whether they are poisoned or no."

Here is the first mention of the "sweat" which later became one of the surest symptoms; though it is the *horn* which is to sweat usually, not the food; so the author must have misunderstood this.

Both passages reflect current medical ideas, reproducing Hippocrates' teaching on the four temperaments, the harmful influence of bile, and the relation between "cold" and "hot". The philosophers of the time consider the Unicorn to be of a "caldissima natura", hot and fiery, which is therefore attracted by the "femina frigida et humida", the coolness and dampness of femininity. Hildegard thinks likewise. In astronomical terms, this means that the sun is drawn by the moon, as masculine to feminine, since opposites attract. This is the Virgin myth transposed into science in the medieval sense, that is, explained with the aid of the elements and the theory of the mutual attraction of opposites. We shall meet the same way of thinking when the medicinal properties of the horn are defined (see Chapter 18).

Abbot Ratgar, the "Raging Unicorn"
Engraving, 1612, Antwerp

This engraving is based on an illustration in the *Life of Abbot Eigil of Fulda*, 9th century

CHAPTER 5
"Physiologus Says ..."

At various times the word "Physiologus" has been mentioned as an important pawn in the Unicorn game and it seems appropriate now to take a closer look at this phenomenon. Physiologus – literally "one well-versed in natural science" or merely "the natural historian" – is the usual term for the medieval books on flora and fauna that carried on the tradition of the ancient natural histories, but with the addition of Christian morality. The continued use of the expression "Physiologus says ..." turned the word into a proper name, which was regarded as that of an original author. When these books were later translated from Latin into various languages they were simply called bestiaries.

The "progenitor" is a Greek manuscript whose author was said to be none other than Aristotle, or alternatively King Solomon. This shows the respect in which the work was held; it was read almost as much as the Bible. The actual author is uncertain but Didymus of Alexandria is thought to be a candidate, a writer during the flourishing of the city between AD 150 and 200. There is no trace of the Alexandrian original; but seventy-seven manuscript copies are known, among them several from the scholarly monasteries of Mount Athos.

There are four editions of the manuscript, variations on a basic theme. The first, which is closest to the Greek original, is found in Syrian, Arabic, Georgian and Ethiopian versions. They form the basis of the Latin translation, which was probably produced about AD 400, that is, more or less contemporary with the Vulgate Bible. Over the centuries this group turned into the popular bestiaries in many national languages, and the crucial point for us is that the books in this group all speak of a "Monoceros" or "Unicornus". We need not concern ourselves with the three other groups; suffice it to say that the Byzantine examples, from which the Russian and Romanian bestiaries derive, make *no* mention of the Unicorn.

Didymus of Alexandria's *Physiologus Graecus* of about AD 200 was a book of some fifty fables on animals, plants and minerals, with a Christian interpretation. The Unicorn is depicted as a swift animal with a long horn on its forehead and hostile to human beings. It cannot be captured, but when a Virgin is thrown to it, it leaps into her lap and she warms the animal with tenderness, so that she is able to carry it up to the king's palace. This fable was not invented by Christian theologians, therefore, but taken from Greek natural history and myth. It had come to stay.

As early as about AD 300 the story appears in detail in a Syrian variant of the basic Greek text.[1] Here again we find a description of an animal which cannot be captured; but if the huntsmen bring out a young and chaste maiden, the animal will approach her and fall upon her. The girl offers it her breasts and it suckles from her and lays its head in her lap. Then the girl puts out her hand and seizes the horn on its forehead, so that the huntsmen can come up, catch the animal and take it off to the king. The story ends in a comparison with the Horn of Salvation which Christ raised for us in Jerusalem through the mediation of the Mother of God, who is a pure virgin, chaste and full of grace.

Some of these texts, earlier or contemporary with the first Latin Bible, have already incorporated the Indian seduction myth that suggests the sexual nature of the Unicorn, although this is absent from the Vulgate. Once the connection with Christ and His mother Mary has also been established, the two animals, originally completely different, cross each other's path. This takes place when the theologians begin to consult Physiologus on the character of the one-horned creature. Isidore of Seville refers to those "who write on the nature of the animals". Physiologus becomes the authority and before long the story of the Virgin slips into a new context – as in Gregory the Great's *Moralia in Job* mentioned earlier.

Some people felt uneasy about the process. At a synod in Rome in 496, Pope Gelasius I condemned the myth of the Virgin as heresy and for a time included the Physiologus itself on the list of forbidden books. But it was too late. The two different genres had been inseparable for too long and had begun to borrow and learn from each other.

We have seen that Physiologus contains some Oriental features, but it is saturated with Christianity as well and speedily takes quotations at first from the Septuagint and later from the Vulgate and the commentaries of the theologians. Time and again one comes across expressions such as: "Ita est Salvator noster" (Thus is our Saviour), "Sic est Dominus noster" (Such is Our Lord), "Iesus Christus spiritualis Unicornis" (Jesus Christ the spiritual Unicorn). These expressions give the effect of being superimposed upon the zoological descriptions, especially during the first centuries; but later the two "cultures" merge. Unfortunately, the natural historians had a tendency to bring the rhinoceros on to the scene, and bred some remarkable hybrids, both literary and figurative.

It is a common feature of the Physiologus texts that they are indeed "natural histories", representing the zoological knowledge of their time; but they are also moral allegories, because everything in nature is a word in God's great dictionary and created for the enlightenment of man. This aspect comes to dominate in the course of time, living up to a pronouncement of St Augustine: "What concerns us is what the animals signify; whether it is true does not affect us."[2]

This medieval thought process is hard to understand in a time like our own, when facts are everything. But to a medieval person it was not particularly interesting how many teeth or toes an animal might have — or even whether it existed. The decisive factor was what it signified in its behaviour. The creature is a mathematical diagram with many parallel lines. Christ and the Unicorn form one of these pairs, and it is the task of man to arrive at a cognition of them and learn from them. If we want to learn about the medieval way of thinking today and enrich our own time with it we must not be blind to this concept of nature, but see animals and plants as *signa* (signs) and not merely as physical existences without any deeper significance.

Naturally the early texts resembled each other, but contained small variations, depending on the different scribes. Some emphasized the importance of chastity in the Virgin and that the animal was actually lured by "the scent of her chastity", and that if it felt deceived it would run its horn through her. Thus the Unicorn could be used as a "virgin test". Others maintained that the Virgin should be naked — even tied to a tree. This is an interesting reminder that Virgin, Unicorn and tree originally belonged together, and that the Unicorn touches tree and Virgin with its horn.

The Arab versions emphasized the erotic aspect of the meeting far more. The Unicorn licks the girl's breasts and is very free with her; the consequences of the suckling are clear and indicate that the girl is no virgin but a concubine. That accords with the Oriental mentality, which traditionally involves the concubine in religious rituals and service in the temple, but it may not have been inadvertent that the Arabs placed the animal in disquieting proximity to the mother of their God.

As the years passed the texts increased at the hands of numerous anonymous authors. The number of the animals included rose to almost two hundred and the stories were expanded. They were merged with folk beliefs, travellers' tales and free fantasizing. Writers and theologians stimulated each others' imagination — and what beasts emerged!

At the beginning of the Gothic period the contrast between the large and small versions of the Unicorn were so marked that it was divided into two types. An example of this is the frequently cited bestiary from Cambridge, which was translated into English by T. H. White:

"The MONOCEROS is a monster with a horrible howl, with a horse-like body, with feet like an elephant, and with a tail like a stag's.

A horn sticks out from the middle of its forehead with astonishing splendour to the distance of four feet, so sharp that whatever it charges is easily perforated by it. Not a single one has ever come alive into the hands of man, and, although it is possible to kill them, it is not possible to capture them."

The other animal is called Unicornus, and is described as follows:

"He is a very small animal like a kid, excessively swift, with one horn in the middle of his forehead, and no hunter can catch him. But he can be trapped by the following stratagem.

A virgin girl is led to where he lurks, and there she is sent off by herself into the wood. He soon leaps into her lap when he sees her, and embraces her, and hence he gets caught.

Our Lord Jesus Christ is also a Unicorn spiritually, about whom it is said: 'And he was beloved like the Son of the Unicorns.' And in another psalm: 'He hath raised up a horn of salvation for us in the house of his son David.'

The fact that it has just one horn on its head means what he himself said: 'I and the Father are One.' Also, according to the Apostle: 'The head of Christ is the Lord.'

It says that he is very swift because neither Principalities, nor Powers, nor Thrones, nor Dominations could keep up with him, nor could Hell contain him, nor could the most subtle Devil prevail to catch or comprehend him; but, by the sole will of the Father, he came down into the virgin womb for our salvation.

It is described as a tiny animal on account of the lowliness of his incarnation, as he said himself: 'Learn from me, because I am mild and lowly of heart'

It is like a kid or scapegoat because the Saviour himself was made in the likeness of sinful flesh, and from sin he condemned sin.

The Unicorn often fights with elephants, and conquers them by wounding them in the belly."[3]

Here are two greatly differing animals from two chief sources. The first passage repeats almost literally Megasthenes and Aelian and thus makes no mention of the Virgin story. From now on this animal is lost to theology but continues in natural history and travel writing, as a rule under the Greek name of Monoceros.

The other animal is a little cloven-hoofed goat or oryx, and its most important function is in the Virgin story as an image of Christ. Here the sources are the theologians and the earlier Physiologi; only the last lines slip into an amusing insert from the ancient source, when the little goat suddenly starts to play the gigantic Cartazon from Megasthenes and go for the elephant.

The two passages clearly show the compilatory method used in the bestiaries, reminiscent of the usual practice in convent scriptoria. In this way the texts proliferate from time to time, and new features are faithfully reproduced: "It is said that . . ." And each time something new and imaginative is said, it enriches the basic theme and creates a colourful treasure chest for the artists of the time.

In the second passage we find "Principalities, Powers, Thrones and Dominations". These are the names of the most powerful of the nine hierarchies of angels that formed God's army. The passage shows how the Physiologus is now engaged in composing a universe, in which angels, devils, virtues, vices and huntsmen take their places in a great cosmic drama ripe for transformation into stage plays and art. The whole universe is set out like a vast stage-set around the Virgin and the Unicorn.

Before long the concepts of the theologians and the natural historians are so enmeshed that they can no longer be distinguished.

Now the Unicorn is assigned another attribute not previously described in Europe: the ability to purify water. As this is an important prerequisite for the understanding of later Flemish tapestries (see Chapters 12–14), I here cite a Greek *Physiologus* from the fourteenth century:

> "An animal exists which is called Monoceros. In the regions where he lives there is a great lake, and there the animals gather to drink. But before they arrive the serpent goes and spews his poison into the water. Now when the animals notice the poison they dare not drink but wait for the Monoceros. It comes and straightway goes into the water, makes the sign of the cross with its horn and thus annuls the power of the poison. And when it starts to drink the water all the animals do likewise."[4]

This is the Christianized animal from Vourukasha, the world sea, which – now with the sign of the cross – cleanses the water of the poison of the evil creatures and consecrates it, so that the other animals can drink. A "holy communion image" or a consecration of the baptismal water is being created. The priest too made the sign of the cross over the water of the font to sanctify it for the baptism and drive out the poison of the Great Enemy. The fact that faith in the power of the horn to nullify poison was growing may have contributed to the popularity of the image. However that may be, the theme rapidly found a place in pictorial art.[5]

We will close this chapter with a short passage from the Danish chapbook *Lucidarius*. It was originally called *Elucidarius* (The Enlightened or The Lightbearer) and was a popular version of the writings of Honorius of Autun. The earliest copy dates from the twelfth century, but the text was so much in demand that it survived the invention of printing and was brought out in a German edition in 1480 and in a Danish one twenty-five years later. It was a continuation of the bestiaries but with an expanded repertoire, and its dialogue between a "master" and a "disciple" made it a popular textbook in geography, natural history and ethics, padded out with a healthy layer of Bible history:

"Disciple: Tell me about the singular animals of the world.

Master: There is one particular animal called Unicorn, which has one horn on the front of its head and is six feet long; its horn gives off a shine like a carbuncle. No one can capture that animal except a pure maiden clean of sin, and if she seats herself before the animal it goes up to her and falls on its knees and lays its head in her lap and falls so fast asleep that she may kill the animal. The panther also does the same."[6]

**Smyrna Physiologus
with text by Cosmas**
Manuscript, *c.* 900, originally
Scola Evangelica, Smyran, cod.
B8 (destroyed
in 1922)

The Virgin, with a Byzantine
crown, lifts her hand in a
speaking gesture and the
Unicorn listens

CHAPTER 6

Pictorial Art in the Middle Ages

So how was all this represented in art? As we have seen, the Unicorn of antiquity was solely a literary figure, and we have no pictures of it before the drawing made by Cosmas the India-farer after his journey to "Ethiopia" about AD 500. The original is lost, but travel descriptions were copied again and again with their illustrations, and Cosmas's Unicorn has survived in copies in the Vatican and the Biblioteca Laurentiana in Florence.

The Laurentiana copy, from the ninth century, shows a type of antelope with a long upright horn which corresponds to the author's own description (see fig. on p.23): ". . . and all his strength is in his horn." This archetype, which agrees with the ancient concept of the animal and may possibly have been inspired by the Persian bronze figures, was repeated in manuscripts and mosaics up to the year 1000.

The Unicorn must have been associated with a Virgin from as early as the sixth century, for from the Carolingian period – between 800 and 1000 – there exist a dozen or so illustrated manuscripts, both psalters and Physiologi, which roughly copy earlier sources. In all of them it is Cosmas's great antelope with which the Virgin entertains herself.

In the earliest surviving illustrated Physiologus manuscript, the Greek one known as the Smyrna Physiologus from the tenth century, as also in two psalters from Mount Athos and Moscow, we see the Virgin with the Unicorn. She sits upright on a chair or stool with long unbound hair, sometimes adorned with a crown or diadem, amusing herself with a Unicorn. The animal is large, so large that it can look the Virgin in the eye and certainly could not leap into her lap. It has to content itself with placing a great foot on one of her knees. It has a long curved horn, smooth or ridged, standing vertically on its head, and looks now like a horse, now an antelope or oryx with a tufted tail. Some examples have hoofs, but most have claws on all four feet. They are thus in line with the ancient image and are muscular creatures, doubtless dangerous to their surroundings and certainly not easy to catch.

Nevertheless, the wild animal is peaceful; there is an intimacy between Virgin and Unicorn. It either wears a collar, or she stretches out her hand to it, blesses it or offers it her breast. She is not afraid of it. But she is no ordinary virgin: in some cases a medallion hangs above her head showing a Byzantine Madonna and Child, which indicates the symbolism, and below there may be a St John Chrysostom in the attitude

Theodore-Psalter
Miniature, 1066, British Museum, London, Ms. Add. 19352 fol. 124

A noble lady blesses a Unicorn. The artist, Theodore the priest, has placed a golden medallion depicting Mary and the Child, linking the Incarnation to the Unicorn myth. Below, the Greek Church Father John Chrysostom, with the inscription: "Chrysostom spoke concerning the Unicorn"

Opposite
Berne Physiologus
9th century, Burgerbibliothek, Berne, Ms. cod. 318, f. 16v.

The earliest illustrated Latin text depicting a Unicorn

mergit intenebris peccatorem · perfecti autem
& cauti nonadpropinquant ei · Qualiserat ioseph
apudmulierem aegyptiam · qualiserat helias
Iezabel arguens · Qualiserat susanna inmedio
seniorum · Bene ergo similataé mulier huic pisce ·

DE ANIMALE UNICORNIUM

Inpsalmo sicdicit · exaltabitur sicut unicornis cornum meum · phisiologus deeodicit · quodminor sit
animal · Est autem animal simile edum mansuetum
ualde unicornu hab& supcaput · & nonpotestuenator
adpinquare ei ppt quoduualde fortissimu hab&
cornum · quando tam tripudiando discurrit sicmo
do conprehenditur · proicitur anteeum uirgo cas

PICTORIAL ART IN THE MIDDLE AGES

47

of prayer. The Chludoff Psalter includes the words "John Chrysostom speaks of the Unicorn as the Son of God" or "John Chrysostom spoke of the Unicorn." In the Pantocrator Psalter, where the Virgin reveals her breast, Psalm 92 is again cited: "Thou shalt exalt my horn like the horn of the Unicorn." It is clear that the artists were fully aware of the identification with Christ.

In most of the early illustrations we look in vain, however, for a halo around the woman's head. This is particularly evident in the Physiologus. Here the woman is subordinate to the Unicorn and performs a service in the universe of natural history. She is chaste and up to a point can be *compared* with the Madonna; but she does not yet *represent* Mary, and it is clear that a differentiation was made between them.

The earliest group of Latin Physiologi contains two renowned illustrations that reveal new features: the Berne Physiologus and the Brussels Physiologus. The Berne manuscript, from the ninth century, is the earliest illustrated Latin example (see fig. on p.47) in existence. Here the

woman stands upright before a goat-like, delicate blue-grey Unicorn with a shorter horn, sickle-shaped like a moon. The woman, dressed in classical drapery, stretches forth her hand and holds it gently by the mouth. Around them nature is suggested, for the first time: a slope which allows the smaller animal to assume a suitable height, and trees indicating "silva" – a forest. The text states that after taming the Unicorn she will lead it quickly to the king's residence. We see only half of the story, but there is enough to give a satisfactory impression of the whole.

We can see what the whole looked like from the slightly earlier Brussels Physiologus. Both may have had a common origin in Carolingian art. Two pictures, one above the other on a single page, tell the story, in a delicate Carolingian line drawing, in which concentric lines indicate the curves of bodies without shadows. In the top picture a king sits enthroned in his hall. He gestures to a servant to usher in a maiden and the servant holds her by the wrist. She looks behind her and stretches her free hand with a friendly movement towards a Unicorn emerging from the forest. As before, she touches its muzzle and entices it to go with her. In the lower picture Christ stands just beneath the king and speaks to two Apostles. According to

The Stammheim Missal
c. 1150, Abbey of St Michael,
Hildesheim, coll. Baron
Caspar von Fürstenberg

A strictly ritual birth scene is
surrounded by Mary's chastity
symbols. Ezekiel points down
at the "Porta clausa", which is
flanked by Gideon with his
fleece and, on the right, the
Virgin seated with her
Unicorn

Opposite
**God Creates the Animals,
Hortus Deliciarum**
c. 1150, facsimile in Odense
University Library, Denmark
(original burned 1870)

The wild Unicorn of
antiquity with its black sickle
horn has taken a place
opposite the lion, still
untamed

the text he quotes these words from Matthew's Gospel: "Discite a me, quia mitis sum
et humilis corde." (Learn from me, for I am mild and humble of heart.) At the side
appears the usual representation of the Virgin, sitting on a stool and caressing the
Unicorn. It could almost be an illustration to the ancient story of Gazelle Horn!
The Virgin tames the animal and is able to lead it to the king's residence. Christ, the
parallel, is present himself and speaks of his humility: again, the basic figure and
symbol are in the same space. There are still no huntsmen or pursuers. Dare we conclude from this that a seated woman with a Unicorn at this period can refer to the
whole complicated context?

During the following centuries the woman with the animal is one of the most
highly regarded single motifs in Europe. The Unicorn is Christ and in alliance with
an innocent Virgin is a symbol for chastity. In an endless series of capitals, vault
bosses, textiles and book covers, the woman sits in state with the Unicorn, she grasps
its horn, puts her arms around its neck, or the animal lays its head "in sinu" – on her
breast – or "in gremio" – in her lap – and becomes more and more gentle and
amenable. The manuscripts are numerous and varied: to begin with there are the
many bestiaries, in which the Unicorn is primary and the Virgin an adjunct to the
animal. There are the psalters, in which the emblem may be in the margin or beside
the relevant psalm, especially Psalms 77 or 92 (whereas Psalm 22: "Save me from the
lion's mouth . . ." was illustrated with Christ on the cross). Finally, the motif occurs
in Gregory's *Moralia in Job*. Here it plays a part in a complicated whole, representing
Christ's Incarnation and is placed together with a birth scene, perhaps prompted by
the line "Will it take sustenance at thy crib"?

In the beautiful Floreffe Bible of 1165 a whole page is divided in two: above is a
birth scene watched over by angels. Below, the Virgin sits between two enthroned
persons: on the left the Evangelist Matthew holding his symbol and, on the right, Job
with his cheek on his hand regarding the Virgin, who has her arms around a little
animal. The sickle-shaped horn has slipped right down on to its nose, reminding us
of the unfortunate cross-breeding with the rhinoceros. From a cloud above her head
the hand of God appears, holding a scroll on which are the words to Job: "Nunquid
alligabis rinocerotum ad arandum loro tuo?" (Canst thou bind the Unicorn with his
band in the furrow? (Job 39, 10)). As this illustration is on the front page of the
Gospel of Matthew, the Virgin with the animal is directly linked to Christ "born of
woman", and in this way the motif is quietly associated with the Annunciation itself.

In the almost contemporary Stammheim Missal of 1150, the page of illustration
is still further divided up. Mary lies in the central panel beneath the crib and around
her is, as it were, a wreath of strange figures, symbols of her virginity: at the top
kneels Moses before the Burning Bush from which God peeps out, and on the left he
himself stands pointing at the crib and the child. Below stands Ezekiel, indicating
the closed door he saw in a vision, and opposite is Joseph with his Jew's hat. At the
bottom, the portal is flanked by Gideon with his Fleece and the Virgin with the
Unicorn, now with a slim horn on its neck. In this ensemble the animal takes its place
among symbols of chastity, and we can see that it is a dynamic symbol whose
meaning changes according to the context: the first picture illustrates the Incarnation
of Christ linked with a commentary to Job, the second shows the virginity of Mary.
In both the Unicorn appears, but with slightly different connotations.

THE UNICORN

These pictures lead us to another theme beloved by the medieval scholars, the motif of Mary in the *Hortus Conclusus* (enclosed garden), or as in Germany, *Maria im Rosengarten*, which in the Gothic period developed with the intensive cultivation of Mary's innocence. Preoccupation with the spotless purity of the Madonna, amounting almost to an obsession at times, was nourished by the sermons of Bernard of Clairvaux and his commentaries on the Song of Solomon, from which many of the symbols derived. The theme itself comes from this source, where the bridegroom speaks to his bride and praises her in the most vivid and poetic words he can find:

"A garden enclosed is my sister, my spouse; a spring shut up, a fountain sealed." (Song of Solomon 4, 12)
"A fountain of gardens, a well of living waters, and streams from Lebanon." (Song of Solomon 4, 15)

Here already the most important elements are present:

The garden with the sealed and the open fountain. Mary is at one and the same time the bride and the garden, and she is placed in the circular or more often square garden, whose wall or wattle fence is furnished with a gate. Moreover she is surrounded with a number of emblems taken mostly from descriptive passages in the Song of Solomon, or other passages in the Bible which indicate her immaculate state: the well with running water refers to the profusion of the Gospel streaming through Mary in the figure of Christ.

The Utrecht Psalter
1413, British Museum, London,
Ms. Add. 10043, fol. 4v.

The gentle white Unicorn
stands directly under the hand
of God. Its antithesis is not
the lion, but the monkey

The spring shut up and *fountain sealed* refer to the inviolable virginity of Mary.

The ivory tower describes Mary's radiant beauty: "Thy neck is as a tower of ivory" (Song of Solomon 7, 4).

The closed gate. Another important symbol was taken from Ezekiel 44, 2. The prophet Ezekiel is taken in a vision to the outer east gate of the Sanctuary, which he sees is closed, and the Lord says: "This door is to be closed and must not be opened! None may enter through it, for the Lord God of Israel entered by it; therefore it shall be closed." A clearer description of Mary's virginity could hardly be imagined, and this "porta clausa" or "conclusa" is found in almost every single enclosed garden, with a proper lock.

The Burning Bush comes from Exodus 3, 2. The Lord reveals himself to Moses in a bush "burning with fire", but it is not consumed. Yet another symbol of Mary's virginity.

The pot of manna or *golden urn* is from Exodus 16, 33: "And Moses said unto Aaron: Take a pot, and put an omer full of manna therein, and lay it up before the Lord, to be kept for your generations." Mary is the golden container of the saving manna. As a rule the illustration shows a bucket or crock with round discs, the traditional shape of the oblate, for the communion bread is the manna of the Christian.

The Ark of the Covenant symbolizes Mary, who carries the Word of God within herself.

The Staff of Aaron (Numbers 17, 1–10) An altar carries twelve staves – one for each tribe – and the central one, Aaron's, carries either a white dove or a flower.

Gideon's Fleece is taken from Judges 6, 33–40: Gideon lays a fleece on the ground at night in order to test God's word. The next morning everything is drenched with dew, except the fleece, thereby symbolizing the purity of the Virgin Mary in the midst of a sinful world. The next night the opposite is the case: only the fleece is wet. Now Mary has been sprinkled with God's heavenly dew, as the Magnificat says.

Flowers. Lastly, the garden teems with flowers, all reflecting Mary's virtues, such as purity, humility and queenly dignity: roses, lilies, violets, columbine, iris and daisies.

Another theme appears at this time. This is the Unicorn in the Garden of Eden. Ambrose's statement that the Unicorn was the Son of God, who had been close to the Father from the beginning (see p.32) and Albertus Magnus's description of the cosmic power which raged against Sodom provided artists with new motifs. The Unicorn is even present during the Six Days of Creation and thus takes its place in Eden itself. From the ninth century onwards art varied the motif in endless permutations. The Unicorn stays close to God when the animals are created. It is present when Man is created and receives its name from Adam at the same time as the other animals. It looks on during the Fall, and stirs up the waters of Paradise with its horn as a sign of salvation to come.

A good example is the image of Creation in Herrad of Landsberg's great picture book, the *Hortus Deliciarum* (Garden of Paradise) of 1170 (see fig. on p.51).[1] The Lord walks over the world sea surrounding Eden and, with outstretched hands, he creates animals on all sides: peacocks, oxen, horses and swans garland the rocks around Him. At His left hand sits the Unicorn with a black horn, and opposite sits the lion. As early as this, the antagonistic relationship between them is established; but in Paradise they must keep a good countenance. As the accompanying German verse says: "Der lewe und das Einhurne borgen beide ir zorne – swenne si dien stimme uernemen ir grimme schylen si hin legen . . ."[2] (The Lion and the Unicorn hide their rage – as long as they can hear Thy voice, they leave off their ferocious scowling.) In the *Hortus Deliciarum* the Unicorn is seen as a savage animal that rages against sin and in this book's Judgement Day picture it has a human foot protruding from its jaws. This interpretation corresponds to the view of Christ presented in the earliest theologians.

In the Utrecht Bible of 1431 we see the milder type preferred by the Gothic period: God blesses his animal with a kindly hand on its horn, and behind Him is a different kind of antithesis, this time the slightly shady ape scratching its backside. The Christ creature is confronted with sinful Man's ugliest caricature, the ape, which gradually replaces the lion as the symbol of the Devil.

When Adam gives the animals their names, he plays Orpheus and calls long rows of creatures to him, and the first among them is the Unicorn (which also receives its name from Adam). Sometimes the ape brings up the rear of the troop. The Unicorn is also given special preference by appearing at the creation of Eve. The reason for this is not hard to find: Eve was the first woman and it was through her disobedience that everything went wrong. The Virgin Mary was the new Eve who by her very ∩be-

The Temptation of Adam and Eve
in *La Bible Historiée de Antoine Vérard*, Paris, 1499, Metropolitan Museum of Art, New York

Stag and Unicorn stand facing a monkey with an apple. The picture has many stylistic features in common with the Verteuil tapestries and may be from the same studio

dience was to restore humanity by receiving the Unicorn into her body. Following the strong desire of the time to join up the threads in God's great pattern, the animal of atonement was often placed together with the cause of the Fall, Eve. In a miniature from 1400 God creates Eve from the man's side, and above her head rises the Unicorn. It hovers like a vision above our first ancestress, the maidenly Eve. Woman and animal meet for the first time. The picture takes on its full significance when we remember the other illustration: the little goat which jumps into another Virgin's lap.

There are two murals in Denmark in which the Unicorn takes part in the Creation, in the churches of Gjerrild and Hyllested, in the Djursland area of East Jutland. They are both thought to have been painted by an artist known as the Brarup Master, about 1500, and are part of a large Creation cycle in the vaults of the nave. At Gjerrild God is busily engaged in creating. He strolls among the trees of his garden, and large birds with feet like maple leaves take off from His hands. Beneath His right hand, raised in benediction, stands a Unicorn with short legs, almost touching a tree between it and the Creator.

At Hyllested we see the Garden of Eden where Adam was created, as part of a large illustration of the Creation. In the north vault compartment Adam sleeps, stretched out at full length with his hand under his cheek, on a large yellow mound of clay. The Lord has one of his ribs in his hand, and Eve is already growing out of it. Below Adam there is a Unicorn. Its long tail is knotted and swung back almost to its neck. Its horn is turned down and its jaws open to resist the three baying hounds approaching from the left. The leading hound has its tongue hanging out and wears a spiked collar; this aggressive pack makes us think of the depictions of Unicorn hunts. The scene could be interpreted as the Unicorn already defending the first human beings against the attacks of the Devil; but as the hound seems to be attacking the Unicorn itself, it may also mean that the animal is looking at the hounds that will one day drive it into the Virgin's lap, in atonement for the folly of the parents of mankind. The combination of the images is certainly most unusual.

As the mystical adoration of the body and blood of Christ gradually increased during the Gothic period, to be explored further in the next chapter, the images slowly changed from the lucid, easily comprehended scenes in the Garden of Eden into complex allegories that filled the picture with literary symbols, often taken from the action and properties of church dramas. As time went by, the reader came to need an almost encyclopaedic expertise to understand them. An altar frontal from Zurich of about 1480 demonstrates such an allegory.

A strange ritual is being enacted in an enclosed Paradise Garden: Adam – man and hunter – pierces the Unicorn with a spear. Eve – Ecclesia/Church – catches its

The Creation
Vault painting, *c.* 1500, Gjerrild church, Denmark

Opposite
God presenting Eve to Adam
Miniature, Boucicaut Master, *c.* 1410, Bibliothèque Nationale de France, Paris

Within the peaceful circle of Eden, God joins their hands and the animals bow their heads in reverence; the spring of Paradise flows out before the feet of God, so that the animals can drink

Left
The Creation of Eve
Vault painting, *c.* 1500, Hyllested church, Denmark

Eve's creation is acclaimed by the animal, with its raised hoof and lowered horn

God Creating the Earth, detail
Workshop of Raphael, *c.* 1515, Vatican Museum and Galleries, Rome

Let us conclude this chapter with a powerful image of God the creator from the Renaissance. With outspread hands, He causes animals and birds to creep up out of the earth. The Unicorn lifts horn and hoof, as always in Italy, in the figure of a horse

blood in a chalice. Gabriel is there with some hounds, and around the outside we see a number of symbolic animals: the pelican gashes its own breast so that the blood flows, a lion resuscitates its young with its warm breath, and carnations grow in the flowerbeds. Everything points to blood sacrifice. The scene is like a digest of the mythological drama of the age, which portrays the Fall of Man, his burden of sin and resultant craving for cleansing blood and final redemption. It is given words in the accompanying verse: " . . . but He is wounded on account of our sins – and by His blood we are saved."

These few examples taken from centuries of illustration to the story of the Creation must suffice to show how perception of the biblical drama alters – and the Unicorn with it. The animal changes from the powerful opponent of the lion to the gentle creature beneath the Creator's blessing hand, white and pure compared with the ape – and further to the sacrificial animal whose blood flows for the salvation of mankind. The variations are countless, but they are never fortuitous.

THE UNICORN

CHAPTER 7

The Unicorn and the Huntsmen

In the pictures we have been considering there is an absence of pursuers. It is the Virgin herself who leads the Unicorn to the king's castle, gently and without violence. Although the natural historians describe various scenes in which *exploratores* (scouts) or *insidiatores* (trappers) carry off or slay the animal, there is no trace of this in the illustrations. About 1100, however, this theme began to be illustrated as well. The first examples are found in marginal illustrations, where the Unicorn leaps through the branches confronted by a single huntsman, who raises his bow and takes aim at it. Before long a linking of this hunting theme and the virgin scene develops to cover the event described in Physiologus: "... and at that moment the huntsmen come and seize the prey."

The maiden is seated in a landscape, as a rule leaning against a tree. The animal, still quite large and with a long sabre of a horn, seeks refuge in her lap, while one or more huntsmen approach. In the earliest pictures they seize the animal by the hind legs or put a noose round its neck, which does not indicate an immediate kill but a means of taking it away. Later they attack it with axe, sword and lance and, as time passes, one version came to dominate, in which a huntsman pierces the animal's flank with a spear, and the bleeding animal sinks down on to the Virgin's lap, with its head on her breast. Naturally this combination does not occur by chance. For this is the *Pietà*, in which Christ lies dead in His mother's arms after the Crucifixion, and she laments over Him. The interpretation is emphasized by the tree that often grows immediately behind the animal, between the Virgin group and the pursuers: the Tree of Life, closely connected with the Unicorn itself (see fig. on p.58).

However, it is not easy to make a completely precise interpretation of the motif. The problem is, who exactly are the huntsmen? You might think it was straightforward: surely the idea comes from the accounts of huntsmen who place a virgin in the forest so that they – "The King's Men" – may capture the animal and take its horn. But who are the king's men in a Christian context? We might think that they are simply the wicked murderers of Christ, that is, the Jews. Although some of the earliest Physiologi state this, later medieval scholars did not see it the same way. For at that time there is a tendency to justify the divine sacrifice. The huntsmen are not shown as Jews; on the contrary, they are Christian knights in armour, sometimes accompanied by a Moor. The motif of the blow with the lance runs parallel with the

Unicorn Hunt
Illumination in a bestiary,
c. 1250, British Museum,
London, MS. Harley 4571,
fol. 6v

An initial depicts the maiden
sitting with the animal among
three trees; three men kill it
with sword, axe and lance. The
scene is framed by geometrical
symbols for the divine and the
earthly, respectively the circle
and the square.

Longinus legend, in which the soldier mentioned in the Gospel of St John (John 19, 34) is seen as a saint precisely because he pierces Christ's side with his lance and thus releases the stream of sacred blood which is God's great gift to man. The lance itself becomes a noble relic and is central to the Legend of the Holy Grail.

The sum of all these details is a manifestation of the growing cult of the Body of Christ, the worship of the Sacred Blood, which leads naturally to a glorification of the action which is a requirement for the salvation of the congregation, that is, the piercing of Christ's body. The action is a necessity, and he who executes it is a tool in God's hand – not a criminal. Here we may return to the words of Honorius of Autun: "He who placed himself in the Virgin's body has been found by the huntsmen", that is to say, "He has been found by those who love Him". This means that the pursuers really are "The King's Men", in the sense that they are God's tools and must carry out the ritual. The King is God and the huntsmen are His warriors,

THE UNICORN

who seek salvation and therefore crave the blood. In the spirit of the time they could almost be called knights of the Holy Grail! This is why, where a negro is shown, he swings an axe, whilst it is a knight who gives the ritual blow with the lance. The negro symbolizes the "other races" who may also seek grace.[1]

This also sheds light on the role of the Virgin. Strictly speaking, she is an erotic seductress, a Delilah who only pretends to protect the animal and is secretly in league with its enemies. Yet she too is a tool. Often God himself is present, so that everything takes place under His approving eye, without intervention. Sometimes she anoints the animal as the huntsmen arrive, like a consecration to "The Sweet-Pain Death", or as in the *Pietà*, when Christ's body is anointed before burial. The true solemnity of the scene must also be seen as a guar-

Unicorn Hunt
The Ashmole Bestiary
c. 1210, Bodleian Library, Oxford, MS. Ashmole 1511, fol. 14v

antee that what we are witnessing is a sacred ritual pleasing to God, where no vulgar wickedness would be tolerated. Here Christianity has succeeded in a thorough conquest of the old myth, and in ritualizing every jot of it.

The scene expresses the Gothic cast of mind and its evolution is definitely to be set at about 1200 – one of the earliest examples is an archivolt figure on the west portal of Laon Cathedral. From then on it becomes a commonplace in cathedral sculpture, manuscripts and wood carvings.

Many of the manuscript illustrations are of a high quality. In the Ashmole Bestiary of about 1200 we find high art: on a golden ground the scene unfolds like an allegorical ornament, in which every single detail has its definite place. Two huntsmen stand amidst three stylized trees, one of them – a Moor – raises his axe, and a "white man" pierces the animal with his lance. The Unicorn, as it leaps on to the Virgin's lap, arches its back in sudden pain, and from its tautened lines the rhythm spreads through the picture; from the pain centre in its flank emanates the triangular form of horn–axe–spear. But there is no excitement. Here, as in other cases, there is not only a close relationship between the Virgin and the animal, but also between the Virgin and the huntsmen, who exchange serious and approving glances. She loves the animal and she suffers, but she bestows it on those who seek its blood. The ritual is totally removed from the world of reality. It takes place in a transcendent golden sphere, in which each movement submits to the strict patterns of the geometric scheme, restricting emotions.

In Richard de Fournival's famous *Bestiaire d'Amours* of the fourteenth century, the animal is pierced by a woman.[2] At first glance this seems absurd, but the woman stands for Amour, Divine Love or Caritas. As in the Crucifixion scenes in which Christ is pierced by Ecclesia (The Church) or Caritas itself, both female figures, we are nearing the intellectual position which explains the sacrificial death of Christ as a result of the virtues of His heart: Faith, Hope and Love (Fides, Spes and Caritas). They hunt Him to death. When His side is pierced, and the water (of Baptism) and the blood (of the Eucharist) pour forth, Ecclesia is born.

It is as if after years of circling around the motif with many approaches and variations, the solution had at last been found, emerging complete and obvious in its exact and perfect form. Odell Shepard writes:

"Beginning in Physiologus as an allegory of the Annunciation alone, the story came to comprehend in one rich and compact symbol the total life and death of Christ and to shadow forth the whole divine plan of redemption. In its final form it is one of the strangest and one of the most compressed symbols or allegories ever devised."[3]

For our understanding of the Sacred Hunt (see Chapter 8) the scene is an essential prologue.

As many members of the congregation would have been familiar with the image of Mary and the Unicorn on her lap, it was natural for popular ballads and songs to reflect the mythic material. Image and text inspired each other. The songs often possess an intensity and poetry, showing how devoted medieval people were to Mary right up to the Reformation. Here was a scene consisting of familiar and well loved events: the hunt in the forest, the young woman with her animal in the verdant scenery of springtime:

The quarry no hunter could catch
nor with art or cunning snatch
or the whole world subdue.
Our blessed Lady with no thought of harm
ensnared him gently with her sweet arm
as the Scripture tells.
The savage Unicorn hast thou tamed
made willing and patient as a lamb
Thou Maiden without compare . . .

So runs Per Raev Lille's Song to Mary.[4] Well versed in the *Lucidarius*, he continues: "The fierce panther hast Thou subdued . . ."

dicitur: propter incarnationis eius humilitatem ipso
dicente. Discite a me quia mitis sum et humilis corde.
Similis est hedo unicornis: quia ipse saluator factus est
in similitudine carnis peccati. et de peccato dampna
uit peccatum. Unicornis sepe cum elephantis certa
men habet. et in uentrem uulneratum psternit.

Incis dictus: quia in luporum genere numera
tur. Est enim bestia maculis distincta: ut pardus.
sed similis lupo. Huius urinam conuerti in duri
ciam preciosi lapidis dicunt dicunt qui ligurius
appellatur. Quod et ipsas linces sentire: uel docu
mento probatur. Nam egestum liquorem arenis

CHAPTER 8

The Sacred Hunt

The Göss altar frontal
c. 1240, Österreichisches
Museum für Angewandte
Kunst, Vienna, inv. T.6902

The embroidered
antependium depicts the
Annunciation

Around 1300 a group of motifs featuring the Virgin Mary and the Unicorn were about to be combined into a new synthesis: 1. The traditional western *Annunciation* scene with Mary and Gabriel; 2. The *Hortus Conclusus* of the Song of Solomon, with its numerous symbols – a scene especially beloved in nunneries; 3. The familiar juxtaposition of *Mary and the Unicorn*, in which the animal is both Christ and a symbol of chastity; 4. The *hunting scene*, in which the pursuers pierce the animal in the maiden's lap as a symbol of the "questing congregation", who gather around the *Pietà*; 5. *Honorius's sermons* on the Annunciation to Mary, which linked the Unicorn with the Annunciation.

The combination of these motifs into a new and inspired unity was not brought about by certain artists making up a jigsaw puzzle with the existing pieces. In a world full of symbolic personifications, animals and plants, where people are preoccupied with damnation and salvation, associations form of their own accord and emerge in new patterns. This is what occurred in the religious houses. When the Berne Physiologus states that the Unicorn was driven to its death partly by its father, and partly by its love and the virtues of its heart, it was but a short step to shift the emphasis from the searchers who *find* the animal in the Virgin's arms, to the active hunters who *drive* it there.

Who does this? None other than the Angel Gabriel in alliance with His own virtues.

It looks as if the synthesis occurs in a female world. The trail leads to the German nunneries, where the Unicorn had long been stabled, and where Mary in her garden was so beloved. The stage, as it were, was set. We saw what Hildegard of Bingen added to the story in the twelfth century. Now we can bring at least three new women into its development, all of them consecrated nuns. They were Chunegunde of Goss, Mechtilde of Magdeburg and, perhaps most important of all, a member of a Low German order, whose name we do not know. We will begin with Chunegunde.

In Vienna there is an embroidered silk antependium of about 1240. It comes from a nunnery at Goss in the Tyrol. Mary stands in a medallion opposite the Angel Gabriel, who enters from the left. Below his wing and close to an eight-petalled rose, the sign of Salvation, stands a little Unicorn with one forefoot raised. The dove hovers above. Around the border we read the angel's greeting to Mary: "Ave Maria,

voluptatū meaꝝ. Da gl᷑m hō q̄
k̄chon̄s mr̄is mee, ac tubmilū ge
rn̄tis mee. Tūr ꝑot ꞯala. Veve

gracia plena" (Hail Mary, full of grace); and below, "Chunegundis Abbatissa me fecit" (Abbess Chunegunde made me). This does not necessarily mean that the abbess embroidered the cloth with her own hand, but rather that she was responsible for its making. It is the earliest picture known of an Annunciation with a Unicorn, but he is still very small, a symbol like the flower, placed with the angel like a modest footnote. We do not know of any painted source, but we may attribute the birth of the motif to about the middle of the thirteenth century.

It is unusual for a new motif to appear "by itself" in pictorial art, but we know how this happened in the following case, by way of the written word before the final visual form, again in the German-speaking area. The university library at Göttingen has in its possession a Low German manuscript, a *Prayer Book for Ladies of the Order*, of 1480. Among other things it contains a dialogue in Latin between a nun ("Sponsa Christi" – "Bride of Christ") and the Angel Gabriel. The two discuss "Kristi Menschwerdung", or the mystery of the Incarnation:

"Thou bride of Christ, look around thee, as they say, and take note of the beauty and delight of this garden. For it has as many merits, as many creatures, as many wonderful things, as there are stars in the heavens. Now I shall describe something of the chase in this garden: the rhinoceros is the swiftest, the Unicorn the most chaste and the panther the most beautiful quarry in this garden. God the Father had made this garden out of the pleasure of His divine heart. And God's son was fired to love this garden and attracted by the loveliness of its flowers. For in this garden there was a Maiden, wonderfully lovely, graceful, gracious, deliciously beautiful and joyous. But the Son of God grew too pleasure-loving in his attraction to this garden, after He had been given permission to play in it. According to the Eternal Father's plan he entered the garden to play among the flowers. And I, Gabriel, was sent by the Lord, and as a hunter I took four hounds with me. One was called Mercy, the second Truth, the third Righteousness, the fourth Peace, and I also had an ingenious and melodious instrument, which sounded more delightful than any melody from psaltery and cither, and with which I encouraged the hounds to run. And lo, while the swift rhinoceros or the chaste Unicorn leapt spiritedly and played among the lovely flowers of this garden, the Lord's breath blew in this ingenious and delightfully sonorous horn, which I put to my mouth. And it sounded sweet to the Maiden's ears and also to the ears of the Unicorn. But the melody from this horn sounded thus: 'Hail Mary, full of grace, the Lord is with thee.' And they both stood and listened. Then at once the speedy hounds began to run and chase after the noble animal. And lo, He fled and ran to the Maiden's lap desiring to rest there. And straightway the graceful and beautiful girl enclosed Him in her womb. And thus was the Son of God captured in the beauty and flowery scent of this garden. Many sinners come running unwittingly into this garden and say: 'Hail Mary, full of grace.' And at once they are captured by the grace of Mary, which they had least expected and believed."[1]

The text is accompanied by a hand-coloured drawing, representing the classical Hortus Conclusus, in which Gabriel with a horn to his mouth approaches Mary with three hounds. In the garden we find, predictably, the tower of David, the Burning Bush, the altar with candles and the well, also a badly drawn peacock, a symbol of immortality. At the bottom of the picture stands the little nun outside the locked gate with the inscription: "Ortus conclusus, soror mea sponsa" (The enclosed garden, my sister and bride). The picture is a somewhat clumsy copy of a well-known type, generally found in engravings and is therefore not in itself new. The type of illustration is of about 1400, but the text itself, which does not completely correspond to the picture, is several decades earlier. This then takes us back to the time when St Bridget of Sweden received her revelations and carried on long conversations with Mary on similar subjects. This was a time when revelations were

The Sacred Hunt
Coloured drawing from a prayer book for ladies of a religious order, *c.* 1480, Universitätsbibliothek, Göttingen, 8°Cod. MS. theol. 291, fol. 291

"fashionable", when little sisters were permitted to peep through cracks in the heavenly wall, and when many new kinds of picture emerged, inspired by these very visual experiences.

This remarkable text shows the same combination of garden and Virgin as appears in the Song of Solomon, and the picture merges the familiar Annunciation scene, with Gabriel, with the traditional animals. The rhinoceros and panther are mentioned as well as the Unicorn, being among the animals who lay their heads in maidens' laps, as in the *Lucidarius*, although they are never present in the illustrations. So the idea of the hunt and the reason for it are present in literature at the end of the fourteenth century, after which the image formed, although we do not exactly know how or when.

What then do the four hounds Mercy, Truth, Righteousness and Peace, mean? One of the sources is Psalm 85, 10, which states: "Mercy and truth are met together – righteousness and peace have kissed each other." As early as the twelfth century a discussion arose on how God's righteousness and mercy could reach agreement with each other. The question was given the form of a drama, the *Litigatio sororum*, or dispute of the four (heavenly) sisters. This had the four sisters, the Cardinal Virtues, meeting before the throne of God for their dispute to be decided: Truth and Justice will sit in judgement and punish human beings for their evil deeds, while Mercy and Peace will pardon them. The dispute ends with God sending Gabriel to Mary, so that the conception of Christ may provide the solution: the Son will reconcile the contradictions through his sacrificial death. God says: "Hasten to my delightful Paradise! Hasten to my shining gate [Mary]. Hasten to my worthy dwelling." As Gabriel hesitates, God goes on: "Do you not know that the bush burned and yet did not burn out? I shall come to her in the form of a dove."[2] Then Gabriel sets off with the four sisters in the form of hunting dogs, tied together two by two as the psalm dictates. Sometimes there are only three hounds, because the three theological virtues were chosen, Faith, Hope and Charity, as a particular demonstration of Mary's virtues. When there are only two they are Mercy and Peace.

Bernard of Clairvaux linked the virtues to the Passion in the mid-twelfth century, in commentaries on Psalm 85. He also says in his sermons: "The sweet heart of Jesus is pierced through by Love, and He is nailed to the cross with the nails of the divine virtues."[3] The idea soon gained ground; it was dramatic and visual, and in the German religious houses a cult grew up centred on the personified virtues, who took the place of the men wielding hammer and nails at Golgotha, or assisted at the Deposition and Burial. In psalters and on altarpieces we can see the remarkable depiction of Christ on the cross surrounded by small female figures creeping around on its arms, nailing down His hands and feet. Some fine full-page illustrations in the Besançon Psalter show this going on. In 1271 Mechtilde of Magdeburg describes how the virtues nailed Him, and how God himself was driven out of Heaven. Mechtilde is one of the theologians whose writings associate St Bernard with this pictorial theme developed from the literature towards 1400.

Another author who contributed to the development was the remarkable priest Conrad of Megenberg (1309–1374), who had studied in Paris and Vienna and later became a canon of Regensburg Cathedral. He was a mystic, composing among other things music for the mass, and renowned for executing miraculous cures during the

Mary with the Unicorn
Central panel of an altar frontal, *c.* 1420, Erfurt Cathedral

performance of the liturgy. In 1350, during the Black Death, he wrote the first real "natural history" produced in Germany, *Das Buch der Natur.* To a certain extent it was translated from an earlier predecessor; but it was of a new and meditative character that corresponded to the particular mentality of the century. The book described the Unicorn:

"The animal signifies Our Lord Jesus Christ, who – before he became a man – grew indignant and wrathful over the arrogance of the angels and over men's disobedience on earth, then God sent the dearly-beloved girl with her chaste purity, Mary, into the wild forests of this sick world, so that He leapt from Heaven down into her chaste, pure lap, and there he was captured by the brutal huntsmen and the Jews and was shamefully killed; but afterwards He rose again and ascended to the palace of the heavenly king, where He joined all the saints and the community of the host of angels – a sight beautiful to behold."[4]

The text, very reminiscent of Albertus Magnus, mentioned previously, contains gnostic ideas regarding the heavenly host which merge here with the usual imagery of Physiologus. As in Megasthenes, He is taken to the "palace" and shown forth to the hosts of heaven. The cosmic performance is taking shape.[5]

One of the earliest great altarpieces with the completely developed motif is in Erfurt Cathedral, *c*. 1420. On the high altar there is a triptych, whose side panels show the Crucifixion, Descent into Hell and Resurrection. With the Incarnation of the central panel, it displays the whole Atonement story in concentrated form. Mary sits on the grass in the centre of a circular garden with a large, shining Unicorn on her lap. It shines because it is covered with gold leaf, so that it appears quite flat and magical. A small Gabriel appears from the left with two hounds. The hand of God in the sky is sending a child to Mary and small angels sing under the trees. A row of joyful male and female saints with shining haloes and holding golden beakers sits in the background, while outside the fence kneels a bishop, perhaps a benefactor, and young maidens. Here in truth is a muster of young girls "of good family", as Hildegard advises. Banners fly through the garden with the good news, Gabriel's banner, for instance, says: "Ave Regina coelorum . . ." (Hail, Queen of Heaven) – a greeting we shall meet again, eighty years later, in the Verteuil tapestries (see Chapter 13). Gabriel appears, as in most other places, dressed in priestly vestments, an alb and a magnificent cope, and in addition to his horn he carries the lance that will in time draw blood. He is the future Ecclesia, guardian of the four Virtues.

In the Franciscan monastery in Lübeck there is a fresco of the Annunciation in the refectory (*c*. 1440), which includes ambiguities of the kind that were never far from the motif. The hand of God sends down a little child to Mary, while the Unicorn leaps simultaneously into her embrace, pursued by Gabriel. The dove hovers at the top. It is not clear what the Unicorn actually represents in the midst of this wealth of Annunciation symbols. Is it Christ, penetrating her womb? If so, why is there a child on its way from Heaven? Is it more likely to be the Holy Ghost, causing her to conceive with God's "horn"? Then, why the dove? In one or two other cases the baby arrives riding on the Unicorn's back and, obviously, a composition such as this does not occur without some idea behind it.

The true nature of the Unicorn probably made it difficult to play the part assigned by Christianity. As a sexual animal it is most suited to represent God's virility – the Holy Ghost – but through the Septuagint it was identified with the Son. While the Trinity is a unity, in art it is often shown as three figures, and the medieval artist must have given some consideration to the problem. If we are to try to find a reasonable interpretation of the various combinations, we might arrive at the following possibilities. The Unicorn is Christ, as the theologians say – and it lies in Mary's lap. But the Unicorn is also the power of God, and the horn plays the same role as the candle which the priest lowers over the font at the consecration of the baptismal water. The horn cannot evade its basic symbolic value. The presence of a child might lead us to perceive the Unicorn as the spritual nature of Christ, the spirit that is one with the Father – for the Unicorn is often called "Spiritualis Unicornis" – and the child as His corporeal nature. The scene would then become a portrayal of Christ's two natures. This hypothesis is particularly tempting when the child, with the cross before it, actually arrives riding on the animal. The problem has still not been solved.

We do not know what the very first Sacred Hunts looked like, but by about 1420 the classical form of the motif is in existence and then appears in examples on altar-pieces, in mural paintings, drawings and engravings, and even in embroideries, all over Germany. From there, its offshoots reached Scandinavia. We need mention only the altar in Lübeck Cathedral and its derivatives in Denmark and southern Sweden, and as far off as Hattula in Finland.

The motif is rarely found in Italy; but there is one example in Verona, a fresco in the church of San Giorgetto, painted by Falconetto in 1514. Mary sits like Danaë in a large garden and receives the child, who slides down to her from God in a stream of gold. The garden is full of the usual symbols with their names inscribed; but here they unfold in rich Renaissance form: the closed gate is a triumphal arch from an-tiquity with classical decorations. Outside, Gideon is there with his fleece saying: "He descends like rain on my fleece", a sentence clearly applying to Danaë, which shows that the motif re-ceives a particular nuance in Italy, where people were so familiar with ancient allegories that it was natural to interpret the classical Danaë with the golden rain as a symbol for Mary.[6]

The Sacred Hunt
Wall painting, *c.* 1500,
Søndersø church, Denmark

The theme did not appear only in pictures. It is found in Thuringian poems and plays that cast God as a "Heaven hunter", who must chase his Son "into place"; and from the Santa Maria nunnery at Zerbst there are stage directions for a procession at Easter mass and a play from 1507. A "Hortus" was assembled and was the starting point for a procession in which many figures were carried through the town: the Virgin Mary, the Child Jesus, Gabriel, the Unicorn and besides the four hounds, a tower, Aaron's lantern and Gideon's Fleece, while a hymn was sung to the chaste Virgin who took the eternal one-horned one into her lap. All this formed the conclusion to a play about the Fall and a representation of the dispute of the four sisters: Fall and Re-demption!

Others varied the theme in different ways. Thomas of Cantimpranensis's popular *summa* of the legends of Mary, of about 1205, tells this version: a king (God) had two sons. One (Lucifer) killed himself, the other (Adam) fell ill. The king wished to save him and sent for a doctor, who advised him that the blood of a Unicorn would heal the wound. The most beautiful girl to be found should sit in a garden surrounded by six other girls. They are the Virtues, namely: Secrecy (because Mary prays behind the closed door), Shame, Wisdom, Faith, Humility and Obedience. Four swift hounds with Gabriel the huntsman drive the Unicorn to the maiden, who takes it into her womb. Here are the dispute among the Four Sisters, the Hortus Conclusus, virtues

The Garden of Earthly Delights (detail opposite)
Hieronymus Bosch, *c.* 1504
Museo del Prado, Madrid

and the Unicorn as healing power, united in an allegorical story of the Atonement.

There are Annunciation scenes in three places in Denmark, at Søndersø and Gislev churches on the island of Fyn, and in the convent at Elsinore. Søndersø near Odense has an Annunciation scene on the north wall of the north transept, from about 1520. Gabriel comes from the left with his horn to his mouth and three elegant hounds energetically making for Mary. Issuing from their mouths are the names Pax, Caritas and Fides. On Gabriel's long scroll, folded in several places, is written: "Ave – Gratia Plena – Dominus te cum" (Hail to thee – full of grace – God be with thee) and above Mary is her reply: "Ecce Ancilla Domini . . ." (Lo – I am the servant of the Lord . . .). Mary spreads her hands in astonishment and casts her eyes down. Over them both hovers God in a flaming halo, who sends down a little child with a cross and crown of thorns to the Virgin, accompanied by the dove. Immediately below the child is a vase holding three lilies, on a low shelf.

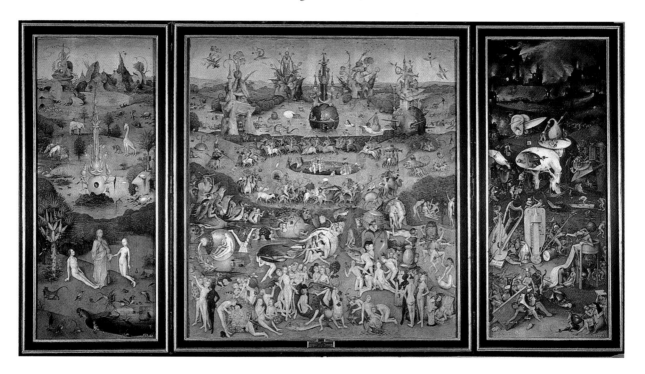

The backdrop to the picture is remarkable. A doorway behind Gabriel opens on to a garden, and a parquet floor in the foreground indicates Mary's chamber. Behind her is a dark panel with nine rectangular niches, whose significance is unexplained. Beneath them are four "cushions" or square pieces of material hanging stretched out on the wall, alternately dark and light. This clearly emphasized row of squares must refer to something – perhaps the Incarnation and the conditions of earthly life, perhaps the four Evangelists – but the exact meaning is unclear.

There is another problem in this picture: where is the Unicorn? The stage is all set for the arrival of the animal: the angel blows his horn, the hounds race up, and Mary does not look up for the child but directs her eyes on to something at knee height.

Unicorn in border of a
manuscript of the Saga of
Olaf Tryggvason
Reykjavik, Iceland

There is enough room by her knees for the Unicorn; but it is not there! On the other hand, there is a strange bulge in her dress and a suggestion of a back and a leg, and a head might peek up out of her mantle. How is this to be explained? Is it an error by a restorer's hand? Or did the artist misunderstand the original he copied from? We cannot know. It has been suggested that the animal has already crept up under Mary's robe;[7] but that would be an innovation to bring us up short. It is all the more strange because Swedish and Finnish examples are quite normal and do not have similar variations.

At Gislev, not far from Søndersø, there is an Annunciation in the chancel by another master, posing the same problem. Mary sits outside a Gothic church and Gabriel approaches from the left in his long, flowing robe. He leads no fewer than six hounds, although unfortunately their scrolls are blank. Can these be the six Virtues from the legend? Mary is already crowned and God sends her the child from above, but her eyes are fixed on the angel or the many scrolls which carry Gabriel's words and her own, and here she does not seem to lack anything. There is no room between the hounds and Mary, which indicates that no other animal was planned as part of the scene. It seems odd that in one picture Mary is not in need of anything but in the other she is. We must acknowledge that the problem has not been solved.

In the church of Our Lady in the Carmelite convent at Elsinore there is a remarkable painting of about 1480 on the vault of the south aisle. A little Unicorn looks up out of the calyx of a flower, immediately opposite a young woman sitting in a similar calyx, her hands folded in prayer. She has no halo, but may well be Mary. Whether this can be called an Annunciation is questionable, for the entire painting is extraordinary. Everywhere the upper parts of figures grow out of well-rounded calyxes, rocking in the wind like decorations on little iced confections. The Unicorn grows bafflingly out of a gaping mask, like a feather in its hat, just one of many strange heads and flowers all over the vaulting: animals grow out of the mouths of masks, jesters out of flowers. In a manuscript, you would find these creatures and caricature masks in the margin, and they are to be seen in contemporary manuscripts and other art from Lübeck and Scandinavia. Christ's family appears in flowers moved by the wind in the churchof Skive, as well as on altarpieces in Lübeck. We are approaching the end of the medieval period, and these figures are contemporary with artists like Hieronymus Bosch. In his remarkable painting, *The Garden of Earthly Delights*, the central panel probably relates to the period before the Flood, when the children of Cain (black) mated with those of Seth (white) and lived in a perverted world of untamed indulgence, carrying on with animals, whoring and gorging themselves. Around the circular lake human beings ride on pigs, camels, stags and so on — mostly on male animals with well developed horns and antlers, and the whole picture bristles with agressive phallic symbols. Here the Unicorn takes its natural place among other potent male animals, as an obviously sexual creature.

The Sacred Hunt has its source on German soil. It spreads like an epidemic through Thuringia, Lower Saxony, Mecklenburg, Silesia, Carinthia, the Alps, the Black Forest, Alsace, Limburg and Holsten, with provincial eruptions in Denmark, Skøne in Sweden and Finland. Why?

Shall we make a guess that it is because the soil is the particular environment of nuns, a setting for intense meditation on the maidenliness and motherhood of the Virgin Mary? It is not hard to understand. Here is a milieu in which women of all ages live in close proximity, their minds dominated by the sacred mysteries; where it was not unknown for a nun to believe that the Holy Spirit had made her pregnant, or that Christ had come into her bed at night. Their thoughts circled around the Conception, Birth and Motherhood — all experiences they themselves were denied absolutely. We know from other similar situations what this can lead to: the imagination incubates erotic symbols and images that satisfy the soul and holds up the beloved motifs before the physical eye — among others, the little goat with the pointed horn which hops up on to the Virgin's lap.

Today we cannot comprehend the intensity of mid-European Mariolatry in the years leading up to the Reformation. Was it by chance that the persecution of witches increased in the same period and that the witches flew to Bloksbjerg to flock around a horned god with a goat's beard and cloven hoofs, just at the time when their pious sisters were praying in the solitude of church and cell before the image of the white Unicorn?

CHAPTER 9
The Gyrstinge Altar Frontal and Danish Mural Paintings

The Gyrstinge altar frontal
Painting on wood (prior to restoration), *c.* 1525, Nationalmuseet, Copenhagen, inv. no. D1257

The Gyrstinge altar frontal
As the frontal is seriously damaged, the scene is clearer in a drawing made in 1909 for a Danish edition of the popular book *Lucidarius*

The National Museum in Copenhagen possesses an altar frontal in wood from Gyrstinge church, near Sorø in Sjaelland, of about 1525, portraying the Sacred Hunt. In the midst of a spacious landscape the Virgin Mary is seated on the right under a delicate tree. Gabriel approaches from the left with his horn and two hounds. A Unicorn, only slightly larger than the hounds, has jumped up to place its forefeet on Mary's lap.

Nothing in the figures departs from tradition, but the landscape of the background is new and strange. We have become accustomed to seeing the chase take place in the enclosed garden with all its symbols; but here is an open landscape stretching into the distance and divided into two components: on the left – behind Gabriel – is a high cliff surmounted by a castle, behind Mary a forest in front of which is a lake or river crossed by a bridge. Two people, apparently a rider and a pedestrian, meet on the bridge. Above the bridge God himself, seated on clouds, turns towards the Virgin Mary. Over the middle ground leaps a swift animal, either a deer or a hare.

A report from the National Museum following a recent restoration of the frontal gave a detailed description of the picture, and noted that it "departs from tradition by placing the Virgin Mary in open country."[1] The explanation given – which, no doubt, is correct – stated that around 1520 the old iconographic patterns were being abandoned: the enclosed garden was felt to be dated, and the new landscape painting of the Renaissance was starting to appear in Scandinavia in this century of Titian, Raphael and Albrecht Dürer.

Is this merely a "pure" landscape painting, then, with no connection with the motif it frames, as the report assumed? Surely not. We must not infer that symbols disappeared from pictures at a stroke merely because nature was now depicted realistically. The realism can be deceptive. It was in this very century that artists took up what is known as the *paysage moralisé*, the moralizing landscape, which scrupulously comments on the action of a picture and refers to an inner meaning. There are many intimations of Annunciations and Burials of Christ,[2] even if they are sometimes hard to interpret.

The landscape of the Unicorn is difficult to interpret too, but I shall make an attempt at it. The contrast of forest/castle is not unique in the imagery of the beast,

THE UNICORN

and we shall meet it later on in the Verteuil tapestries (see Chapter 13), where the landscape is very fascinating. The polarity is also present in literature, which provides important clues to its meaning. In Karen Blixen's story "The Roads around Pisa" a little smelling bottle is a vital requisite.[3] A landscape is painted on one side. This is very carefully described: it is a landscape divided in exactly the same way as on the altar frontal into forest/castle, with a connecting bridge. It appears from the story that the landscape is a symbol of the two sexes – the male and female, with "the third" in the middle, which is the actual theme of the story.

Henry James makes use of similar symbolism in *The Turn of the Screw*.[4] The governess in charge of the motherless children sees the ghosts of two dead servants who have had a strong and apparently baleful influence on her charges. She always sees the manservant in the castle, usually on the top of the tower, while the woman rises out of the lake or stays in the woods. Here is the same sexual division in the same contrasting scenery, and each time linked to fate and profound psychological processes.

That the Renaissance was aware of this contrast is clear from an engraving after the alchemist Lambsprinck (see fig. on p.76). A stag and a Unicorn face each other in front of the same two landscape elements. According to alchemical lore the deer is the feminine element, "soul" or *anima*, and the Unicorn the masculine, "spirit" or *spiritus*, which is attracted by its opposite (see fig. on p.159). The landscape is defined as "Substantia humanae", the conjoined psychological substance of the human

**Unicorn and Stag Meet in
the Forest**
Illustration to an alchemical
textbook *Musaeum Hermeticum*
by Lambsprinck, published
1678, Bibliothèque Nationale
de France, Paris

The Unicorn represents *spiritus*
and the stag *anima*

The Sacred Hunt
Engraving by unknown
artist known as "The
Monogrammist", *c.* 1470–80,
Universitätsbibliothek,
Göttingen

Gabriel arrives with the four
hounds: Love, Truth, Humility
and Righteousness

being, but divided into masculine and feminine. Perhaps that is why God is enthroned on the Gyrstinge altar frontal just above the connecting bridge on the
central axis. The tree, the forest and the water are behind Mary, opposite the constructed castle with its tower and spire with the strange horns. It is then possible that
the leaping animal in the middle ground can be interpreted as the deer, the *anima*.[5] So
we must still keep the scene's erotic aspect in mind. We have here a Virgin and an
animal which runs around with an unequivocal sexual symbol in the centre of its
forehead. The age said it in its own "scientific" language, and it is probable that the
picture tells it in the landscape.

The Gyrstinge frontal is among the last examples of the Sacred Hunt in the
sphere of official ecclesiastical art. By about 1550 the motif is played out, perhaps
precisely because of its ambiguity, now more and more understood – and because of
the Reformation. A large number of the most important nunneries were closed and
the motif was banned indirectly even in Catholic circles. The Council of Trent, active
between 1545 and 1563, one of whose functions was to stake out the limits for the
choice of motifs and style in ecclesiastical art, forbade motifs with unusual or offen-
sive content, and the atmosphere of the time would include the Unicorn in this cat-
egory. Many frivolous Unicorns were now leaping around on Italian frescoes,
painted by decorative artists in the late Renaissance style. Nude courtesans caressed
its long horn with the frankness afforded by the new age. In an astonishingly short
time the Sacred Hunt had vanished.

It is perhaps possible to identify yet another reason for the breaking open of the
Hortus Conclusus; but it is of a formal kind, to be found in one of the most revo-
lutionary events in European art – namely, the development of central perspective in
the course of the fifteenth century. Here we must have recourse to a comparison of
images: let us look at one of the traditional images of the Annunciation in the
Hortus Conclusus, from the second half of the fifteenth century. We observe a
whole, enclosed, world from a superior viewpoint; it is a self-contained circle. We see
a well organized cosmos "from above", which allows us to identify all the symbolic
objects, spread out within it: lambskin, tower, altar with candles and God in the
Burning Bush, and we understand that everything is connected. The holiest things
are larger than the less significant; thus, the light of Christ is larger than the other
candles, and Mary is larger than God in the thornbush, for God is here a subordinate
symbol. It is not space, but spiritual pre-eminence which determines the relationships of size.

The relationships are quite different in the woodcut on p.78: the angel, the animal
and Mary still have the same size, but we are no longer in a position from which to
embrace the whole scene. We are placed in front of the middle of the image – which
is now actually a stage – in a fixed position before the meeting point of the perspective in the centre of the altar. It is perspective and thereby space which determines
everything. The twelve candles on the altar table now run inwards and end with the
Christ light, which comes at "the end of the table", and everything is arranged sym-
metrically on each side. We do not see very many of the symbols, however, and we do
not see a wall forming a circle. We see a section of wall running out of the picture on
each side, and the few objects for which there is room in the small portion of garden
that we overlook. Our viewpoint cannot take in much.

The Annunciation in the Garden
Woodcut illustration for
Ulrich Pinder's *Der beschlossen
Gart des Rosenkranz Marie*,
Nuremberg, 1505,
Kupferstichkabinett, Berlin

Perspective arranges the world for us, draws us too into it and makes us the centre, but it also fragments it and makes us half blind. The holism has been broken, the sacred geometric figures crack, the world is piecemeal and divided. With this, the scene is disrupted and the Hortus Conclusus no longer has any meaning.

There are about thirty fresco paintings featuring the Unicorn in Denmark and this book is the first to put them in a European context. They are distributed over the greater part of the country but occur in groups, on the island of Møn, of Sjaelland, in South Fyn, and Djursland in East Jutland. All the pictures date from the late Gothic period, between 1450 and 1530, and all are on vaulting or chancel arches. The majority were made during the last decades of the fifteenth century, at the same time as the Burgundy tapestries and the German altarpieces. They are clearly influenced by French heraldry and German images of the Annunciation, probably via Lübeck.

This was the period when the artist known as the Elmelunde Master and his workshop were active. About 1480 they decorated three churches on Møn: Keldby, Elmelunde and Fanefjord, with pictures on every vault. Here is a small elegant Unicorn with hoofs, a long tufted tail and a downward-turned narwhal tusk. It is artistically spotted, and in its Gothic elegance is in striking contrast to the robust Romanesque lions that we know as the symbol for Christ in earlier church art. All the Unicorns on Møn are in the corners of the vaults, like footnotes to a more detailed story, and face other symbolic animals, such as the hare, deer or owl. In two of the churches the dominant story is an Annunciation, at Elmelund there is also a Judgement (see fig. opposite and on p.80). As we have seen, the association with the meeting of Mary and Gabriel is quite traditional.

If we cross the Guldborg Sound to the island of Falster, we find a couple of Unicorns from the same workshop in the two churches at Tingsted and Astrup. They are slightly later, from about 1490, and are again on the vault nearest the choir. At Tingsted the animal is associated with the Three Kings and is presumably intended as a symbol of chastity in Mary or as Christ; but at Astrup it is unusually placed beneath a Flogging of Christ and close to the Man of Sorrows, who is flecked with wounds, and must stand for Christ. This Unicorn is from the Elmelund School, but a coarsened version. Its body is almost identical to those of the Evangelist creatures placed beside it and, apart from tail, hoofs and horn, hardly any characteristics remain.

At Skørbelev (see fig. on p.80)on the island of Langeland and at Gudme on Fyn two strange animals arrest the attention by their unusual appearance. Both are placed in the midst of a chaotic and disrupted universe, in which a plaited cross, flowers, small dogs and unconnected letters are strewn about in apparent disorder. At Skrøbelev, the Unicorn lowers its horn before a crucified Christ above the altar. It is a distant relation of the Elmelunde animal, but more exuberant. It lowers its horn and tries to lift both fore and back legs in the same manner, even though its gait is somewhat muddled. The round spots on its coat are partly painted in but cover only half its body. Despite all this, it would seem that the painter had probably seen the "right" Unicorn on Møn and half remembered it, reproducing it with sincerity and an attractive robust charm.

The Gudme Unicorn resembles an elk with a jagged horn, standing among cosmic symbols like a Christ-symbol, its tail ending in a cross. It is dated 1488. In a confusing setting executed by lo l painters, these creatures are elements in strange ensembles of decoration known today as the "Master Builder Paintings"; they are attributed to the artisans who built the churches. Two small Unicorns chasing each other among stars on the east wall of St Hans Church at Stege must belong to the same group.

In all these examples the Unicorn seems to stand for Christ and is displayed to the congregation almost as His armorial device. The consistent positioning in the eastern vault compartments and the association with Annunciations or Crucifixions and cosmic signs indicates that they retain their significance at least into the sixteenth century – even when they degenerate to the point of being unrecognizable. The form itself loses coherence as the distance from a main workshop increases, and in remote churches it is hard to recognize the heraldically disciplined animal from Møn. Even so, these more distant relations have their own charm.

A number of churches have modest decoration, as a rule on an eastern compart-

Left and overleaf (top)
The Unicorn and Doomsday
Vault painting, *c.* 1480,
Elmelunde church, Denmark

ment, consisting of two animals facing each other and lifting a foreleg to salute a stylized Tree of Life. The type is very ancient. Indeed, it goes back to Levantine models, which were taken over by Romanesque art for tympana and fonts, and later in heraldry, when the animals were employed to guard the shield (see Chapter 16). Sometimes these animals, almost lion-like, consort with coat of arms and Tree of Life in exactly the same manner, saluting and lowering their horn. This attitude towards two very different objects may indicate a weakening of the original significance. It is strange to see the Christ-animal observing a servile attitude towards an aristocratic shield. Despite this, it is noticeable that out of the thirty or so examples in churches, half are in the choir itself or the chancel and eastern vault compartments, facing the congregation. It was still important that people should see the Unicorn!

A lightning tour of the Danish Unicorn population undeniably gives the impression of a province – indeed, a province appended at a late date. The animals appear sparsely, often in diffused contexts; there is a preponderance of heraldic animals – and the quality is often poor. There are surprisingly few Virgin Hunts, considering the period, and there is only one sustained scene, the hunt on the altar frontal from Gyrstinge. The two on Fyn lose the point. If the Danish Unicorns are unimpressive, they are nevertheless acceptable witnesses to Danish participation in the European art scene at the start of the Renaissance, and to the themes that stimulated the imagination of Danish church artists.

From the Reformation onwards, the Unicorn also appeared on the large christening dishes which were used as covers for the open basins of fonts. They are a special group, often imported from the Low Countries, with themes associated with sin and redemption; the middle field of the round dish is often filled with an Annunciation or a Fall. There is a fine example from Toreby on the island of Lolland, made in Holland and dating from about 1625. The centre shows the Fall with the two naked figures in a luxuriant garden, with tree and serpent between them. On the wide border above, the tree seems to grow and change into a Tree of Life, divided into a triple-petalled flower held together by a ring. Beneath are glimpsed the Four Rivers of Paradise. The foliage winds all round the dish and forms a dense thicket with

Sketch of a Unicorn
c. 1500, Skrøbelev church,
Denmark

THE UNICORN

animals leaping through it. On either side of the flower is a Unicorn with a waving mane, more like a rearing heraldic animal than a worshipper. Partly they guard the flower, as if it were a coat of arms, partly they have arrived, running like the hare and the deer, driven by four hounds on the lower edge of the dish. The hare and deer are of course symbols of swift and thirsting souls yearning for the water and the Tree, and are often associated with the Unicorn–Christ. We are familiar with the hounds. This seems to be a conglomerate scene portraying Sin and Mercy and the Salvation of the congregation through water and the Tree. Yet the symbolism is awkward: the four hounds should really be driving Christ towards the Virgin's womb, but are now chasing other animals; the Unicorn, originally Christ, has been duplicated and stands beside the Tree as a heraldic animal. The many cultural layers have gradually blurred the clarity and precision of the original meaning.

Unicorn
Vault painting, 1488, Gudme church, Denmark

CHAPTER 10
The Unicorn of the Troubadours

Young Woman with Unicorn
Tapestry from Adelshausen
church, c. 1310–20,
Augustinermuseum, Freiburg,
inv. 11508

The lady sits with her left
hand raised beneath a tree.
Hardly a chastity symbol, the
animal lays its large horn in
her lap, and she grasps it with
her right hand

The combination of Virgin and Unicorn stimulated a completely different kind of art in France. There the story was coloured by the troubadour tradition. In typically French fashion, artists and writers foresaw the consequences of the Unicorn's erotic nature and openly depicted what was implicitly understood by everyone — and ushered the animal into the sphere of worldly art. Mary with the animal's head in her lap was an image easily transferable to the human plane, and the soulful lover identifies himself narcissistically with the animal. As early as the beginning of the thirteenth century we find the first examples of poetry in which human desire has adopted the motif. Thibaut IV of Champagne (1201–1253), King of Navarre, writes:

Like the unicorn am I
quite astonished to see
the maiden walking towards me.
So seized with sorrow as it is,
fainting it rests upon her lap
and then is slain by guile,
in the same manner they slew me
Amor and my lady, for to see:
they have my heart, I shall not see it more.[1]

Here we are in quite a different world — a man's world, whereas before we were in women's convents — and the interests are not quite the same. Like another Samson, the male is lured by the woman's power, lays his head in her lap and, according to the laws of the *minnesang*, is betrayed or dies in unrequited longing. In this erotic art deception naturally enough plays a larger part than in the cult of the Madonna. It is true that there is an underlying combination of Mary with the Unicorn and the hunting scenes; but the maiden is "La Belle Dame sans Merci", and the point is not that she entices the animal on to her lap but that it suffers at her merciless bosom. Paradoxically, whereas the chaste nuns ultimately depict a scene of consummated love, the French poets describe chastity — either imposed or voluntary.

The route to the motif is decked with anecdotes from antiquity and the Bible about wily women. Delilah, Phyllis and Aristotle, and the absurd Virgil in a basket are adduced as parallels both in poetry and art. On a capital in the northern Spanish city of Pamplona there are several of these motifs, together with a Unicorn–Virgin with a mirror in her hand. As the mirror can be a chastity symbol, like the Unicorn itself, one cannot be sure whether the woman is one of the deceivers, and the mirror denotes vanity – or the chaste opposite. In either case it is necessary to make a careful analysis of the context: studying a group at Saint-Pierre in Caen, Normandy, where Virgil in a basket is opposite a Unicorn group, it is tempting to see the hunt as a positive symbol, opposing the heathen and sinful.

This intercourse can be risky for both parties. The man may die, but the woman risks punishment if she is not chaste. On the love coffers (*Minnekästchen*) used as bridal gifts in Germany and France, there is a threatening atmosphere in the meeting. The scenery is a pure idyll of nature, and Tristan and Isolde sit beside the stream. He gives her a falcon. But the betrayed King Mark lurks in the tree above them, and immediately afterwards the eye moves on to the scene in which the animal is killed in the woman's lap: look, this is what happens! This must be a warning against breaking the marriage bonds for the sake of sexual desire.

After studying numerous coffers it seems likely that the triangle of huntsman-animal-woman depicts a conflict between chaste sexual love and low, brutal lust; which may well be said to be the basic theme of the *minnesang*. One or two examples will illustrate this. On a coffer in the Musée National du Moyen Âge in Paris, a youth hunts the animal with his hounds. A scroll bears the words: "Ich jaghe in trouwen" (I hunt with faithfulness) and the Unicorn replies, ". . . dat en sal nit rouwen" (that thou mayest not repent). On the reverse of the coffer the girl binds the huntsman who has driven the animal to her, in chains. Or the inscription on a tapestry: "He who hunts for sensual pleasure will find sorrow for himself and his way."

Tristan and Isolde
Love casket, in ivory, French, *c.* 1300, Barber Institute of Fine Arts, Birmingham

On the left, King Mark lurks in the tree above the lovers. On the right is the warning against unfaithfulness: the Unicorn is pierced to death in the maiden's lap

The coffers are not unambiguous, however. Where it is clear that the man in the tree or the one who kills the animal is Cupid – and thus the god of love – the Unicorn must be the languishing suitor described by the poets. Here Love is the capable hunter. In other cases we must regard the huntsman himself as the suitor, and the Unicorn as his alter ego, his desire, that speeds ahead but must be tamed – "slain", if you like – by mirror and spear before he can be deserving of his lady's trust. This is a vital question in connection with the Flemish tapestries (see Chapter 11) and it leads us first to the complicated nature of the mirror.

The mirror is an important requisite in the art of this period and it can have several interpretations. It may be an attribute of vanity, narcissism and arrogance, as in Danish Gothic murals. But it is also an attribute of Prudentia (Prudence) and a weapon against evil animals. Here it functions as a means to self-knowledge, or disclosure of the deeper levels, for whoever looks at themselves in it. Physiologus says that wild animals can be tamed by meeting their own gaze in the mirror; indeed, the basilisk perishes if it does so. Perhaps the suitor's desire, the brute kind, is tamed when the maiden lifts up the mirror before him and he sees his own face in it.

The mirror is also the attribute of the Virgin Mary. Here it is the "spotless mirror", the symbol of her purity in which "God saw his image for the first time". In this quality of chastity symbol it is quite naturally adopted by love poetry, in which the knight actually compares his lady with a mirror, "…shining clear, unspotted", in which he can see both his own love and that of his chosen one.[2] For the people of their time, these ladies with their mirrors must have been surrounded by an aura of innocence and inviolability, at least in a poetic context.

One of the loveliest examples of this kind of tamed suitor's quest is represented on an enamelled medallion dating from the fourteenth century. It is delicately framed with Gothic clover-leaf curves, within which sits a maiden with loosened hair. The Unicorn kneels before her and she grasps its horn with one hand. With the other she lifts a round object, reminiscent of the wreaths which maidens in the books offer to their chosen suitor; but here it looks like a shining mirror. It is raised in the middle axis of the picture towards a young man sitting in a tree – like King Mark, in the legend of Tristan and Isolde – who, as in the hunting scenes, is carrying out the huntsman's kill with his spear. At the same time, the maiden receives the long horn into her hand, and the animal smiles. Again, it is not clear whether this is Cupid himself piercing the lover's heart, so that he dies a voluptuous death – or whether it is rather a taming by means of the mirror, by means of which the suitor "kills the beast" and makes himself deserving of the lady's acceptance. He seems closely bound to his animal by the spear, and she to him through the horn and the mirror. This delicate little picture is shot through with rhythms and lines that lead the eye along a continuous movement from person to person.

The marriage coffers contain a wealth of motifs, which really deserve a special iconographic study. If this were undertaken it would shed more light on the role of the Unicorn in French chivalry. The numerous variants may be due partly to the prototypes and imaginative ideas of different workshops and artists, and partly to the requests of clients. Many of the coffers were mass produced, particularly in Paris, and the standard was not always high. There is thus the possibility that motifs were misinterpreted or that their execution was imprecise. Some of the pictures can be

identified as illustrations to the popular romances and ballads of the time, for instance the famous *Roman de la Rose, La Dame à la Licorne* or — as we have seen — *Tristan and Isolde.* But even if we cannot always interpret the pictures, we can sense their bittersweet mood and almost hear the accompanying notes of the lute or the stanzas of the *Minnesinger.*

A typical text, which sets the scene for both *Minnesang* and picture, is Richard de Fournival's book the *Bestiaire d'Amours* from about 1250. It is a "Book of Courtship", which demonstrates the courtly style of the period among the ruling class:

"I have been drawn to thee by thy sweet scent alone, just as the Unicorn falls asleep under the influence of a maidenly girl's scent. For such is the nature of the Unicorn that no other animal is so hard to capture, and it has a horn on its nose which no armour can withstand, so that none dares to attack it – except an untouched girl. And as soon as it feels her presence through her scent, it kneels to her humbly and subjects itself, as if to acknowledge that it will serve her. That is why cunning huntsmen, who know its nature, place a maiden in its path! It falls asleep in her lap, and while it sleeps, the huntsmen come, who would not dare to approach it if it was awake, and kill it. Just so has Love treated me cruelly, for I was the proudest man in the world in regard to Love, and I thought I would never set eyes on the woman I would care to own . . . But Love, that cunning huntsman, he put a girl in my path, in the sweetness of whose scent I fell asleep, and now I die the death to which I was condemned . . ."[3]

Here is almost the perfect text for our medallion!

CHAPTER II
The Flemish Tapestries

**The Ornesbury Psalter:
Hunting the Unicorn**
Bodleian Library, Oxford,
MS. Douce 366, fol. 55v

For a hundred years — from about 1380 — the duchy of Burgundy enjoyed a re-markable cultural burgeoning under three great Valois dukes: Philip the Bold, Philip the Good and Charles the Bold. It was a chivalrous culture, bordering on an age when gunpowder, bullets and printer's ink would turn the knight into an anachronism, and armies of mercenaries dissolve the personal bonds between feudal lord and vassal.

In this declining feudal culture a bizarre knightly romanticism throve against the background of the all-too-harsh reality of the Hundred Years War and signs of decadence in chivalry itself.[1] It was a nostalgic dream of a time when everything had been so much better. The dream was based economically on the extremely material-istic market towns of Flanders, from where the dukes could requisition the means to run their courts. They did not imagine that those very towns represented a new age of bourgeois capitalism which would put a definitive end to the dream. But for a time the knights were able to turn dream into reality in the form of tournaments, the poetic worship of woman and other rituals — and to an expenditure on art without parallel. They competed with the North Italian merchant cities in splendour and threw a cloak of beauty and colour over a raw and brutal world, whose daily realities contradicted both art and ritual. The dream produced remarkable effects.

Serious dukes had the Arthurian Legends read aloud to them, burst into tears and declaimed selected passages of the *Roman de la Rose.* They were addressed as "Sir Lancelot" and, what is more, played out the chosen roles to the last detail, becoming Don Quixotes two centuries before time. In the *Book of the Good Knight, Deeds of M. Jacques de Lalaing,* from 1449, we read of a young nobleman who constructs a pavilion beside an artificial spring or fountain which he calls "La Fontaine des Pleures".[2] Within it sits the wax figure of a young lady with a Unicorn carrying three shields: one white, one violet and one black, dripping with white tears. A tree stands at the side, dedicated to Charlemagne the Great, one of the famous "Nine Worthies" or heroes. Jacques had sworn to conquer thirty knights in noble jousting before he himself reached the age of 30 and on the first day of each month he awaited a chal-lenger who would throw a gauntlet at one of the shields, thereby choosing the weapons. Each of the ceremonial combats, in which no blood was to be shed, would be rounded off with a banquet in the bishop's palace at Châlons-sur-Seine, when all

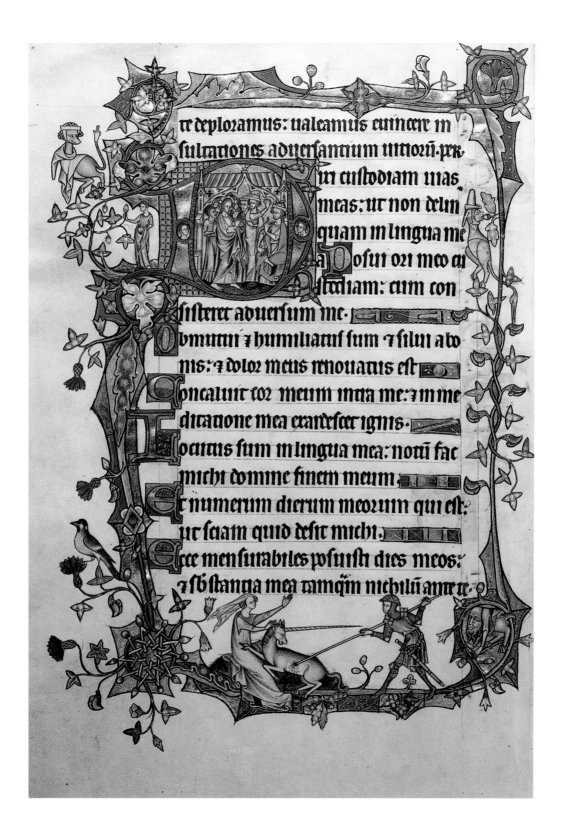

the laws of chivalry were observed. Ironically enough, the young knight fell in battle when only 32, with a bullet through his head. The new age had spoken.

The Unicorn throve in this environment and became a fashionable animal. It possessed all the qualities in high regard. It had long since shouldered its way into the coats of arms of various families and, in company with the Hortus cult in Germany and the triumph motif in Italy, a Unicorn cult developed in Burgundy and France, which – as we saw – could not be imagined there without the specialized troubadour lyric, and which was reserved solely for the noble ruling class.

Here the Unicorn may well be Christ, but he is also the lover who feels himself to be a defrauded animal in the arms of a merciless lady. Both in literature and painting a composite of Christ, lover and heraldic animal appears, which sometimes makes it difficult to see whether it is the lady who guards the Unicorn or the Unicorn who guards the lady. In the romance *La Dame à la Licorne* of about 1300 both heraldic animal and Saviour are involved.[3]

The beautiful daughter of the king of Friesland is so virtuous and good that Christ (or Cupid) presents her with a Unicorn and the title of the "White Lady, Guardian of the Unicorn". She loves a brave, but poor, knight who rides around accompanied by a lion, but she is given in marriage to a nobleman she does not love. After the usual misunderstandings, the lady is carried off by a wicked nobleman and taken to his castle. Her lover determines to set her free and they both flee over the moat on their animals – he on the lion (Courage) and she on the Unicorn (Chastity). The wicked nobleman dies of rage, after which the knight honourably delivers the princess to her rightful owner. In this fable lion and Unicorn figure side by side as companions to man and woman, almost as in the Flemish tapestries discussed in the following chapters.

At the same time it seems that the Unicorn is now given the status of the Ch'i-Lin in China: it becomes a wedding-animal. It takes part in the festivities and brings gifts to augur a good future, and it is present in the bridal chamber on hangings and in tapestries. In July 1468 the wedding of Charles the Bold and Margaret of York was celebrated in Bruges. We know a good deal about the event because the captain of the duke's guard, Olivier de la Marche, gave a description of the festivities. Among other things he describes a *tableau vivant* which was performed between the soup and the meat course at the great dinner:

"The first to enter the hall was a Unicorn, as large as a horse and fully arrayed with a silken cloth on which the arms of England were painted. On the animal was placed a very fine leopard, painted to the life; in one forepaw it held a huge English banner and in the other a splendidly worked marguerite flower. When the Unicorn had circled the tables to the sound of trumpets it was led before my Lord, the duke, and then one of the ducal stewards plucked the flower from the leopard's claws and kneeling addressed the duke: 'Most mighty, noble and victorious prince, my honoured and adored Lord! The proud and awe-inspiring English leopard, come as a guest to this noble company, now personally presents for the delight of Your Honour himself, thy realms and subjects, a marguerite of noble birth.' Thus my Lord received the noble Margaret, and the Unicorn returned from whence it came."[4] On the same occasion the Unicorn's horn was physically present, hung up over the table to protect the grand company against sudden death during the meal. As the author writes: "The appointments in the great hall included at each corner large Unicorn horns with decorated points."

In the Bodleian Library there are a number of examples of the use in Flemish–Burgundian art of "drôleries", i.e. the borders of interlaced ornamentation and small drawings used in the late Gothic period for Books of Hours and Bibles. Like certain reliefs on cathedral portals they depicted an "inverted world" filled with grotesque juxtapositions of medieval symbols. This is the contribution of art to the carnival's world of mockery. In a Book of Hours from *c.* 1480, originally attributed to the Master of Mary of Burgundy's workshop, now given to "The Nassau Master", a series of little drawings depict a "monkey tournament" that turns the ceremonial deeds of the knights topsy-turvy and moreover has the monkey dominating the Unicorn. The two animals must originally have been taken from the polarization of the creation pictures; but here the ape rides on the animal of chastity, which corresponds to later representations of savage hairy women riding it. One of the pictures shows an elegant lady with the tall pointed hat of the period (hennin), kneeling behind the Unicorn to drape a tournament blanket over it, while a monkey fastens the hooks in front of the animal (see fig. opposite). The other shows the animal ready for the contest with an armoured lion and a monkey on its back. Other pictures show two Unicorns clashing, with apes on their backs and monkeys on the backs of both Unicorn and stag. There is a sense of constantly increasing ambiguity.

These are the surroundings in which we must envisage the tapestries described in the next chapters. Many more or less fragmented wall hangings have come down to us which bear witness to the high standard of contemporary craftsmanship and to the beautifully appointed rooms in which the ruling classes moved. From among them we shall choose the two most distinguished sets of tapestries, the series in the Musée National du Moyen Âge, at the Thermes de Cluny in Paris, called the *Lady with the Unicorn* – popularly known as the Red Series – and that in the Metropolitan Museum of Art, New York, known as the Verteuil Tapestries – or the Blue Series.

Lion and monkey on a Unicorn's back
Probably the Nassau Master, *c.* 1470, Bodleian Library, Oxford, MS. Douce 220, fol. 159

CHAPTER 12
The Lady with the Unicorn

Sight,
The Lady with the Unicorn
"The Red Series", *c.* 1480,
Musée National du Moyen
Âge, Cluny, Paris

The Red and the Blue Series of tapestries are some of the loveliest flowers in the Burgundian garden of art. They stem from Flanders, where quantities of standards, silken sails, tents and decorations came into being under the direction of distinguished artists, who considered these things a regular part of their work. The weavers' workshops in Brussels were particularly highly regarded, and it is possible that both these series originate from there.

The Paris tapestries were rediscovered in 1841 on the walls of the sub-prefect's dusty offices in the castle of Boussac at Creuse. It was the writer Prosper Mérimée who first drew attention to their value. In 1844 Georges Sand saw them and wrote about them in her novel *Jeanne* and in articles, in which she correctly dated them to the end of the fifteenth century on the basis of the ladies' costumes. Yet they remained at the castle for a long time, threatened by damp and mould. Not until 1863 were they brought to the Thermes de Cluny in Paris, carried by the wave of Romanticism. Careful conservation has now restored them almost to their former glory.

The series consists of six separate pieces, not equal in size, varying between three and four metres each way. Common to all of them is their composition, with a sitting or standing young woman as the central figure, elegantly dressed and of high social rank. She is placed on a little dark blue island, studded with flowers, and is flanked by a lion and a Unicorn, who take turns to guard her shield and standard. Her coat of arms is a rose-coloured cloth divided by a blue diagonal strip bearing three yellow sickle moons. The animals are surrounded by trees and the whole island is on a red ground of *millefleurs*, a carpet of small flowers on which play rabbits, dogs, monkeys and birds.

To start with let us look at the five pieces, which since the age of the Romantics have rightly been known as the *Five Senses*. This popular theme is traditionally presented, as follows: *Sight* is a young woman with a mirror, *Hearing* shows her occupied with a musical instrument, in *Taste* she is feeding a parrot, her sense of *Smell* is aroused by flowers, and finally *Touch* is demonstrated by the lady holding the flagstaff with one hand and with the other lightly touching the Unicorn's vertical horn.

In all the pictures the lion appears as a slightly stylized heraldic animal, indicating a heraldic tradition, although its almost human features express a fascinating and rather diabolic mimicry, to which we shall return later. Above all the scene is dominated by the Unicorn. It is invariably near the lady's left-hand side – the side of the heart – now reclining, now standing and always attentive to her actions. It radiates a self-consciousness which gives it a different dimension from the lion. It thinks its own thoughts and could leave the scene if it so wished. But it stays there. Its attitudes are those of devotion, and the intimacy between lady and animal is reflected in her hair, which is plaited above the brow in a little "horn", ending in a tuft precisely like the one on the Unicorn's tail. It is as if the two poles of the animal have merged into a hieroglyph above her forehead, which binds them together. Over all the pictures there is a refined grace, bordering on decadence.

This atmosphere emanates glowingly in *Sight*, an image that has particularly delighted writers and the general public, and is frequently reproduced. It portrays the classic Virgin scene, but in a worldly guise. The lady plays the part of Mary. She sits in the middle of her island with the Unicorn at her side, and he has placed both

forelegs in her lap on the blood-red lining of her dress, while in obvious satisfaction he studies his face in the mirror that she holds up before him. The resemblance to the enamel (see fig. on p.85) is so striking that there is no need to repeat our reflections on the mirror or the goodwill of the animal. The fashionable standing mirror bears remarkable resemblance to a Gothic monstrance, which can hardly be accidental.

But the picture is ambivalent! The scene is sacred – and it is profane. The animal is poised in the tension between the red dress lining and the mirror. Desire is barred by taming, just as the ermine at her feet signifies chastity – but the numerous leaping rabbits imply fertility. If the motif originates in the Virgin Mary type, the ambivalence is the contribution of French culture. The mirror is appropriate to both worlds. *Sight* is the simplest picture in the series. Everything is concentrated on the meeting of the lady with the Unicorn on the dark blue island.

An almost sacred mood emanates from the sense of *Hearing* as well. The lady plays on an organ, aided by her maid, and the animals turn their heads to listen. The lion and the Unicorn double as gilded statuettes on the end posts of the organ, as if guarding the portals of a church.

A new animal appears in the sense of *Smell* (see fig. on p.94): the lady is plaiting a garland of red and white carnations, and a monkey steals flowers from a basket behind her and sniffs them; but she is unaware of it. This is also the case in the sense of *Taste* (see fig. on p.95): she takes an almond from a bowl to give to the parrot on her hand, but does not notice a monkey sitting by her foot eating a nut, and another above her head.

In the fifth picture, depicting the sense of *Touch*, there is a strange mood, hard to verbalize (see fig. on p.97). The young woman stands erect, holding the flagstaff herself, the symbol of family and power, and with the other hand she holds her Unicorn's horn. Both monkeys have moved up to the top of the picture – and both are firmly chained up. Similarly the other animals are now wearing collars and the lady's long, loosely hanging belt looks like a chain, as if the whole picture has the chain or bonds as its leading symbol. The Unicorn looks anxious. It pulls down the corners of its mouth and for the first time we see its tufted tail turned down towards the ground.

We notice that in the four preceding pictures the lady holds the requisites necessary to the given sense, but she does not carry out the "action" of the sense. The animals do that for her. In *Sight* and *Hearing* it is the Unicorn who looks and listens, and in *Smell* and *Taste* it is the monkey who sniffs and eats. This is important, for it raises the animals above the decorative level and gives them significance. Not until the sense of *Touch* does the lady rouse herself to take hold of flagstaff and horn. What is happening?

One senses a hierarchy, a hierarchy of the senses, in which we move downwards from sight–hearing, via smell–taste, to touch. Can we use this supposition for an interpretation? To seek an answer we must return to ancient philosophy, and first of all to Plato. In several writings, particularly the *Timaeus*, he develops his theory of man and the cosmos.[1] To Plato, existence is a great staircase leading upwards to The One and the ideal world behind that of the senses. The material world, in which man is fitted to live, is composed of the four elements: earth, water, air and fire, in precisely that order from the lowest – earth – to radiant fire and the sun itself. The soul is

Hearing,
The Lady with the Unicorn
"The Red Series", *c.* 1480,
Musée National du Moyen
Âge, Paris

THE UNICORN

chained to a body which is also composed of the elements, and it experiences the material world through the senses, which, although necessary, can confuse and divert the soul from the reasoning faculty which alone can bring order into its chaos. A constant war is waged in us between the senses and reason.

Five senses are necessary, but they are not of equal value. Like so much else, they are arranged in a pattern. Although Plato does not go so far as to state an order of precedence, he makes it clear that some are nobler than others. During the conversation that Socrates holds with Timaeus, he has Timaeus explain the matter. God gave us sight first of all the senses and placed the eyes uppermost in the head, which is nobler than the body. The eyes emit light themselves, which meets the sunlight's fire, and is thus joined with the highest of the elements. And God bestowed sight upon us in order that we might see the order of reason that is revealed in the movements of the heavenly bodies, and thus create order in ourselves. For if we had never seen

Smell (left) and *Taste* ,
The Lady with the Unicorn
"The Red Series", *c.* 1480,
Musée National du Moyen
Âge, Cluny, Paris

the movements of the heavenly bodies and from them learned the laws of number and geometry, we should never have attained to philosophy, for mathematics and astronomy are the forerunners of philosophy. Therefore above all the eye gives us intellectual benefit and is the greatest blessing for us, for not one word would have been uttered about the universe if we had not been able to observe the stars and the sun and their movements in the heavens.

In fact, the blessings of the ear are of the same type. Harmony and rhythm grant us clarity and peace. Speech and music are available for those who do not merely seek superficial pleasure, but allies against the disorder in the mind that threatens us. And since sound comes to the ear through vibrations in the air, the sense of hearing is naturally conjoined with the element of air.

Smell and taste are also pleasurable, but of a more material kind. Both are concerned with the nourishment of the body and demand physical contact. Taste depends on the sensitivity of the tongue and occurs when it meets with things that are dissolved; smell depends on the nose's receptiveness to vapours. Smell and taste are concerned with substances that vary from solid matter to liquids and vapours, that is to say, with half-formed material, and thus border on the nature of water.

Since the head is nobler than the body, owing to its spherical shape, the sense of touch, which is diffused over the whole surface of the body, is of a lower kind. It informs us of the solid form of material and surface, of texture and weight. In addition, it lures us towards sensual pleasure and can lead soul and body into depravity. It corresponds to the lowest element: earth.

Medieval thinkers were in complete agreement with this order: to the Christian mind it was no surprise that light was the highest expression for God and sight a prerequisite for the ascent of the soul towards the spiritual sphere. Music with its harmonies was the preferred art of the Church because it showed us the order of numbers and thus God's order, and the idea that the more earth-bound senses could lead man astray was of course a commonplace. Sometimes the five senses were linked with animals at this time, and the monkey, which was symbolically negative, represented the sense of taste and, in the scene of the Fall, was positioned sometimes behind Eve actually eating an apple.

A clearer light is now shed on the five scenes of the tapestry. *Sight* is so spiritual that it can refer to the Virgin Mary herself. *Hearing* is symbolized by church music, while the three other senses include the monkey. The sense of *Smell* must have a higher position than *Taste*. It has an airier character and in this scene there is only one monkey. With *Touch* we come to the sense that more than any other can chain human beings to instinctive urges and bring them close to the animal. Now the lady seems very much aware of the monkey, which has hold of one of its feet and scratches its chest; her eyes, wide open, are directed on to it, and her dark figure, the standard staff and the white horn form three vertical, static accents on the surface. The Unicorn is conscious of the danger and looks anxiously at his lady.

The sixth picture may hold the key to the meaning of the whole series. Here the lady stands in front of an open blue tent, spangled with shining drops or flames. In front of it stands the little maid, holding out a casket to her mistress, who seems to be taking from it a heavy necklace. For the first time her neck is bare. What is the lady doing? It has usually been assumed that she is naturally picking up the gift she has

received from her suitor. A reasonable motif for a wedding tapestry. For that is what it is, isn't it? Or is it?

Now doubt asserts itself. We note that it is not the same young woman in the six pictures. Their costume and, not least, their faces definitely show six different girls. Moreover the suitor's coat of arms is missing, although it is normally seen on wedding tapestries. What seemed at first an obvious explanation has lost credence and now it is thought that the lady is not about to don her necklace but rather has taken it off, and is putting it into the casket wrapped in a cloth. The elegantly falling rhythm from left to right in the picture also supports this view.

This brings us to a new problem in the universe of the picture: the inscription on the tent. Above its entrance are the words in large letters: "A mon seul Désir V". Colourful pavilions with the owner's device and coat of arms were almost prerequisites in the knightly theatre of the age, as an expression of the owner's personality. So

THE UNICORN

all the symbols on them are significant. The phrase is apparently perfectly simple and, while it was still considered to refer to a wedding, it seemed obvious to translate the words, "To my sole desire", and understand them to be addressed to the beloved. Perhaps they should be understood in a completely different manner, however. It is also possible to construe them as, "A – Mon seul désir – V". In this case, A and V might be initials (a member of the de Viste family?). The three remaining words, in the middle, would then stand alone as an exclamation or appeal.

We have evidence of a similar series featuring the senses, this time copperplate engravings, which about 1559 belonged to a Cardinal Marck of Liege, with the inscription "Los Sentidos" (The Senses). This also comprised six pictures, of which the last, which we know only from its inclusion in an inventory, bore the inscription, "Liberum arbitrium" – Free Choice! It refers to the morally conscious person who voluntarily renounces the pleasures of the senses in order not to sink down to the chained state of the animal. Through reason one chooses the "Highest Good".

Free Choice! My sole Desire! Now the interpretation can be simplified, and others have had the same idea. Jean Cocteau created an introduction to a ballet inspired by the Paris tapestries, *La Dame à la Licorne*. Here the lady lives with her Unicorn in a tent, where she is visited by the knight on the heraldic lion, and the Unicorn rightly feels betrayed. When it looks in the lady's mirror it sees only the image of the knight, and in anger it pierces it with its horn. The scene ends in the lady regretting her fall and, looking up, her eyes meet this very motto, "Mon seul Désir", and these three words only – in the form of a complete statement with no distracting preposition.

Now we may ponder on whether the word "desire" can refer to the soul's desire for spiritual liberation or for God. Phrase and action must link with each other. If, cautiously, we interpret the action of the lady as the voluntary denial of the chains of the senses because she wishes to pursue her desire for the "Highest Good", then the tapestry is a series of moral images, governed by Neoplatonic thought. It would then be consonant with Botticelli's contemporary works. His *Birth of Venus* and *Primavera* convey Neoplatonic ideas beneath the most sophisticated aesthetic guise. We should not forget that Burgundian art competed with Florentine art not merely in elegance but also in the use of profound allegories, and that Neoplatonism was common property for intellectual Europe. I know of no work of art that is more reminiscent of certain of Botticelli's paintings.

Several observations confirm the interpretation. The lady is part of an apotheosis. She stands beneath a canopy of blue and gold – the colours of Mary – whose heavenly blue emphasizes the golden turban which forms a halo around her head. The flames, which in Botticelli indicate blessed souls, rise in harmony with the lines of the pavilion, the moon and the Unicorn's horn. And the four trees, that throughout the series accompany the figures in constantly changing places, also speak the language of symbolism. The oak stands for strength and perseverance, the meaning of the orange tree revolves around fruitfulness – the bride wears white orange blossom – the holly stands for the Passion and the pine is a Tree of Life. It is not insignificant that the pavilion in the last picture is firmly tied to the two noblest trees, the holly and the pine, instead of to traditional heraldic animals. This pavilion is protected by God.

Lastly, we must not forget the animals and birds. Several animals have been mentioned, but among the wealth of fauna three birds occupy a special place, high up in the picture: a heron (crane), a falcon and a magpie, three birds prominent in the bestiary and love poems. Let us look at the parts they play. In *Sight* they are completely absent. The Unicorn dominates the scene and we are introduced to the dramatis personae, the lady, the lion and the Unicorn. In *Hearing* the falcon chases the heron, which flies up to the very top edge of the picture. The falcon is a noble bird which sits on a knight's hand and fetches his prey. In Christian symbolism, it can descend on the prey, like the eagle, and stand for Christ, who seizes the soul to carry it with Him. The heron is traditionally a symbol for the alert Christian soul, which keeps itself awake on watch by carrying a small stone in its lifted claw. These two birds also appear in the symbolism of the worldly knight and can be seen in pictures of Burgundian "love gardens", where a falcon hunts a heron in the centre of the picture above the courting couple, or a knight and his lady exchange a falcon and a heron as gifts. The two birds come to signify *spiritus* and *anima*, and thus express the masculine that pursues the feminine.

In the sense of *Smell* the heron is placed precisely in its classic guarding position above the negative magpie, which is above the monkey. In *Taste,* falcon and magpie meet, as if good and evil confront each other. The drama rises in the strange *Touch* picture. The heron flaps in great excitement above all the chained animals: its neck feathers bristle and its small round eye seems to shoot lightning flashes of anger or fear, while the falcon flies off to the far right, further away than usual.

Then in the last picture the heron seems to capitulate to the falcon. It leans over backwards with feet upwards and shows neither fear nor anger. The flying falcon carries something in its claws: two black ribbons flutter behind it with two gold rings. It resembles the sling that the falconer uses to restrain his bird — a ribbon which is obviously to be placed on the heron, which seems ready to receive it.

One thing is certain: the little bird drama played out above the figures is of vital importance to understanding the whole. The Christ-falcon, that desires to bind the soul-heron to itself, is a commentary on the Unicorn, which guides the lady, who now exchanges the heavy chain of the senses for the leading-string of Christ before a pavilion tied to the sacred trees. The picture is again in the sign of the chain; but this time it is God's!

The Unicorn plays a similar part to Hermes, leader of souls, in Botticelli's universe, as the spiritual guide, Reason, which directs the powers of the picture. It is gentle, white and charming, but make no mistake: the Unicorn is a powerful spirit and not without demonic force. It has Pan's sharp cloven hoofs and a flame in its tail, and its horn can pierce through the elephant. It is the animal that Job was unable to keep by his crib, which started its career as a huge monster with roaring voice and sabre-shaped horn, before the nuns tamed it and the knights gave it a coiffeur. But the tapestry repressed its past just as the age repressed reality, and it is precisely these repressions that give the pictures their attraction and their scent of decadence.

The lion is interesting too, although here it seems to play second fiddle. Its lively face registers humour and it finds music somewhat boring, seems content when the Unicorn is worried and slightly ironic when innocence rules. We are never certain of what it is thinking.

We want to know who originally owned this masterpiece. As far back as 1833 the bourgeois family of de Viste from Lyons was suggested. Like many other such families, its members made careers as officials in the king's service in Paris and gained high positions through their efficiency. A favoured candidate has been one Jean de Viste, whose distinguished memorial brass in the Celestine church in Paris shows that, despite remaining a commoner, he had attained high social standing. This may therefore be a work of art commissioned by a "nouveau riche", who wished to reflect a noble image and so could not have enough standards and pennons on his tapestry. He may have ordered it between 1484, when he inherited the right to use the family coat of arms on the death of his father, Aimé, and 1500, the year of his own death. This fits the style of the tapestry perfectly.

The lady used to be as his daughter Claude, depicted receiving her bridal jewels; but she was not married until 1513 and, as we noted, there are six different ladies. The theory has therefore been abandoned. Likewise, another old idea that the tapestry was a gift to the third wife of Charles the Bold, Margaret of York, has been dropped. Scholars, who have been inclined sometimes to connect great names with great works of art, were reluctant to let go of the idea; but today it is thought that the owner was indeed Jean de Viste and that he commissioned a magnificent "moral" tapestry for himself.

Behind him, however, an assembly of humanists and theologians had created the ingenious allegory, and behind them were ranged long bookshelves, where centuries of words had been amassed: from the Bible, the Church Fathers and the philosophers: Isidore, Honorius, Plato and Aristotle, Pliny and the bestiarists, to Ficino and the French lyricists. A thousand years of meditation and writing are met in this universe and piled up in one transparent layer over another, until everything is double, triple, polyphonic in meaning to the limits of the possible. So it is not surprising that it is hard for us to fathom them and that we are left feeling we have only half uncovered their depths. Much uncertainty still surrounds these tapestries. We know neither artist nor designer, nor even the correct sequence of the pictures, and we are tempted to go on improvising further explanations. Here I have tentatively given them a Neoplatonic setting.

Rainer Maria Rilke was enchanted by the tapestries, which he described in *The Notebooks of Malte Laurids Brigge*. He puts them in a different order and does not attempt to interpret them; but he immerses himself in their life and atmosphere. He was especially interested in *Sight* and wrote a sonnet about it in his *Sonette an Orpheus*:

Oh, this is the animal that never was.
Though they knew nothing of it, still
They loved it for its grace, its gait, the full
Curve of its neck and clear quiet gaze.

It never had been. But out of their love
A pure animal rose. They left it space.
And in that light and well protected place
It raised its head with ease and did not have to be.

They nourished it, not with corn,
But only with the potency to be,
And this gave to it such a wealth of power

That from its brow a horn grew up. One horn.
In whiteness it approached a Virgin, to see
Itself in the silver-mirror and in her.[2]

In 1990 a German scholar, Gottfried Büttner, offered a new interpretation.[3] He too saw Neoplatonic ideas in the tapestries and detected extremely important agreements between them and Botticelli's *Primavera*. He saw the role of the Unicorn as a Hermes, that is to say, a guide for the lady's soul, a 'psychopompos'. But he did not think the series had any connection with the five senses!

His conjecture is completely different: he notes that the lady, whose appearance alters between one tapestry and another, changes because she grows older. In some scenes she is young and smooth-skinned, but she apparently matures and acquires a more lined and longer face with bags under her eyes and a solemn expression. At the same time her coiffeur changes: from being covered with a close-fitting cap, it has a tall upright tip that grows more and more like the Unicorn's horn, until the tip finally becomes a diadem ornamented with precious stones.

Naturally this gives rise to a completely new sequence, which has nothing to do with the hierarchy of the five senses. It is ruled by the Platonic idea of the ages of man, divided into a seven-yearly rhythm, denoting the first three bodily development from birth to the 21st year and the next the spiritual maturation of the adult from 21 to 50 years of age. If we retain the old designation, the course of the sequence runs as follows:

1. Smell. The child's innocence develops among flowers and lambs. The girl is young and smooth.

2. Taste. The transformation of puberty is indicated by restless gusts of wind, the animals are agitated, and the animal nature of the monkey is about to awake.

3. The apotheosis with the blue tent. The woman is now an adult, and her free will shows itself: she takes the first step towards spiritual development and relinquishes her jewellery. But the monkey suggests that nature cannot be completely subdued.

4. Hearing. The sound of the organ arouses a responsiveness to spirituality. The Unicorn has seized the standard for the first time, and the lady's plait is arranged around her forehead.

5. Sight shows increasing spiritual awareness. The lady is now alone in her absorption. Her mirror catches the face of the animal and she sees God 'as in a mirror' and meditates on his image. Her plait spirals like the horn.

6. Touch. In this picture the lady is oldest, fully adult and conscious. She has matured in relation to the animals and stands now as their ruler with standard in hand, leading the Unicorn by grasping its horn as a sceptre. The top of her coiffeur is now like a crown. She has definitively conquered all the lower instincts: the wild animals and apes around her are all in chains and subjected to her awakened gaze.

To Büttner the tapestry series is a true work of the Renaissance. It is concerned above all with the development of the human individual, becoming an almost modern *Bildungsroman*. Moreover he stresses that *Sight* has lost about 40cm from its border at the bottom end beneath the island, and from older pictures it can be seen that there was a monkey here together with a fox, a pair of rabbits, a heron and a magpie. This seems to indicate that the monkey – as an inevitable part of the amplitude of God's work of creation – was probably originally present in all the tapestries. This being so, it is interesting to speculate on what it was doing in the various pictures, and where its place was in the hierarchy; also how many there were in each tapestry. There is no doubt that lion, Unicorn and monkey form an extremely important trio (just as do falcon–heron–magpie) whose deeper meaning we do not yet know.

Büttner's theory is interesting. Nevertheless I distance myself from it to a certain extent because he does not give any consideration to the interplay of the birds above, nor to the quantity and threatening placing of the monkeys in the final picture, while he puts the apotheosis with the blue tent in the centre of the series, where it seems most awkwardly placed. Moreover it is difficult to exclude the five senses! But there is absolutely no doubt that we should take note of the lady's changing age and her coiffeur. The tapestries continue to keep their secrets.

There is an opportunity to examine the association of lion, Unicorn and monkey in a tapestry of the same date and perhaps even from the same workshop: about 1500 a brother-in-law of Jean de Viste commissioned tapestries of St Stephen for the cathedral in Auxerr, where he was bishop. These depicted of the death of the saint by stoning in several pictures, of which the last one is extant. In this the saint lies dead, surrounded by stones, and his soul is carried to heaven by angels. A circle of animals keeps watch around him. Here we see the well-known stag, a porcupine, with lion, Unicorn and monkey, the three last gathered in front. The monkey wears a wicked grin. Why?

CHAPTER 13
The Chase

The Start of the Hunt,
The Hunt of the Unicorn,
the Verteuil Tapestries,
"The Blue Series", *c.* 1500, The
Metropolitan Museum of Art,
Gift of John D. Rockefeller, Jr,
The Cloisters Collection
(37.80.1)

One day at the beginning of the 1850s a farmer's wife called at the château of Verteuil (Charente) to see Madame Elizabeth de la Rochefoucauld and ask if Madame might be interested in some old curtains that her husband had been using for a long time to protect his potatoes against frost in the winter. Madame replied that she might as well take a look at them – and the curtains were produced for inspection.

They were the Verteuil tapestries – the Blue Series – which now returned to their old family owners after some sixty years in exile.[1] This masterpiece consists of seven tapestries, worked in silk and wool with occasional silver thread. Today, one of them is just a narrow fragment divided into two strips; and the first and last pieces are somewhat different from the rest. They were either used for a different purpose or made by another artist; but iconographically they seem to belong, and will be discussed here in the order that has always seemed natural.

A "heading" to each piece will show the sequence:

1. *The Start of the Hunt.* The first picture may be by a different artist than the rest. The figures are slightly stiff and the proportions and structure not completely convincing. As in the final picture, the scene is set in *millefleur* surroundings – not unlike the Paris series – and this creates an unreal atmosphere around the figures, who move in an enchanted forest outside time and space. They are accompanied by the letters A and E, bound together with a knot, which occur five times in each picture: in the four corners and the centre, where they are hung up in a delicate tree. A group of young men is out hunting in this flowery forest. The leader is a knightly youth with a feather in his hat, who stands immediately beneath the central tree, so that his feather touches the letter A. He is accompanied by his huntsmen; all carry horn or spear, and two of them lead the eager pack of hounds. A small scout has climbed up a tree and waves them into the forest. The quarry is discovered, the chase can begin...

2. *The Unicorn Dips his Horn into the Stream.* After the peaceful introduction we find ourselves in the midst of the hunt. The company, now twelve persons strong, has gathered in a circle around a fountain, whose centre pole bears the two letters. Four lions' heads gush out water on all sides, from where it is carried through a lion mask on to the ground, where it gathers into a stream. A crowd of animals has assembled around the flowing water: a pair of lions in the foreground, a spotted leopard, a weasel or stoat, a stag and a hyena; on the edge of the basin itself a pair of pheasants has come to rest and they look at their reflections in the water, beside two fluttering goldfinches. Snipe and duck move in the thick undergrowth, in which can be seen red roses round the well.

In the centre of the picture, in front of the well, the Unicorn kneels to dip its horn in the water. This is the event that the other animals are all waiting for and which arrests their attention. One of the huntsmen on the left points to it, and the eye is led from his hand through the Unicorn to the jackal which lurks in the lowest corner. The distinguished youth lifts his index finger to command silence. The hounds are held back. For this is the moment of the water cleansing!

We are looking at one of the most significant pictures in the series, and its symbols are as subtly blended as those in the Legend of the Grail. We know the well: it is Mary's well from the Hortus Conclusus or the Well of Paradise, with the column of the Tree of Life, the flowing waters of the four Evangelists and the spotless mirror of the water in which the birds can see themselves. The "twosomeness" of the pairs of birds on the edge of the basin, and the red roses, refer to both Mary and to love.

After the water has run on to the ground the Unicorn must cleanse it, just as Moses cleansed the water at Mara with his staff, or as the taper is lowered into the baptismal font. This is also the establishment of a Holy Communion ceremony, in which the other animals approach to drink of the consecrated water. These animals belong to Christian symbolism and are also heraldic. In front is a group of significant creatures: opposite the Unicorn itself stands its counterpart, the stag, which is a symbol of both Christ and the soul, next panther/leopard, the pair of lions and the weasel, which as a snake-slayer is an ally of the Unicorn. These animals are in opposition to the negative hyena in the corner. With its thin body and lowered, hissing head it is the Judas in this gathering, the carrion eater. It is an ill omen for the Unicorn to be already confined here between hunters and hyena.

The twelve "Apostles" of the hunting party and the animals are an expectant congregation. They tell us something very important: the hunters are not unambiguously wicked murderers, but take part in a ritual drama which is preordained. They are instruments in a divinely ordained plan.

3. *The Unicorn Leaps the Stream* (see fig. on p.108). After this hour of initiation, in which the animal is given sanctuary, the hunt for the precious quarry starts in earnest. In a new bipartite landscape the Unicorn leaps for its life over the stream pursued by hounds and hunters. One of them blows his horn, another releases the hounds. Four ugly faces close in on the hunted animal, all with spears aimed at it. They exactly resemble the four negative "temperaments" that surround Christ on the way to the Cross in altarpieces of the period by painters such as Bosch, Memling and Dürer.

THE UNICORN

THE CHASE

THE UNICORN

The Unicorn will not be captured, however. Although it is surrounded it cannot be stopped, for "It is a strong and swift animal and cannot be taken alive."

The animal's strength is indicated by the dominant oak tree, but its fate is seen in the holly which grows up around it. Above the oak crown, the letters this time are F and R, while A and E are still in the corners and on the collars of the hounds. The two unusual letters have quite obviously been inserted later in an appliquéd piece of sky, and we shall return to this.

4. *The Unicorn Defends Himself* (see fig. on p.109). The Physiologus continues: "It fights with horn, hoofs and teeth . . . it gores even the elephant with its horn." Now the pursuers have to hold back their hounds to save them; but the Unicorn has torn open the stomach of one hound which twists itself into the air with a marvellously well observed movement, and the man behind is close to being struck by the kicking hoofs. Alert and powerful it wards off the pack, and the hounds crouch and slink away.

One or two figures stand out: on the left a young huntsman blows his horn. On the scabbard of his sword are the words: "Ave Regina (C)oelorum" – a variant of Gabriel's greeting to Mary, which we met with earlier on the Erfurt panel (see fig. on p.67). This is in fact Gabriel himself, who has joined the hunt and now wishes to drive the Unicorn to its fate. Just above him an old man comes on to the stage. He is dressed as a peasant, carries a water bottle in one hand and a staff over his shoulder, pierced through something that looks like a loaf or a sponge. He is obviously bringing provisions to the company. Beside him stands a huntsman with an axe, pointing, as if requesting something, at the central tree, an apple tree, as if encouraging the old man to cut it down. This huntsman belongs in part to the worldly plane of the hunt, in part to the two invading figures, who like unreal guests from the religious sphere now enter the chase to direct its course. The little scene may indicate the approaching sacrifice: now the Tree of Life is to be axed and the ritual brought to its end. The unobtrusively threatening action on the left side of this picture is linked visually, through the tilted movement of the Unicorn and its horn, which also is piercing something (the hound), to the watchful crane in the lower right-hand corner. As before, the crane is the Christian soul watching through the hours of the night. Reed mace (the sceptre) and thistle and holly (the crown of thorns) are still rooted; but they are present and drawing nearer to the animal. There is no doubt that we are approaching the climax. The young nobleman, who clearly plays a special part in the drama, is uppermost on the right. He is passive, does not seem to take a direct part in the chase itself, but stands still, observing the scene unfolding before him.

5. *The Unicorn and the Virgin Mary.* It is unfortunate that this scene in particular – the Virgin Hunt itself – is only a fragment. Only two small strips remain from the climax of the story, but we can glean something from them. The left-hand strip shows a holly tree and a man blowing a horn (apparently not the same Gabriel as before). The animal is being driven towards an enclosure, which it is just possible to see is square – an earthly Hortus Conclusus. The fence is edged with red and white roses, and within are parts of a dog's tail and collar: the pursuing hounds have already made their way inside. An apple tree again stands on the central axis.

THE UNICORN

THE CHASE

On the other strip, which must have been joined closely to the first, is the Unicorn's head with teeth bared as if in pain. Two hounds attack its back and drops of blood trickle from it. Just behind its neck can be seen the tip of a delicate hand caressing its throat, and a piece of brocade sleeve which is almost a mirror image of the lady's sleeve in the first picture of the Paris tapestry. Beside this stands a lady of the court, with raised hand, casting a sideways glance at the huntsmen. Her twisted mouth and strange look give her an unpleasantly Delilah-like expression, which bodes ill. Treachery is abroad here! Everything takes place in luxuriant vegetation, which in itself contains the whole story: a forest of apple tree, holly and roses.

6. *The Unicorn is Killed and Brought to the Castle* (see fig. on p.111). The picture is divided into two halves: on the left the animal is killed in the forest with spear and teeth, alone among its enemies. On the right the castle, which appears behind the action in the distance, appears in the middle ground surrounded by a moat, which is nothing other than the stream that runs through the pictures from the water-cleansing scene. This shows that the castle too is in consecrated water.

A procession of gentlemen and ladies emerges from the open gateway. In front an aristocratic gentleman with his lady advance to meet the huntsmen coming from the forest leading a horse. The dead Unicorn is slung over the horse's back, with blood dripping from its neck, round which is a wreath; this is apparently of holly, but on closer inspection it is seen to consist of oak leaves. A huntsman holds its horn as if it were a sceptre, and points to the lance wound in its flank. The lady looks at her husband, she points to the animal with one hand and holds a rosary hanging from her belt with the other. Because of the condition of the preceding picture we cannot see whether she is the lady who captured the animal; but considering her age and married state she hardly qualifies. Perhaps we should not ignore the young woman whose face mysteriously appears behind the barred window of the tower! Why does she stand there in hiding, observing what is happening so intently? The wound of the animal and her glance lie along the same line – the diagonal of the picture. I think the two belong together.

We can also see how the eye is led along lines that move into the picture from the middle of its left-hand edge, running along a spear to the huntsman pointing at the wound in the Unicorn's neck. From here another spear leads down to the lady's rosary, while another line through the arched neck of the horse leads up to the young woman standing behind her lattice.

The picture is not without its puzzles, but the meaning of the whole is unquestionable: deprived of its strength through its encounter with the woman, the Unicorn is overcome by its pursuers. They take the precious booty to the king's castle, where its value is understood. It is received with reverence like a relic and worshipped through the rosary.

7. *The Unicorn in the Hortus Conclusus.* This is not the end. In the last tapestry, on a dark ground with a wealth of vegetation like a tropical forest, sits the resurrected Unicorn, now in a circular mandorla, the heavenly Hortus, among white lilies and red carnations. As in ancient pictures of the tamed Unicorn, it wears a wide green collar and is chained to a pomegranate tree with ripe fruit, symbols of both love and

The Unicorn in Hortus Conclusus, **The Hunt of the Unicorn, the Verteuil Tapestries,** "The Blue Series", *c.* 1500, The Metropolitan Museum of Art, Gift of John D. Rockefeller, Jr, The Cloisters Collection (37.80.6)

eternal life. The fruits are opening so that the kernels can be seen, and the red juice drips down and lies like drops of blood on the white skin of the animal. This time the initials A and E hang from red cords in the tree's crown and the animal's gold chain is plaited into them. The chain is a "chaine d'amour", which binds the suitor to the tree (the woman), as Christ is eternally bound to the Tree of Life. Through consecration, death and annihilation the road leads to Resurrection and new life – for God himself as for the individual human being, here the seeking suitor who attains the life of love. In these remarkable tapestries the Unicorn becomes a grail, which one desires in order to share in its power. Perhaps, as in the caskets, it is at the same time the "alter ego" of the young knight, his desire, which must undergo every ordeal and be tamed before he can claim his reward.

The riches of these tapestries cannot be appreciated fully without taking into account everything that has preceded them in Europe: the particular interpretation of the Unicorn offered by Christianity, the Virgin in the garden with the suffering animal wounded in the flank, and the animal that cleanses the poisoned water. To this must be added the animal world of the bestiaries, the love lyrics and possibly the special undertones of alchemy. In the tapestries all this is blended together into a poetic universe transformed by masterly craft. Never has the animal been more exquisitely realized nor had a more powerful individuality; from picture to picture one admires its beauty and strength and suffers with it in its bitter death. Only an age that was enchanted by the worldly aesthetics of the cult of chivalry and at the same time engrossed with the mystical worship of the blood of Christ could create such a consummate synthesis. What could follow this? We seem to be at the summit of the Unicorn's history, and simultaneously facing its conclusion.

We shall not deal in depth with the problems surrounding the history of the Verteuil tapestries. As with the Paris series it is evident that a work of this quality was intended for the wealthiest ruling class. The letters A and E provide a clue and, as usual, many theories have been adduced, often linking the series to well known persons. The most important of these (from 1942) claims that the tapestry was made for Anne of Brittany, who was first married to the mad French King Charles VIII (1491–1498) and then to Louis XII (1499–1515). So the married couple in the last picture should be Anne and her second bridegroom Louis, whose marriage was solemnized on 8 January 1499. The style fits the date and there is undeniably a marked likeness between the faces and contemporary portraits of the pair; but such likenesses could depend upon common stylistic features. In fact the "Anne" in the tapestry seems too old, as she was only 22 when she married, and the "Louis" does not wear the chain of the Order of Saint Michael, as was his custom.

A more tenable candidate might be found in the Rochefoucauld family, later owners of the tapestries, but no member of that family seems to have had – or to have married – anyone with the initials A and E. Perhaps the letters are not initials at all. Could they be alpha and a mirror-image omega, thus standing for Christ, who is present throughout the story? Or might they – as is often seen – be an abbreviated device?

We recall that in the third picture there were two other letters – F and R – entwined on a section of sky. This was inserted later and may perhaps refer to François de la Rochefoucauld, who died in 1516. Later on we find the tapestries listed in inventories of the Rochefoucauld family in 1680 and 1728, after which they turn up during the French Revolution. In a letter of 2 December 1793, one of the committees set up to investigate the possessions of the nobility advises that they should be spared because they do not show any undue signs of "royalism", but contain only stories. We sigh with relief for once, until we find that the tapestries disappear for half a century, only to turn up again as winter protection for the farmer's potatoes. Then they returned to the Rochefoucauld family. They were subsequently purchased, in 1920, by John D. Rockefeller who greatly prized them and hung them in his own home until 1937, when he presented them to the Cloisters, the recently founded medieval outstation of the Metropolitan Museum of Art in New York, where they remain today. Their odyssey had finally come to an end.

It is generally thought that the tapestries were designed for a bridal chamber, and that the large, almost square pictures of the chase were wall hangings, whereas the resurrected Unicorn on the narrower pieces was for another use – perhaps as a bed covering or indeed the "sky" above the bridal bed, a sophisticated idea indeed. Who the personages are, however, and whether all seven pieces originally belonged together remain the tapestries' own secrets.

The two series date from the same period as the Sacred Hunt in Germany, but are of superior quality in manufacture. Their patrons belonged to a highly cultivated class that had the best artists of the time at its disposal – not always the case in provincial German convents. The sets have in common their environment, their balance of theology with the symbolism of love, and their refined style. This includes the flowered ground and the wealth of finely observed natural details, an inheritance from Gothic manuscripts and centuries of studying the symbols of nature, and also the expressive faces of the characters, depicted with great psychological insight. The Unicorn found its classical form here. It is disciplined heraldically but realized more spiritually than ever before. The little snow-white creature seems a guest from a higher plane of reality, which of its own free will visits our world and enriches it with its beauty.

The French King François I was the godson of François de la Rochefoucauld family and may have been familiar with the great Unicorn Hunt at the castle. His son, Henri II (1447–1459), could also have known it. At all events, a series picturing a Unicorn was ordered for him and his mistress, the famous Diane de Poitiers, at that period virtually queen of France. The artist was the goldsmith and engraver Jean Duvet (1485 – after 1561), who also created patterns for tapestries and was associated with the tapestry workshop opened in 1530 in Fontainebleau by the king's father. Today only a series of six engravings remains (see figs on pp.116–17); but their proportions and style seem to indicate that they were an introduction to a suite, or that there did exist such a set of tapestries, which incidentally gave the artist the sobriquet "Master of the Unicorn". This must mean it was a well-known work.

In these six engravings Christian allegory and worldly flattery of the ruler blend into a higher unity, no doubt a continuance of the medieval ideology – but with a marked air of the Renaissance that had become established in France with François's import of Italian artists. We are unmistakably on the way into a new era.

The six engravings have been ordered in different ways, but we can begin with the princely couple, who sit conversing beneath a canopy in the open air (not depicted

The Hunt of the Unicorn
Engravings by Jean Duvet,
c. 1550, British Museum,
London

From top to bottom, left
to right: 1. *The Unicorn
Dips his Horn into the Water*;
2. *The Unicorn Kills a Hunter*;
3. *The Unicorn and the Maiden*;
4. *The Trionfo and the Unicorn*;
5. *The Unicorn is Brought to the
Castle* [The first engraving in
the series, depicting a princely
couple, is not shown]

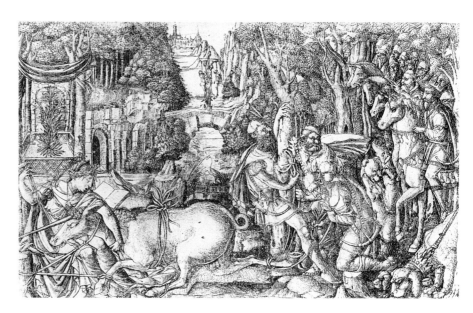

here). The king – clearly represented by a portrait – holds sceptre and crown, Diane – "dame, reine et maîtresse" – is surrounded by her hounds like Diana goddess of the chase herself; she bends over the king almost protectively – he was considerably younger than she was. She has a classical profile and wears the costume of antiquity. A kneeling servant proffers the fewmets (excrement) of the Unicorn wrapped in a cloth, to indicate the size of the prey. A hunt is underway, commended by the goddess of the chase herself, and the participants have gathered with their hounds. In the very detailed picture a monkey in a tree is to be seen on the right, possibly as a negative element in contrast to the princely couple.

Another introductory picture may be the Unicorn undergoing the water cleansing, as in the foregoing tapestry, although some place this picture as the final one in the series.[2] But as usual, the thirsty animals are deployed around the poisonous water waiting for the miracle. The Unicorn, as big as a horse, stands in the centre of the picture, stirring the water with its horn. The animals wait in two disciplined rows along a straight channel: panther, lion, peacock, stag and wild boar – carnivores and herbivores in a patient affiliation. The setting is no longer a *millefleur* paradise, nor is it dense forest; instead it shows a "world" landscape with ocean and city, forest and mountain in a vast panorama seen in depth perspective. Now the animals are placed in a kind of cultivated park landscape, and it is no surprise to find a classical column with a naked sculpture rising behind them.

Now the hunt begins, and this time the prey not only impales a hound but pierces a naked hunter in the groin; and not only that, fallen horses and naked men lie around in a semicircle after an absolute blood bath, while a few hurl stones in an effort to stop the animal. The king seeks the shelter of the trees and, fleeing on horseback with the remainder of his men, glances back at the battlefield.

We know that an unchaste maiden was pierced through by the animal's horn. But that men should be speared as well is remarkable and scarcely paralleled in art. It can be found in a few margin drawings and in moral allegories, but the theme has not yet been interpreted. However, I shall return to it later.

Meanwhile one must resort to the old stop-gap: the girl whose innocence is guaranteed here by the lily growing out of a square hedge above her head, like a final remnant of Mary's "Hortus Conclusus". She has lured the animal with her lute, and it is sound asleep in her lap. It is thoroughly bound up with ropes, which the hunters are busily winding around the nearest trees. As usual, the open central axis is interesting: here we are looking into the inward-running river and immediately above the animal we see, a pair of herons (soul birds) and above them a gallows on a bridge from which hanged figures dangle helplessly from their nooses. Furthest back a tower can be glimpsed. This is not by chance. At the far right a king sits astride his horse expectantly on the end of a line of horsemen. But these bear no resemblance to the earlier naked hunters. On the contrary, they are clothed and look more like philosophers and scholars, passively regarding the strange booty.

The picture seems to be divided into three vertical zones: the woman, who catches the animal opposite the king and his wise men (?) who observe the action, and the central part depicting action and capture, execution and death, but on a bridge, indicating a transition between two states. Could the savage naked men in the previous picture be a contrast to the king's closest advisors, who had first to be stamped out as the expression of heathendom, materialism and lower instincts, while now the king is on his way into a spiritual sphere?

The last two pictures are dedicated to the triumph of the Unicorn. Here it is acclaimed as triumphant even more than in the old tapestry. There the slain animal was carried to the king's castle, slung over a horse's back; here it is alive and resting on a large carriage at the feet of the king and the glowing maiden, who is crowned by the king's hand. The animal wears a collar and a bridle, and gladly allows itself to be reined in by a putto. Now at least six hounds, which previously had taken part in the attack, draw the carriage. The four leading ones, slim and noble creatures, may possibly be the four renowned Virtues we know from the Annunciation, and which now not only draw the Unicorn but also the maiden, who here seems to play Castitas – Chastity – in her triumph. What we see here is a classical *trionfo*, like those from Italy, which we shall look at soon. The artist is influenced by Albrecht Dürer's engraving of the triumph of Emperor Maximilian of about 1515, and by his depictions of German towns, seen here in the town in the background.

Finally the magnificently adorned animal is led to the "castle", driven by the royal couple, Henri and Diane, he dressed in classical armour, she in the costume of antiquity and holding a lyre. The significant central section is occupied by the two personages and the animal, being crowned with oak leaves by a putto. Cloths are spread before its feet, and a crowd of horn-blowing men and women with palm branches follow the train, which is making for the left-hand side, in which there is an altar with the lighted candles of the Trinity. In heaven the Unicorn (and the princely couple) are blessed and greeted by Jupiter himself, with the eagle at his side. But what are we really looking at?

We see that the persevering princely couple – with the aid of chaste Diana – have captured the animal, which of course is Christ, and are now taking it to their castle – but at the same time it is the entry of Christ into Jerusalem and at a deeper level, the victory of Christianity over Judaism. For the crowd is received by King David playing his harp, and in the top left-hand corner the two tablets of Moses can be glimpsed. This indicates the New Jerusalem. In 1550 a contemporary writer notes: "Jupiter signifie et denote nostre Dieu, créateur de toutes choses, la lune [denote] l'Église."

This is a Neoplatonic attempt at a synthesis of Christianity with the gods of antiquity: Jupiter with the eagle is God with the Holy Spirit, who greet the Son; Diane de Poitiers is Diana the moon goddess, with reference to the Church itself, and Mary, who has indeed "conceived" or captured the animal. And the animal is crowned with the oak leaves of Jupiter – not with the usual thorns of Christ.

As early as the 1540s Benvenuto Cellini suggested to his patron, François I, the idea of building a fountain in which the king himself should crown the work as a nude Jupiter surrounded by virtues and muses, and in the king's gallery his mistress was for a long period figured as Diana, goddess of the chase. This explains the crescent moon over the town and over Diane's brow, and the oak leaves over that of the animal! The earthly royal couple represent the ancient and the Christian gods on the earthly plane – and lead Christianity on to victory in their kingdom!

The dating of Duvet's Unicorn engravings is uncertain. One date that has been suggested is 1562; but this sounds unlikely. The artist complains of infirmity as early

Henri II's Triumphal Entry into Rouen, c. 1550
Facsimile by P. de Merval,
1868, Rouen Library

The king is seated in a massive
triumphal carriage drawn by
two Unicorns, in the Italian
fashion. Fame on a rolling
wheel crowns him. There is
a raised platform with
balustrade, built like a Roman
triumphal arch, and maidens
in the costume of antiquity
applaud him with music
and song

as the 1550s, then already about 70. As the king in the series is crowned, the picture
must have been commissioned between Henri's accession in 1547 and his death at the
ill-starred tournament in 1559. This suggests a date of origin in the 1550s, around the
time when Duvet also created his renowned Apocalypse. It is not known why the
picture of the entry of the Unicorn was not completed – the top right-hand part is
empty.

There is thus half a century between this and the Verteuil series; and they illumi-
nate each other in a most interesting manner. What we see in the engravings can shed
light on several puzzling details in the tapestries. They have several scenes in
common, including the water cleansing, the maiden capturing the animal and the indomitable Unicorn. Both are hunted by a particular male person, and both are
brought back to the castle and received with honours. The authentic portraits in the
engravings indicate that the couple in the tapestries also represent actual personages
– princely or noble – who are to be acclaimed, and not abstract types. And the oak
leaves of the slain animal indicate a Neoplatonic background there as well. In both
instances the Unicorn is the grail that is conquered by the power-holders, who wish
to possess its power. Moreover, in both instances we find the numerous animals from
the *Physiologus* and possibly the four hounds. But there the similarities end!

The gods and heroes of antiquity have taken over the arena previously occupied
by Gothic knights. Nakedness is developed. The dead hunters derive from the paintings of Mantegna, Michelangelo and Rosso; they are the armour-clad heroes Adonis
or Hercules, and of the Iliad. The virgin is a powerful Diana with a classical profile.

THE UNICORN

The costumes are "antique", but also closely resemble the masquerade costumes which were in fact designed by Rosso and Primaticcio for the festivals and *trionfi* of the court then being developed in the strictly laid out parks among winding water channels and shrubberies. Here the animals are civilized and made into pawns in the human beings' game. That is perhaps the reason for placing the water cleansing last, in order to show that now the animal is to serve culture. It becomes a ditch-cleaner for the upper class. At the same time the poetic universe in the old tapestries is replaced by classical pathos and weight. A certain self-solemnity rests upon the closely packed scenes. The animal must first and foremost pay homage to the power of living princes and Christian virtue. They possess the grail and are substitutes on earth for the heavenly powers. The sacredness of the animal held good; but it was stabled, and what we are witnessing is the first step towards absolute monarchy and worship of the king as god.

Costume Sketch
Primaticcio, c. 1540,
Nationalmuseum, Stockholm

In the elegant Fontainebleau style, a lady is depicted riding on a Unicorn, which indicates her chastity. In French court masquerades the medieval myths were casually blended with the gods and heroes of antiquity

CHAPTER 14
Man Takes Centre Stage – The Renaissance

With Jean Duvet's series we have crossed the threshold between the late medieval retention of semi-Gothic art and the Renaissance. And that is a big step. It does not only mean that central perspective creates depth in pictures, that new ideals of beauty reshape figures and that the gods of antiquity with their symbols take the place of the saints of the Church and the heroes of chivalry. The philosophy of life itself is changed. The human being places himself in the centre and constructs a new world around him that is not godless, but which begins to be ruled by reason and not merely by the authority of the Bible.

Where the surrounding world is interpreted anew, the Unicorn must keep pace. Among other things, it assumes what could be called national overtones and is elaborated very differently from country to country. In the early Middle Ages the Unicorn, like so many other symbols, was common European property and had more or less the same significance everywhere, but this gradually changed. Differing surroundings needed different qualities in the animal, and we have seen already how the German convents created their own version, the French knights of chivalry theirs. The Sacred Hunt never really won a place in Italy, where the chastity of the animal was used in another way, which seemed natural to a land with quite other traditions.

There it was given a part in the *trionfi* tradition. We have already met the animal as a participant in *trionfi* – now as draught animal, now as the one that itself receives homage: but the idea stems from the early Italian Renaissance. What then is a *trionfo*? To explain this we need to go back to the Rome of antiquity and its imperial triumphal processions. For centuries the Romans had strolled around among the ruins of triumphal arches and read the histories of the triumphs of Pompey and Caesar. Standing on the *biga* – the two-wheeled chariot – and crowned with laurels by Fama (Fame) or some other divinity, army commanders and Emperors had themselves transported across the Forum to receive the homage of the soldiery and the people. This could still be seen in the reliefs on the Arch of Titus. The idea survived both in literature and visual art; but now it was no longer potentates who held *trionfi* or triumphs. They were replaced by the resurrected ancient gods or by medieval personified virtues and other allegories. From the thirteenth century to the High Renaissance the transportable stage of drama and festival, the triumphal chariot, is an important feature of Italian urban culture.

THE UNICORN

Procris and the Unicorn
Bernardino Luini, mural
painting, *c.* 1520–22,
National Gallery of Art,
Washington, DC, Samuel H.
Kress Coll.

About 1370 the poet Petrarch published a book which more than any other was to inspire pictorial elaboration of the triumph motif. He called it *Trionfi*, and in it described a dream in six scenes, in which the author sees six allegorical figures successively defeat each other, all concerned with his loved one, Laura.[1] The poem begins with the triumph of Cupid (Love); but he is conquered by Pudica (Chastity), who in the figure of Laura rejects desire. But Laura herself is vanquished by Death. In turn, Death is conquered by Fama (Renown), who is defeated by Time – and at the end Eternity becomes the final victor, giving the poem a religious dimension, since Petrarch hopes to be reunited with Laura in Paradise.

The poem consists of a series of dramatic scenes, and only a few are *trionfi* proper. But when the book was illustrated during the fifteenth century, the episodes were represented as a series of triumphs in which the competitors were carried in vehicles inspired by the real calvalcades that traversed the streets of Italian towns on festive occasions, which we know so well from descriptions and paintings, not least from the Florence of the Medici.

The Triumph of Chastity
Illustration to a manuscript of Petrarch's *Trionfi*, c. 1500, Biblioteca Estense, Modena

In the centre Castitas balances on top of a column, surrounded by four cupids. At the bottom left, the Unicorn performs the water-cleansing ritual and further up, hounds chase a Unicorn into the lap of a maiden, an earthly chastity symbol. The procession is directed from the sea by Venus Celeste riding on a fish

The leading characters are carried along on high tribune-like wagons, standing or sitting with their attributes in their hands. The vehicle was drawn by the character's symbolic animals and accompanied by a "court" corresponding to its characteristics: young women, scholars, warriors, monkeys, etc. It might be a blinded, naked Cupid with wings and bow, drawn by four white horses and accompanied by all his "victims", for instance Anthony and Cleopatra or Tristan and Isolde. In the Petrarch illustrations, we see Death swaggering on his chariot with scythe and hourglass, drawn by black buffaloes through a dead forest landscape, while the heavy wheels crush human bodies below and black devils fly off with their souls above. Castitas (Chastity) sits with a bound Cupid at her feet and myrtle in her hands, her wagon surrounded by young women carrying a banner with her symbol, the stoat. Before the vehicle walk two white Unicorns with corkscrew horns, hooves and a tendency to goat beards. In the manuscript in the Biblioteca Estense, in the upper centre of the picture, Castitas balances on top of an ornate column surrounded by four cupids. At the bottom left, the Unicorn performs the water-cleansing ritual while other animals drink. Further up, hounds chase a Unicorn in to the lap of a maiden who resembles the other maidens and must be an earthly chastity symbol. The procession is directed from the sea by Venus Celeste, who rides on a fish.

This is a newly created type. From now on Castitas's chariot is drawn by Unicorns – or she actually rides on one. The theme passes from the books to the painted Italian bridal chests (*cassoni*) whose rectangular front sides were well suited to a *trionfo* design, and in this way the virtue of the bride could be suitably acclaimed.

Castitas might be the central figure, but there were others. In about 1470 Duke Borso d'Este had a series of pictures of the months painted in the great hall of the Palazzo Schifanoia in Ferrara. The leading planetary god for each month came riding along in his chariot drawn by his symbolic animal: thus Venus, with Mars the god of war chained by the foot, was drawn by swans, and Pallas Athene (or Minerva), the protector of marriage and domestic virtues, is drawn by two Unicorns. She is accompanied on one side by maidens weaving, sewing and playing music, and on the other by conversing scientists and philosophers. Here is a perfect division of the sexes in the enlightened spirit of the Renaissance. Antiquity illustrates the virtues, and the Unicorns, these remnants of the medieval universe, move into the service of a new age.

In a celebrated book, *Hypnerotomachia Poliphili* (*The Dream of Poliphilo*), published in Venice in 1499, four woodcuts illustrated the following *trionfi*: Europa and the Bull drawn by centaurs, Dionysus drawn by six lions, Leda and the Swan drawn by elephants, and Danae, receiving the golden rain in her lap, is drawn by no fewer than six

Pallas Athene Drawn by Unicorns
Mural painting, *c.* 1470, Palazzo Schifanoia, Ferrara

In the great hall of Duke Borso d'Este, the chastity of Pallas Athene is hailed

Danae in a *trionfo*
Illustration in *Hypnerotomachia Poliphili* (*The Dream of Poliphilo*), 1499, Venice, fol. 85v, 86r

Below:

Battista Sforza, Duchess of Urbino, in an Allegorical Triumph of Chastity
Piero della Francesca, Uffizi Gallery, Florence, *c.* 1470

This is the image on the reverse of Piero's portrait of the Duchess of Urbino

"atrocissimi monoceri" (very wild Unicorns). The company in which the Unicorn here finds itself shows that the identification with Christ is faltering. The animal has entered a humanistic context by turning into a mere chastity symbol, and the animal which originally belonged to the Virgin Mary can now be hired out to grand ladies eager to emphasize their virtue. That they retain a faint air of the Madonna herself is inevitable – and flattering.

A delightful example of the worldly use of the symbolic animal appears in Piero della Francesca's pair of portraits of Francesco da Montefeltro and Battista Sforza from about 1470. On the reverse of the duke's panel a *trionfo* is pictured, in which he himself is drawn by horses. On hers there is a similar vehicle, in which she takes her place as Castitas, while Cupid drives a team of Unicorns. As this is a wedding procession, pointing to a married life, Cupid is not trampled underfoot as occurs sometimes in a cavalcade with Castitas, and the Unicorns with the gilded horns are not white, but of a warm brown hue like that of a horse. Foremost on the wide carriage three significant virtues ride in state: Fides (Faith) with his chalice, Caritas (Divine Love) with the pelican pecking its breast until it bleeds, and presumably Spes (Hope) hidden behind. All the good spirits from both Christianity and antiquity stand guard around the Duchess of Urbino. Interestingly, a living and named personage is enthroned on the carriage, taking the place of Caritas. The Unicorn serves them both.

The idea caught on and spread northwards. In Germany Emperor Maximilian has himself depicted by Albrecht Dürer on a triumphal car like a Roman Emperor. In France, Henri II makes a simlar entry into Rouen (see fig. on p.120). This development of the *trionfo* theme quite naturally finds a place in portrait painting. Several variants can be seen almost side by side: around the year 1500 the Venetian Giorgione (*c.* 1477–1510) paints an allegory of Chastity in almost the old spirit. A classically beautiful young woman sits in the open air with the Unicorn's head on her lap: not the Virgin Mary, but not an individual person either; a lyrical picture executed in the soft Venetian style, in which nature and human melt together in delicate harmony.

From here it is a short step to association with a saint famous for her chastity. Just as Agnes has her lamb, so Justina (Giustitia) is provided with a Unicorn. The painter who depicts the saint with palm branch and sacred animal, with the donor of the picture, is easily tempted to give the saint the features of the donor's mistress, as happens in Moretta's delightful picture of *St Justina of Antioch with a Donor, c.* 1530.

Allegory of Modesty (or Chastity)
Attributed to Giorgione, *c.* 1500, Rijksmuseum, Amsterdam

Moretta da Brescia (*c.* 1498–1554) has placed the two figures in a northern Italian landscape with a large Unicorn in the lower left-hand corner, incidentally with the black horn set on its forehead by Pliny and Megasthenes, in accordance with the natural history of antiquity.

The Unicorn is also found simply as a chastity attribute in portraits or images of ladies, in the same way as the ermine. In these cases there is very little left of the Unicorn's association with Christ. One famous example is Pisanello's medal for Cecilia Gonzaga of Mantua (1448). The lady is naked and above her is a crescent moon; a large shaggy Unicorn lays its head in her lap. Another is a Florentine engraving in the form of a medal, *c.* 1470, known as "Marietta", in which the lady caresses the animal, which seems to be enjoying the situation enormously!

One of the most interesting variations can be seen in France, executed in the fashionable Fontainebleau style: here the court painter François Clouet (*c.* 1516–1572) created an intimate type of picture that became very popular in higher circles (see fig. on p.130). It is based upon Leonardo's *Mona Lisa*, then in the possession of the French king, with the bust of a lady, her arms resting on a shelf. The subject is now the king's mistresses, and they are seen at their toilet, posing in their bath in the right foreground of the picture. The room opens out into depth, layer after layer, behind opened curtains, first on a wet nurse in the middle distance (in Flemish style) with a child and from there to the back of the room, with a fireplace and a brightly lit girl bringing a large pot, the preferred symbol of the time for woman. At the furthest point – exactly above the child's head and at the point where many lines meet, rises the little white figure of the Unicorn, resting beneath a tree. It is not alive in nature, but like an item of heraldry, embroidered on a chair back as a last remnant of the famous tapestries. Here the woman's luminous colour is repeated and measures the distance into the depth with its small format, like a centre of innocence, from which everything else spreads out towards us.

This picture was admired so greatly that several ladies were permitted to pose in the boudoir; the workshop used it for several years and variants of it are found in different museums. This painting has for long been regarded as a portrait of Diane de Poitiers, but is now thought to represent Charles IX's mistress Marie Touchet (*c.* 1570) – later on, Henri IV's lady, Gabrielle d'Estrées, takes her place in a similar setting. The Unicorn has come into the boudoir. If the women's changing faces indicate the passage of time, the Unicorn takes its place as a timeless symbol: *spiritus*, innocence and enigma.

Young Woman with Unicorn
Raphael, *c.* 1505, Borghese Gallery, Rome

The young woman, sometimes called Maddalena Doni, is depicted as innocent. The modest size of the Unicorn shows that it is to be seen solely as an attribute

Opposite
St Justine of Antioch with a Donor
Moretto da Brescia, *c.* 1530, Kunsthistorisches Museum, Vienna

The saint with her martyr's palm is seen with the chaste animal kneeling at her feet, while the benefactor regards her with adoration. The painting is actually of Prince Alphonso Ferrara and his mistress, Laura Eustacio

Mariette
Florentine engraving, *c.* 1470
British Museum, London

The unknown lady tries to place a collar around the animal's neck and to tie it to a tree whilst nonetheless caressing it

In these associations the Unicorn still holds status as a positive symbol. It is true that its significance as Christ is weakened; but it continues to represent chastity and is the amiable servant of the superior human being. But the Renaissance rediscovers other aspects of the animal, which have been underplayed. Let us try to look at this other side and find the cause of the interest that emerges around it.

Diane de Poitiers
François Clouet, *c.* 1570,
National Gallery of Art,
Washington, DC, Kress coll.

The lady, probably Charles IX's mistress Marie Touchet, sits at her toilet like a Mona Lisa while a wet nurse suckles her child. In the background, a Unicorn is embroidered on the back of an armchair, directly above the baby's head

CHAPTER 15

King of the Wilderness

We have accompanied the gentle Unicorn and seen it associated with Mary and maidens for so long that we might easily lose sight of the other side of the animal, the one that went cavorting around in the Book of Job and in Megasthenes. Now and then the theologians recalled it: "Guard against the Demon!" or "The Unicorn is the savage Saul." There was also the constant reminder in Psalm 22, in which the horn threatens man and the Unicorn becomes the symbol of Death. In the Physiologus man could not stand its "mugitus horrendum" (terrifying roar) and risked being gored by its horn. Tertullian said it would toss the nations to the ends of the earth. Moreover, the unchaste Unicorn persevered, not least in the Arabian Physiologus, mentioned earlier. This variant came to Europe during the Crusades, and we saw how French artists refined and developed the erotic motif in courtly style.

In the course of the sixteenth century something crucial happened to the Unicorn. It was in that century that Europe moved from a medieval view of the world to a modern one, from that of a universe interpreted theologically towards one interpreted scientifically. Little by little, material phenomena began to be explained with the aid of physics – that is, by the laws of nature – and spiritual things by a psychology that pointed the way towards new potential in the human being himself or herself. The existence of the subconscious was recognized and understood in a new manner, preparing the way for a Shakespeare. It was a slow process, but in the long run it turned everything upside down.

Obviously, such changes were bound to affect mythical animals; not least those linked with theology, such as the dragon and the Unicorn. But this did not take place all at once. We have already seen that the Unicorn was growing more and more complex. For several centuries it had been interpreted as a symbol of chastity related to the Virgin Mary, indeed, as Christ himself, the humble of heart. It was impossible completely to disregard the sexual aspects that smouldered in the animal; but they were underplayed on altarpieces, and it was not discussed. As soon as the animal was associated with earthly human marriage, as in the French caskets and the tapestries, these characteristics began to set up a tension in the significance of the animal. Mary was drawn into a sophisticated erotic conversation. She became a courtly lady, dressed in the latest fashion, who took the hoofs of the animal into the folds of her red dress. Hoofs and monstrance met on her knee.

At the end of the fifteenth century we find mention of the Unicorn in several – originally Italian – books on virtues and vices entitled *Fiori di Virtù* (The Flowers of Virtue). In these it represents "intemperanza" (licentiousness and intemperance):

"Intemperance can be compared to the Unicorn, which is an animal that takes such joy in being with a virginal girl that when it sees one it goes to her immediately and falls asleep in her arms; but then the hunters come and capture it; which is impossible to catch, were it not for its desire."[1]

This theme was adopted by Leonardo da Vinci , who also described the animal as wild and ruled by "intemperanza". In some *Frammenti letterati et filosofici* he depicts the Unicorn thus:

"The hunters always mentioned the Unicorn as a puzzling creature.

'Is it an animal or a spirit?' they asked each other.

For this strange little horse, which had a horn in the centre of its forehead, appeared now here, now there, yet no one ever succeeded in taking it by surprise.

'It is a wild, weird being,' said one hunter. 'Perhaps it is a messenger from hell sent up here to spy on us.'

'No, it is too beautiful to be an evil spirit. It is more likely an angel', said another.

A young girl, sitting a little way off beneath a pergola spinning her wool and listening, could not help smiling. For she knew the Unicorn well; she knew everything it was possible to know about it, because it was her friend. And as soon as the men had gone, the animal came out from behind a bush and ran up to the young girl.

It lay down beside her with its head on her lap, and there it lay gazing at her with adoring eyes. For this wild animal, which escaped with such ingenuity from every ambush, had a weakness for young girls. It loved them all, and when it discovered they were alone, it approached fearlessly to admire them at close quarters.

After this first meeting it grew as tame as a domestic animal and always stretched forth its muzzle to be stroked.

But this strange affection was to be its undoing, for at length the hunters realized what was going on, and one day they set up an ambush and killed the Unicorn."[2]

Woman with a Unicorn
Leonardo da Vinci, drawing,
c. 1480, Ashmolean Museum,
Oxford

The striking feature about this passage is that Leonardo makes absolutely no mention of the theological interpretation (apart, perhaps, from the girl spinning wool), but returns the animal to the bestiary as an ambivalent creature which can be both devil and angel, and through its desire is imbued with the seed of self-destruction. It is almost a prelude to Shakespeare's lines in *Timon of Athens* (see p.167). Leonardo drew three small sketches of the young girl with the Unicorn. In one, she sits under a tree, to the trunk of which she has bound the animal with a long leash, while she points to it with her right index finger and looks out at us. In a variant she is just touching its muzzle. When the Unicorn itself is seized by desire, it is not far from the synthesis of ancient and Christian motifs cultivated by the Neoplatonists. The Virgin and the Unicorn became a parallel to Leda and the Swan (also depicted by Leonardo) and the scene might even express a hint of sodomy.[3]

The illustrations to the books of virtues and vices also give the scene a touch of the boudoir: the lady combs the animal's mane with a large comb and caresses it fervently, and the animal grows bigger, very amorous or the opposite: it assumes a demanding expression, with open mouth and teeth, and a thick growth of hair.

The theme is developed to the full in the frescoes of the Castel Sant' Angelo in Rome. The great council chamber was decorated about 1545 by the painter Perino del

THE UNICORN

Vaga and his school in the frivolous Mannerism of the time. Here are stark naked young women treating Unicorns in just the same way that their predecessors in Hellenistic art had treated satyrs: caressing their horns, pulling their beards and seductively alluring them to direct the horn into their lap. The old expression used reverently by the theologians about Christ, who places himself "in uterum virginis" here takes on a robust significance. Now the animal is plainly acknowledged to be a phallic creature, like the erotic *meraviglia* figures favoured by Mannerism.

This may be the most significant reason for the decline of the Hortus Conclusus. The image had become too loaded. As if by tacit agreement, it vanished and was no longer to be found in religious art by the time of the Council of Trent (1564–1563). Like so many other symbolic subjects, the animal had been drawn into human consciousness as an element of human temperament, or as representing powerful natural forces, which the alchemists could attempt to tame, but which was no longer suitable company for the Virgin Mary. The development came first and most strongly in Italy; but changes were taking place north of the Alps as well.

In Germany the motif developed interesting connotations of life before civilization. Unicorns are kept as a kind of domestic animal by wild men of the woods, who ride them, milk them and take them into their families. In engravings and woodcuts we see wild women, naked and with long hair or clad in crude skins, riding the animals or caressing them, like Madonnas in negative. Tapestries in Zurich show young people or shaggy wild men living in the depths of forests with spotted Unicorns bearing great curved sickle horns. The mood is almost bucolic, the figures make free with each other and the line drawing is crude. Here the Unicorn is really an illustration of the dark side of humanity. In company with the undeveloped consciousness of primitive man the animal dwells in the forests, where Pan holds sway. The forest is the negative Hortus Conclusus, unfenced formless nature in contrast to the tamed and fenced one of Reason's square or the sacred circle. The dark side develops in parallel with the light, just as virtue and vice complement each other. Not surprisingly, it is in the sixteenth century particularly, when awareness of the subconscious was growing and instinctive urges being charted, that we find engravings and drawings depicting battles between primitive people and Unicorns.

This wild state of nature, the primeval forest of the instincts, is not an unqualified evil, however. It is dangerous, but also fruitful and vitally nourishing for humanity. This emerges in a strange story, originally part of the legendary material of the Arthurian cycle of legends, popularly known as *Le Chevalier du Papegau*.[4] King Arthur himself discovers a square red tower without a door on a deserted coast. Colour and shape forewarn us that we are confronted with symbols: the earthly and material. Here lived a dwarf who was abandoned in this desert place by his wicked master, the Lord of Northumbria, with the nobleman's pregnant wife. When she died, the dwarf was left alone with her infant son. In despair, he took the child into the forest seeking shelter, and came on an enormous hollow tree. Inside it were some newborn kids with tiny single horns on their foreheads. Very soon their mother arrived, as big as a horse and with fourteen large udders. She too had one horn, as sharp as a razor. The dwarf was terrified, dropped the child and fled; but when the baby cried the animal grew gentle and offered it her udder. When the dwarf returned in fear and trembling she offered him her milk as well. They both stayed on in the

Wildman on a Unicorn
Drawing from the *Playing Cards* of Master E.S., *c.* 1461, Kupferstichkabinett, Basle

THE UNICORN

tree and the Unicorn nursed the child and killed game for the dwarf with her horn. The boy grew up and became a mighty warrior, who later helped his father to build the red tower in which they now lived. King Arthur recounted this story after his homecoming to Camelot.

The tale is a beautiful illustration of the richness of Arthurian allegory: the knights of the Grail and the king constantly see and experience myths, veiled in anecdote. Here the Unicorn is nature's primordial female power, wild but nourishing and with its dwelling in the very marrow of the tree. The defenceless mite can appeal to its mercy and by drinking in its strength can grow to gigantic size, construct an earthly citadel and live in peace. The entire story takes place in natural surroundings and on the powerful animal's terms. Male and female, tower and tree. . . We recognize these oppositions from various strange landscape backgrounds in the biblical scenes of the period; and the story of Mowgli could be illustrated with the paintings of the Danube School, in which the Unicorn sleeps on the forest floor among semi-barbarian people. The Renaissance has begun.

So it is not altogether unexpected when Albrecht Dürer, in an engraving of 1516, shows the rape of Persephone with the aid of a really wild animal, which comes galloping with thunderous gait out of the thicket with a downturned sickle horn in its forehead and shaggy legs like a devil, perhaps the wildest Unicorn since antiquity. Its behaviour is in striking contrast to the good manners of the French guardians of maidens. This pictorial type is widespread during the Renaissance in central European areas, particularly in southern Germany and Austria.

To descriptions of these untamed creatures of nature can be added the story of Barlaam and Joasaph, a Buddhist legend involving the Unicorn, from about 600 BC. This had a remarkable career in Europe, showing how Oriental and Christian motifs constantly merged with each other. The story tells how the young Buddha is "enlightened" about the human condition and human vanity by a wise hermit, who teaches him in ten parables. As early as about AD 800 this was elaborated into a *novella* in Greek by Johannes Damascenus, now as a Christian parable with the title *The Edifying Story*. The name Buddha – actually Bodhisat, which means "The Enlightened" – became Joasaph in Greek, while the wise hermit Bhagavan became Barlaam. In 1250 the theologian Vincent of Beauvais rewrote this *Parable of the Unicorn and the Lovers of the World (Children of the World)* in a popular version which later became part of the *Golden Legend*, and the story was so widely distributed both in Latin and the vernacular that the two Indian figures ended up among the Roman Martyrs, in 1583.[5]

Joasaph was brought up in isolation as a wealthy king's son, ignorant of the reality of the world around him. One day he steals out of the castle garden and is horrified to meet a leper, a poor beggar and a funeral cortège. He wanders in the forest in despair, but then comes on the wise hermit Barlaam, who converts him to Christianity (!), partly by telling him ten parables. The legend runs:

"There was once a man called Barlaam who lived in a desert near Senaah and who often preached against the vanity of the world. He spoke thus to a man who was fleeing in haste from a Unicorn which threatened to devour him. He fell into an abyss or well but succeeded in grabbing hold of a bush, although he could not get a proper foothold.

As well as the ferocious Unicorn staring down on him from the edge of the well, he discovered a terrible dragon spitting fire, waiting for him to fall with open jaws. From the narrow ledge he clung to, four

The Rape of Persephone
Albrecht Dürer, engraving, 1516, Kunsthalle, Hamburg, B.73

The wild Unicorn thunders through the landscape with its great, serrated horn. In late medieval Germany, the huge animal of antiquity appears again as an expression of human sexuality and inner power serpents hissed at him. A pair of mice, one black and one white, gnawed at the roots of the bush he still held on to, while the bush itself was about to break. But when he raised his eyes he saw honey drip from the branches of the bush, and forgetting all about his situation he now gave himself up to the sweetness of the honey."[6]

Barlaam explains that the Unicorn is Death, who threatens human beings everywhere. The well is the world, filled with every kind of evil, the bush is the life of man, slowly devoured by the constant attrition of the hours of day and night, which are the black and white mice. The four serpents are the human body formed of the four elements, which separate if they are disturbed. The dragon is the bottomless gape of Hell that threatens to engulf man. The honey is worldly pleasure, to which man foolishly gives himself up, forgetting all danger.

This wise tale, which shows that human beings are the same in every age, was illustrated many times. The earliest manuscripts emphasized the man's flight, but,

The Man in the Tree
Vault painting, *c.* 1380, Vester Broby church, Denmark

THE UNICORN

rather than into a well, he escapes up a tree; the two mice gnaw at the roots and a dragon lurks in a hole below. This version is a favourite in eastern icons, which maintain the theme for a long time, and it is thus that it appears in Denmark in one of the earliest wall paintings to feature a Unicorn.

This is in Vester Broby church (Sorø district, Sjaelland) and dates from about 1380. We see the elegantly dressed young man – the child of the world – who has climbed up a tree with spear-shaped leaves and is plucking the round apples with both hands. In earlier illustrations the man sits in a tree too, but as a rule he eats honey. The transfer to an apple tree probably occurred in allusion to the story of the Fall. Down below, a blackish brown and a white mouse or rat gnaw at the tree roots. On the right side, traditionally that of Hell and of the black mouse, the dragon directs its angry open jaws at the man, as if the gates of Hell had moved from the apse or chancel arch up into the vaulting. The Unicorn stands above, close to the light-coloured mouse, touching the tree with its horn. The horn emerges from its neck and has not yet completely developed into the twisted tusk of the narwhal. The composition is sharply divided into a day and a night side, which together threaten the man's equilibrium. The elegant design is in the International Gothic style.

In the opposite compartment we see Death, entwined with worms, threatening a young woman with his weapon. She is looking at herself in a mirror and is thus the feminine counterpart to the youth in the tree: greed and vanity reflect each other and are threatened with destruction. Together they are a *memento mori*, common during the period of the Black Death and epidemics of plague. The congregation must remember the vanity of the world. Bernt Notke's famous painting of the Dance of Death (now destroyed) in the Marienkirche in Lübeck dates from a little later (1460s).

The illustration closest to the textual description is an engraving by the Dutch artist Bolswert dating from 1610. Here we are really gazing down into the flaming depths of Hell with Leviathan; we see the four serpents, the mice, and the Unicorn's threatening horn pointing down at the incomprehensibly carefree man, who hangs on to a branch and licks the honey. Obviously, the moral was still relevant in the seventeenth century.

Barlaam and Joasaph
Bolswert, engraving, 1610

Here the man hangs from the branch surrounded by the four snakes. The mice gnaw, the dragon roars from the abyss and the Unicorn threatens him with its great horn

CHAPTER 16
Shield and Seal

We have looked at the blossoming of chivalry, with all its requisites: colourful pavilions, standards, tapestries and ingenious allegories and devices – and coats of arms. The Unicorn plays an important role in much of this, and now we shall take a glance at its substantial involvement with heraldry. The creature we meet in the tapestries, which seems so natural in its grace and spontaneity, was in part created by the art of the escutcheon.

Once Europeans had encountered Arab culture during the Crusades, they brought various skills back with them: the architecture of fortification, new techniques of warfare and thus new types of weapon. As helmets with closing visors came into general use, it became necessary to create clear outward signs and symbols to distinguish friend from foe. These colourfully designed cognizances adorned pavilions, standards and shields, and helmets – armorial bearings had arrived.

The designs were chosen from geometric symbols, crosses or bars, chessmen and crescent moons, and from the bestiaries: animals with suitable characteristics, such as bears, lions and wild boar, wolves and eagles and, a special predilection, horned creatures like the bull and the Unicorn. The noble lion was an obvious choice; but the Unicorn swiftly vied with it because it was a Christ symbol, chaste, courageous and invincible, and was close to the Virgin Mary. Its qualities were almost synonymous with the chivalrous ideal and it seems probable that the image of the perfect knight and the white Unicorn fed upon each other in a self-strengthening process, contributing further to develop the animal both physically and spiritually, particularly in France. Arthurian literature had already pointed out the parallel between the Unicorn and the knight, when Percival was described as being as faithful as a Unicorn, which must suffer death for the sake of his purity.

This laid emphasis on self-sacrifice and emulation of the Christ who was "humble of heart". It is a Christian chivalrous literature, which, at least in theory, was imbued with the Franciscan spirit. This was so vigorous that it continued unchanged into the Renaissance and beyond. In 1644 Marc Vulson de la Colombière says

"Just as the Unicorn is the enemy of poison, it has the symbolical meaning of moral purity and can be used on the shields of those who detest the vices, which are the poisons of the soul. Just as the Unicorn cannot be captured alive, so it indicates on a man's coat of arms that he would rather die than be conquered."[1]

THE UNICORN

The animal thus possesses qualities which give it the right to a place on the shield. Three of them are especially emphasized: Fortitudo (Courage), Castitas (Chastity) and Fides (Faithfulness), genuine knightly virtues. It was depicted in every possible position: rampant (rearing), courant (running), saliant (leaping), statant (standing) and couchant (resting), and frequently confronted with the lion. Heraldry was one of the most vital shaping powers in giving the two creatures their finished silhouette in European consciousness: they had to be simplified, flattened and given precise lines, like those required of a logo or an advertisement. The lion received its distinctive face in the process, and the Unicorn its snow-white elegant form, more of a horse than a goat, but with cloven hoofs and waving tufted tail. This became the animal that leaps through the tapestries, assuming all the heraldic attitudes. In so doing, the knights created their own masculine parallel to the nuns' little lapdogs. As the Danish writer Christian Elling says: "the Unicorn is emblematic of the highest potency; proud, wild and noble and possessed of a frenzied urge for independence."[2] "Nemo me impune lacessit" (No one provokes me with impunity) runs the motto on the shield of the Stuarts.

One of the earliest coats of arms comes from Germany. It belongs to the Thuringian *minnesinger* Ditmar von Aist. His blue shield bears a silver Unicorn on its hind legs, defending its master with a large, curved horn with serrations. Soon the animal takes its place both on noble and ecclesiastical coats of arms – on the insignia of the Order of the Garter, on tombstones, seals and coins; in short, everywhere that a pregnant symbol could express a man's noble qualities. The Unicorn reached the summit of prestige when it was included in the English royal coat of arms, as a supporter. James VI of Scotland had two Unicorns on his own shield, acquired from France through a marriage in his family during the period of the tapestries, about 1480. In 1603, when he became king of England as well as Scotland, after the death of Queen Elizabeth I, he took one of the Unicorns with him and inserted it opposite the English lion. There the two animals stayed, glaring fiercely and presumably prevented from going for each other only by the shield that they were intended to guard. Their strange love-hate relationship is familiar to the English from of old, as we know from the nursery rhyme:

"The lion and the Unicorn were fighting for the crown,
The lion chased the Unicorn all round the town . . ."

The enmity of the two animals is very ancient and confirmed by Physiologus. Even before AD 1000 they meet in ferocious frontal attack on fonts and in manuscripts, and in Paradise they are hard put not to stare each other out of countenance, as we have seen in the *Hortus Deliciarum* (see fig. on p.51). In fact it is only with a shield of Our Lord Himself between them that they can restrain themselves. It is hard to say whether the biological hostility between herbivores and carnivores is the determining factor, or whether this is the Christ symbol opposing the "roaring lion", the Devil; but the difficulties dogging the two creatures' relationship leave no doubt.

Among the well known families in Europe who have borne the Unicorn on their shields must be mentioned the D'Estes of Ferrara, both Duke Ercole D'Este and his son Borso (1413–1471). Ercole had an emblem featuring the water-cleansing Unicorn, which was also drawn on the spine of his breviary; in frescoes in the Palazzo di Schifanoia in Ferrara, Pallas Athene is drawn by Unicorns. The northern Italian

Coat of arms of the *minnesinger* **Ditmer von Aist**
Illustration from the Codex Mannesse, *c.* 1300, Heidelberg Universitätsbibliothek, cod. pal. Germ. 848

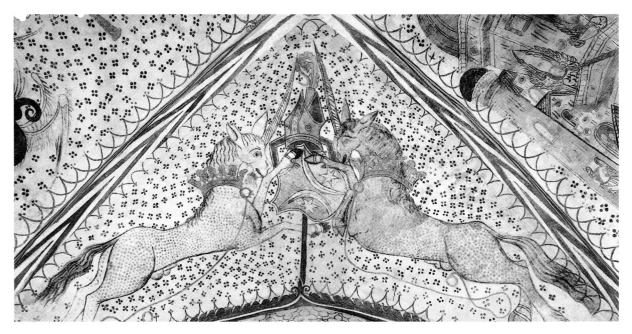

**Bishop Clausen's
coat of arms**
Vault painting, *c.* 1500,
Udbyneder church, Denmark,
Nationalmuseet, Copenhagen

family of Borromeo, which held court on Isola Bella in Lake Maggiore, filled their gardens, the villa and wall tapestries with their armorial animal. The family included both princes and bishops, and with the Archbishop of Salzburg the animal travelled to Austria and later to Heilbronn, where it can still be seen. The Unicorn is on the seal of Ivan the Terrible, and an emblem of Pope Clement III and the Farnese family.

A dozen or so Danish families featured the Unicorn in their coats of arms. In the Aarhus district of Jutland, the Rosenkrantzes of Rosenholm have two and Niels Clausen, Bishop of Aarhus, who reigned from 1491 to 1520, had the Unicorn painted in his smaller churches. Today his shield remains on the vaulting of Udbyneder church. The shield with two crescent moons and two stars is guarded by large Unicorns with crowns around their necks; they are chained by cords with golden rings. In Aarhus Cathedral, where the bishop is buried, two Unicorns are placed among other shield-sentinels in the transept vaulting, a location often reserved for heraldry; but here the shield has been replaced by a Tree of Life, and the animals hail this as if it were a coat of arms.

During the Renaissance the Unicorn made its way into civic circles, not least into town coats of arms, and we see the animal as standard bearer both in the Paris tapestries and in the shield of the painter Hans Baldung, taken from the city arms of his family's place of origin, Schwäbisch-Gmund. From coats of arms and tombstones the Unicorn passed on to the printing trade and became a popular watermark and ex-libris, particularly for apothecaries, doctors, papermakers, printers and publishers. Among well known examples is the watermark of the Albigensians, chosen, no doubt, because of the animal's chastity, while the apothecaries would naturally think of the medicinal qualities of the horn. In 1617 the Society of Apothecaries in London took the helpful animal as supporters for their coat of arms: two rearing Unicorns guard Apollo, the sun god, who has felled a dragon with his bow and arrow, and this main theme is crowned by a rhinoceros. Any alchemists among the apothecaries' customers would have nodded in recognition: for spiritual victory was symbolized for them by the vanquished dragon, and the sun god Apollo was the figure of victory, the Unicorn was *spiritus*. As far as the rhinoceros was concerned, it had always been named with the Unicorn and was also of medicinal interest. One can still sense how the roots of medical science are firmly anchored in medieval alchemy.

So it is not at all surprising that one of the first ex-libris we know of was designed by an apothecary at Wittenberg about 1500; or that the earliest were designed in the likeness of coats of arms. You put your little shield inside your books. The idea caught on and soon there were quantities of personal and imaginative variants, beginning a practice that has lasted to our own time. Well known and unknown people still design interesting ex-libris, making it an interesting genre to investigate.[3]

These examples show that the image of the Unicorn was a European phenomenon, known and treasured by the ruling class. It is also noticeable that with increasing individualism and an ebbing Christian symbolism, the universal significance of the beast begins to fade, so that it could be used to please individual taste. Sailors, for instance, were very fond of it. They named their vessels after it and placed it on the prow as a figurehead. In 1610 the Danish nobleman Mogens Ulfeldt captained a ship of this name and nine years later Jens Munk sought its help in finding the North-West Passage, without success. This maritime theme has continued right up to Hergé's cartoon of Tin-Tin, in the story of *The Secret of the Unicorn*.

Coat of Arms of the Society
of Apothecaries of London

Ex-libris
Drawing by Thomas Arnel,
Denmark, 1969, Archiv für
Kunst und Geschichte, Berlin

CHAPTER 17

"When Someone Makes a Journey…"[1]

Mappa Mundi, detail
Hereford Cathedral, c. 1290,
British Museum, London

The *Mappa Mundi* in Hereford Cathedral is a map of the world from around 1280. Apart from its fascination in showing us how the world seemed to people of that time, it is interesting to see the animals that they believed could be found in various lands. East faced upwards, for this was where Paradise was situated, where the Tree of Life crowned the slightly arched disc that was the world. So Asia was "uppermost", Jerusalem the centre, and the two other known parts of the world, Africa and Europe, had to be content with the lowest half of the world disc, beneath the blue belt of the Mediterranean. Along the edges were depicted the beings who were thought to live there: in Africa we see "dogs' heads", pygmies and strange fabulous animals, not least, along the upper reaches of the Nile, the rhinoceros, standing side by side with the Unicorn. The testimony of many reliable people had placed it there and fixed it firmly. One of the earliest well known travellers was Ctesias, whose statements had been partially confirmed by Aristotle, and the most famous medieval one was Cosmas the India-farer, who had seen the animal in Ethiopia and even drawn it.

One of the most popular books throughout the Middle Ages was known as the Romance of Alexander, a life of the admired Alexander the Great (356–323 BC). Although it is a blend of imaginative biography and romantic tale, it should almost be included in the genre of travel literature. The book was written originally in Greek, compiled from earlier biographies and now-forgotten sources about AD 200 in Alexandria. Julius Valerius translated it into Latin in 320, in the metre that was to become known as the Alexandrine, and then the book set out on a triumphal progress of about thirty-five languages, as a much loved and entertaining novel and travel description, with many variations.

The text describes Alexander's remarkable birth, childhood and adolescence, his taming of his horse Bucephalas, who in some versions has one horn, and his heroic deeds in a series of adventures, which, particularly in the section on his prowess in India, have the stamp of Mandeville's Travels. Here he slays basilisks, fights with crabs as large as coats of mail, conquers the giants Gog and Magog, and is borne up to heaven by griffins. It is therefore no surprise that he meets with the Unicorn. Persian miniatures show his battle with the one-horned Carcadan or illustrate the scene where Alexander and his army stand beside the Red Sea and see a flock of

THE UNICORN

animals with single horns as sharp as swords. They can only be killed with arrows. Some have bodies like horses and heads like stags, and black horns; others resemble oxen and are covered with white hair, and they are as wild as bulls. It is not hard to find the literary forebears, and one realizes too that in an ancient heroic tale it is the wild version of the animal that is of interest.

The book contains another important detail. In Persia Alexander meets the fabulous Queen Candace and makes friends with her, later writing a letter to his old teacher Aristotle telling him about the gifts she has sent him:

> "This queen has graciously sent me
> a beast so proud and nobly formed
> which bears upon its forehead the most splendid carbuncle stone
> and by a pure maiden is tamed.
> But few Unicorns can be seen

la force des tartars. Mais se mistrent a desconfiture et tournarent a fuie. Et qnt
les tartars les virent desconfis. si leur aloient derriere chassant et occiant et abatant
si malement que ce estoit vne pitie a voir. Et quant il les oient vne piece chacies
si ne les vouloient plus suire. mais retournerent arriere es bois pour prendre des
oliphans qui estoient la toms. Et leur comencoit taillier les grans arbres
et mettre leur au tenant pour auoir les. Et aucie tresout ce ne les pouoi
ent auoir: se ne seussent les hommes meismes du roy qui auoient este pris en
la bataille qui miculx les sauoient congnoistre que les tartars. Et ainsi les
prenoient. car les oliphans sont bestes qui ont trop plus grant entendement
que nulle autre beste et en prisrent plus de deux cens. Et de celle bataille en a
uant comencha le grant kaan a auoir moult doliphans. Et en ceste ma
niere fu desconfist ce roy par le sens et par la maistrie des tartars. si comme
vous pouez auoir entendu cy dessus.

Comment len descent grant valee.

Quant len se part de celle valee que ie vous ay comptee adonc
trouue len vne grant descendue. Car sachies que len cheuauche
ij. iournees et demie toutes fois a declin. Et en toute ceste desce
due na chose qui a compter face. fors seulement que il y a
vne grant place ou il tiennent aucune fois grant marche
Car toutes les gens de celle contree y viennent aucunes iours nommez. et tien
nent la leur marche trois iours la sepmaine. il changent or pour argent ₹
car il sont de lor assez. il donnent trois pois de fin or pour .v. pois dargent fin.
et pour ce y viennent marchans de plusieurs parties qui portent leur argent

for what reason I know not
And only those are captured that
have been tamed by spotless maids.
For no man of woman born
can withstand the strength in his horn."

Here the poem speaks the language of Arthurian legend, and the ideals of the age of chivalry are put into Alexander's mouth, together with the mystery of the virgin story. This suggests that the piece is of later date, presumably added in the twelfth century under the influence of the Crusades. The story of the remarkable stone in the forehead appears in several different places at this very time.

The really great period of travel writing, which also had its sophisticated moments, was the twelfth century, when pilgrims and crusaders were abroad in various lands exchanging travel stories. Their curiosity was boundless. Many went to the limits of the known world, to the Sinai peninsula and Egypt, to Persia and even India, where with open minds they recognized the strange creatures described in the Physiologus and enlarged upon them. Theologians at home also wrote about them, such as Honorius of Autun on the Indian Monoceros, and sculptors reproduced their likenesses on the tympana above church portals.

Livre des Merveilles
Marco Polo's travel book, 1375,
Bibliothèque Nationale de
France, Paris

In the same century a remarkable personality, who surely never really existed, lived a fictional life: he went by the name of Prester John. He had about as much substance as the Unicorn itself, for he was said to be the son of the Grail Maiden Response de Sjoje and the knight Fejrefis. As a young man he journeyed to establish great kingdoms in the Far East. He appears in this guise in the Arthurian legends, surely his true setting. As early as 1145, he is mentioned in a chronicle as a "rex et sacerdos", a Nestorian priest-king who had conquered Ekbatana on the far side of Armenia in a three-day battle against Persians and Seljuk Turks. Because of this, he became the great hope of the Crusaders for providing aid against the heathen. There was thus a need to believe in him; he was taken so seriously that Pope Alexander III sent his personal physician with letters to him.

About 1150 some fictitious letters from him to the Byzantine Emperor Manuel and to Pope Alexander were circulated. They were in various languages and were translated into French in Paris as late as 1490. In them appears an account of the Unicorn. After a general description of its appearance, which includes one black and white horn, it tells what happens when the Unicorn meets its enemy, the lion:

"When the Unicorn sees the lion it attacks it; but the lion runs away behind a tree, and the Unicorn, which tries to strike it with its horn, drives it into the tree with such force that it cannot free itself, and the lion kills it."[2]

This story, which is also found in Aesop's Fables, continued in many variants. We find it again in the Grimms' fairytale "The Brave Little Tailor":

"'You must carry out yet another heroic deed before I will give you my daughter', said the king. 'Out in the forest there is a Unicorn which wreaks great havoc; you must capture it.'

'I am even less afraid of that than of the giants', said the tailor. Taking a rope and an axe with him he went out into the forest and told the men who had accompanied him to stay behind. He had not gone very far before the Unicorn came leaping towards him threatening to eat him up then and there. 'Calm down,' he said, 'it's not as easy as that.'

Unicorn Hunt in India
J. Collaert, engraving,
Museum Plantin-Moretus,
municipal print room of
Antwerp, cat. no.III/C. 767

An imaginary hunt for wild
Unicorns. They must be shot
with bows, they are like wild
asses and have black horns

He stood quite still until the creature came right up to him, then slipped adroitly behind a tree. The Unicorn rushed with all its strength towards the tree and drove its horn so far into the trunk that it could not get it out again. 'Now the bird is caught,' said the tailor, put the rope round its neck, chopped the horn out of the tree and took the creature to the king."³

Numerous sources meet here: the tailor plays the role of the hunter, the tree is the Virgin, and the result is the classical one: the animal is taken to the king. Prester John's unknown authors have merely developed well-known legends originating in antiquity and published them as "travel literature", a not unconmmon practice, as we shall see. Sometimes it is a lion which lures the Unicorn into the tree; but the original story uses the hunter.

The Unicorn is also mentioned by such travellers as Marco Polo (*c.* 1254–1324), the famous Venetian explorer who penetrated far into Asia during the 1270s and stayed at the court of Kublai Khan for seventeen years. From there he travelled on to China and then home through Burma and Persia. After his return, he wrote several accounts of his journey, including *Concerning the Kingdoms and Marvells of the East* about 1300, and in 1307 the book *Il Milione*. Among these important descriptions of unknown regions we find also the following on the animal life of Burma, where of course he saw the Indian elephant, but also another animal:

"There are wild elephants in the country, and numerous Unicorns, which are very nearly as big. They have hair like that of a buffalo, feet like those of an elephant, and a horn in the middle of the forehead, which is black and very thick. They do no mischief, however, with the horn, but with the tongue alone; for this is covered all over with long and strong prickles, and when savage with any one they crush him under their knees and then rasp him with their tongue. The head resembles that of the wild boar, and they carry it ever bent towards the ground. They delight much to abide in mire and mud. 'Tis a passing ugly beast to look upon, and is not the least like that which our stories tell of a being caught in the lap of a Virgin; in fact, 'tis altogether different from what we fancied."⁴

This description of the Unicorn is totally unlike the picture we have gained of it so far, and there is no doubt that the animal Polo describes must be the Asiatic rhinoceros, with its low-slung head. For once we see here a genuine confusion with the rhinoceros – made no by a "simple-minded native", but by a highly intelligent white man from Europe! When Polo's books were illustrated a hundred years later, however, in the book *Livre des Merveilles* by the Boucicaut studio (1414), one or two pictures show the animal in its customary, graceful form, and with its traditional opponent: the elephant. All are white and the Unicorn in fact is "almost as large as the elephant". This confirmed the belief that in those distant lands the white animal ambled around the forests among all the other strange creatures. Later Mandeville has the animal in India near Paradise, that is, highest up on the earth disc of the *Mappa Mundi*.⁵

One of the most interesting descriptions is in the *Itinerarium Joannis de Hese*, a travel journal written by one Johannes of Hesse, near Utrecht, who was in Palestine in 1389, according to his own account. He actually witnesses the miracle of water cleansing:

"Close to the field of Helyon there is a river called Marah, whose waters are very bitter. Here Moses plunged his staff into the water and made it sweet, so that the children of Israel could drink. And to this very day the venomous animals poison the water after sundown, so that the good animals cannot drink it; but in the morning after sunrise Unicornus comes, and by dipping his horn in the stream he drives out the poison, so that the other animals can drink through the daylight hours. This have I seen for myself, just as I describe it . . ."⁶

THE UNICORN

What had he really seen? He also maintains that he saw the Gates of Paradise on his journey east; and the truth is no doubt that he had never been outside those of Utrecht. There is an abstract literary feel to his account, which does not give the impression of actual experience. As is also true of Mandeville, the writer sits at home brewing up his travel book with such a wealth of classical and popular ingredients that he can fill many pages and give a fascinating insight into the nature of animals in the later Middle Ages – but also indeed into that of the author! We recognize the Great Ass which allows the good animals to drink, and Moses who cleanses the water for the Jews with his staff, as a typology for Christ's "raised horn". We visualize the Verteuil tapestry of a century later, in which the Unicorn again cleanses the waters, and its equally colourful universe composed of many centuries of cultural deposits.

The most notable travel description of the fifteenth century was made by Canon Bernhard von Breydenbach from Mainz Cathedral. In 1483 he made a pilgrimage to Palestine with the young Duke of Solms. It was quite a company of travellers, for

Ioan. Stradanus invent.   Ioan. Collaert sculp.   Ioan. Galle excud.

29.   Non procul à ripis Asinos venatur agrestes   In fronte: hinc phialæ fiunt et pocula, morbos
      Indus, permissu Regis : cornu quibus exstat   Quæ sanant, vulnus curant, pelluntque venena.

they took with them Brother Felix Faber from Zurich and a Dutch draughtsman Erhard Reuwich, who illustrated their experiences. The detailed travel journal was published in Mainz in Latin in 1486 and soon afterwards in German – at about the same time as the famous French tapestries were woven.

The book is a goldmine. It tells us how problematic travelling was then. They had to wait for a ship in Venice, haggle with skippers and endure a long cramped voyage as the ship battled its way to Jaffa. We learn of wind and weather, food and accommodation, attacks of sickness, and all recorded with a sense of reality which makes us see, taste and smell a voyage through the Mediterranean in the age of Columbus. It also makes us believe what we read, undeniably throwing the story that follows into a certain relief. It makes astonishing reading, partly because to a certain extent it is quite as visual as the rest of the book. Breydenbach and his little company have left Jerusalem to visit St Catherine's Monastery on Mount Sinai and now find themselves between this and Cairo. They stroll around the mountainous region picking thorny branches on the slopes, which they were told had been used to make Christ's crown of thorns. Then they lift their gaze:

"At midday we saw an animal looking down on us from a mountain peak. We thought it was a camel and wondered how a camel could survive in this wilderness, and these speculations gave rise to a discussion among us as to whether there were such things as forest camels. Our guide Kalin joined in and assured us that the animal must be a Rhinoceros or a Unicornus, and he pointed out the single horn growing from the animal's forehead. We gazed at this noble animal very carefully and regretted that it was no nearer so that we could observe it even better. For in many respects this is a singular animal. In particular it is said to be very wild. It bears a single horn about four feet long, so sharp and strong that it wounds or pierces everything it strikes and nails it to the rocks. And this horn has a magical lustre; pieces of it are valued as the most precious stones and set in gold and silver. The animal is so wild that no hunter's art or skill are enough to capture it, but the natural historians assure us that it can be caught by putting a chaste maiden in its way.

When it rushes towards her she shows it her bosom, and it lies down there, bereft of all its wildness and so content that it is defenceless against the huntsmen's spears which now can slay it. But if they wish to take it alive power is of no avail, as it would die of grief on the spot in such circumstances, for it is a proud animal. It is so strong that Holy Scripture compares the strength of God himself with the Unicorn; and it is so unmanageable that it is said of it in Job 39: 'Canst thou . . . etc.' David speaks both good and evil of the Unicorn. It is a large animal with the body of a horse, feet of an elephant and tail of a pig. Its colour resembles that of the yew and it utters a frightful roar. It fights with the elephant and defeats it by thrusting its horn through the soft parts of the elephant's stomach. As mentioned before, it is miraculously attracted to untouched girls. In his book about animals Albertus Magnus recounts how Pompey the Great took a Unicornus to Rome to show to the people.

We stayed for some time at the foot of the mountain where the animal stood and observed us as peacefully as we observed it, for it stood still and did not move until we went on our way . . ."[7]

The strange thing about this description is that the writer tells us nothing of *what* the animal looked like as it gazed at them for so long from the mountain top. After mentioning the horn, which they could obviously see against the sky, he starts to recount the virgin story, copying the Physiologus, and then goes on to describe the animal directly according to the tradition of Aelian and Megasthenes.

Here they stand, these well informed people, and are shown this animal they have heard so much about – and proceed to quote from the classics. This is not the end of the experience, for Erhard Reuwich sets out to draw the animal, with others they have seen on their travels. Beneath his picture he writes: "These animals have been

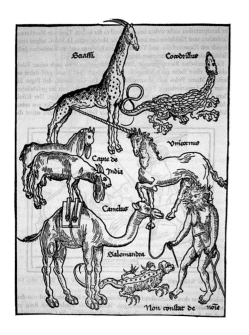

Woodcut illustration by Erhard Reuwich to Bernhard von Breydenbach's travel book *Peregrinatio in terram sanctam*, Mainz, 1483

meticulously portrayed, exactly as we observed them in the Holy Land." So what did he draw? The two goats with drooping ears and the dromedary are acceptable. The giraffe is more problematic; it has acquired goat's horns and is spotted. The salamander is a direct copy of the "fiery salamander" of alchemy, with claws and the stars of the firmament down its back. The crocodile has gone the same way and become something of a dragon. The "wild man" must be a misconstrued ape. Finally, the Unicorn is straight from the tapestries; the impossible horse with cloven hoofs and the long narwhal tusk on its forehead, found everywhere in European art – except on Mount Sinai or in Breydenbach's description. We may consider what controls human powers of observation, how easily we see what we expect to see – and how strongly a prevailing culture limits our construction of the world around us!

In 1503 Ludovico Barthema – also known as Lewis Vartoman – of Bologna travelled through parts of Africa and the Near East. His *Itinerario* describes the Unicorns he saw in the town of Zeila in Ethiopia and in a park near the temple at Mecca. There he found two which had been sent as gifts from the Emperor of Ethiopia:

"...shewed to the people for a miracle, and not without reason for the seldomenesse and strange nature. The one of them, which is much hygher than the other, yet not much unlyke to a coolte of thyrtye monethes of age, in the forehead groweth only one horne, in maner ryght foorth, of the length of three cubites. The other is much younger, of the age of one yeere, and lyke a young Coolte: the horne of this is of the length of foure handfuls. This beast is of the coloure of a horse of weesel coloure, and hath the head lyke an hart, but no long necke, a thynne mane hangynge only on the one syde. Theyr legges are thyn and slender, lyke a fawne or hynde. The hoofes of the fore feete are divided in two, much lyke the feet of a Goat. The outwarde part of the hynder feete is ryght full of heare. This beast doubtlesse seemeth wylde and fierce, yet tempereth that fiercenesse with a certain comelinesse."[8]

Jörg Breu, illustration to Sebastian Münster's *Cosmographia*, Basle, 1550

Now this description really feels like a true eye-witness account – if somewhat influenced by Pliny – and as such it was received. In 1554 Sebastian Münster published his great natural history *Cosmographia Universal* in Basle, and Vartoman's description formed the basis of a drawing of the Unicorn in the beautifully illustrated 1550 edition. The artist Jörg Breu drew the two animals in a cage at Mecca, and we recognize this picture again in Conrad Gesner's *Historia Animalium*, published in Frankfurt in 1551. It is up to modern zoologists to decide which African animal Vartoman could have seen.

Here travel description intersects with natural science, and it is time for us to move on to this last – but not least captivating – part of the Unicorn's history.

CHAPTER 18

Science on the March

If the Unicorn continued to be a tangible reality after it had disappeared from the theological universe, it was due to a great extent to the medicinal qualities associated with its horn. Favoured children have many names and the horn was known by several, originally merged by two definite articles, the Arabic *al-* and the French-Romance *li-*, plus the Latin name for horn, *cornus*. The result was in Italian "Alicorno", English "Alicorn" and French "Lichorne", "Lincorne" or "Licorno", while the Germans kept to their special "Einhorn".

Naturally the imagination worked on the horn. As we have seen, it had a strong tendency to grow: from Ctesias's measurement of about half a metre, via Pliny's one metre to a metre and a half in Solinus and Isidore. In Albertus Magnus it has shot to three metres and the Arab Alkazuin makes it long enough to spear elephants upon, to the point where the whole animal would surely topple over. The colour changes too, from completely black (Aelian) to white with black bark; or the whole horn is polychrome. Some add that the horn gleams brightly like a carbuncle. A light, almost ivory colour was adopted consistently after 1200. The horn with spirals or rings is mentioned for the first time by Aelian and he is followed by Megasthenes, although it is not certain what they mean by this. It might, of course, be some kind of artificial decoration. Otherwise it is not mentioned before the leftward-twisting spirals turn up in art almost as a matter of course about 1200. By then the ivory-coloured narwhal tusk, which bore such spirals, had long since been tangible proof of the animal's existence.

Knowledge of narwhal tusks that had been washed ashore perhaps goes back to the Imperial Roman era about AD 200. Then they were not needed for the Unicorn, which as we know was already furnished with the great "sickle horn", which crowned it right up to the Middle Ages. When the Northmen began to hunt whales in earnest, however, the tooth became an important commodity. In 1126 the historian Arngrimr Jonsson reports on cargoes of teeth in Iceland. After this exporting began, tooth and Unicorn became conjoined in people's minds; medieval traders saw no reason to worry about whether one object was horn, the other dentine. The ultimate Unicorn horn had been found.

Why? Firstly perhaps because the medicinal narwhal tooth, of whose actual origin only very few in the European interior were aware, seemed naturally to belong

SYMBOLORVM
&
EMBLEMATVM EX
ANIMALIBVS QVA,,
DRVPEDIBVS
DESVMTORVM
CENTVRIA ALTERA
COLLECTA·
A
IOACHIMO CAMERARIO
MEDICO NORIMBERG·
Exponuntur in hoc libro rariores
tum animalium proprietes tum
historiæ ac sententiæ memorabiles·
AN° SALV̈T: CIƆ·IƆ·IƆXV·

PIETAS · PVRA

CELI · PVRA · PIA

on the head of the Unicorn, whose horn was recorded to be a preventative against poison; but perhaps other forces played a part. Among the powerful symbols of divine strength was also the twisted rope design, which in the Romanesque period was assiduously carved round the edges of fonts, around portals and stone sculptures, and represented as Samson's twisted lock of hair, the sign of his strength. Now this twisted design was set on the Unicorn's brow as its mark of divinity. It is thought-provoking that on a Persian relief of the king and the fabulous animal, mentioned above, this creature's horn is also spirally twisted (see fig. on p.16). An ancient idea is taken up anew.

It was inevitable that the horn should be assigned medicinal qualities. The account of the cleansing water was easily kindled in a Christianity where staff, taper and lance had always cleansed, fertilized and consecrated. Moreover, Ctesias said that the horn was used against sickness and poison, as was rhinoceros horn. Physiologus said of the stag:

"The stag by its nature hates all poisonous things, and therefore no snake will enter where the foot or the skin or the horn of a deer has been nailed fast to the door."[1]

The Physiologus also claimed that both the deer and the Unicorn attack and eat snakes, and can neutralize their poison. There is war between deer and serpent. It is more complicated than this, however, for there is also a remarkable parallel between them, which it is difficult for those not born in medieval times fully to understand. The serpent is also the symbol of the god of medicine and the "cerastes horn"[2] was hung above the salting tub beside both the Unicorn horn and the left hind hoof of the elk as protection against poison, according to the theory that "evil drives out evil". This had been claimed by a succession of great men, from Galen the physician, "Simili similibus curantur" (Like heals like), to Ambrose, "Venenum veneno excludetur" (Poison is prevented by poison).

Here we have reached an important principle that governed science from antiquity until recent times, namely the "teaching of essences", which maintains that only things like each other in "essence" can cure each other. When the stag eats the snake it becomes poisonous itself and, as the horn is that part of the animal upon which its life depends, and is therefore most receptive to "essence", the poison collects there. It stands to reason that the effect is doubled if there is only one horn, and a horn that is so doubly supplied must be an excellent remedy against poison. When the horn on the table "sweats" in the vicinity of poison, this may be from antipathy, but principally also from "the sympathy of likeness". The result is the same for the owner. He is warned, or the powdered horn will counteract the poison if he has already eaten it.

Hildegard of Bingen said that several parts of the animal could be used as remedies (see p.38), but generally the horn was the important one. It was hung up, food and drink was touched with it, or it was taken in powder form to cure many diseases. Wolfram von Eschenbach's *Parzival* of about 1210 offers a variant. In this poem, a part of the Grail Legend, the knights seek help for the sick King Anfortes, and they believe that the horn of the magical animal might be of use:

"The Unicorn a creature is
who loves the purest virgin sweet
and slumbers in a maiden's lap.
We take the creature's heart
as balm for the king's hurt.
We took the bright carbuncle stone
that grows upon the creature's head
and grows out from under the horn.
With this we rubbed the victim's skin
and placed the stone the wound within …"[3]

Hildegard talked also of the precious carbuncle beneath the horn, in which "a man can see his own face". Clearly this mirroring stone contains in itself the "essence" of masculinity, but on a heightened plane, for one senses that the sacred animal is the bearer of the Philosophers' Stone. Unfortunately the cure did not help in the case of King Anfortes.

Belief in the medicinal qualities of the horn began early in the medieval period and increased in fervour during the Crusades, from the twelfth century, probably because the narwhal tusk had now become generally known and played its part as the "alicorn" all over Europe. More and more people could hold the tangible "proof" of the Unicorn's existence in their hand.

It was worked into the shape of a crosier or chalice, and kept as a relic in church-es or, later, in cabinets of curiosities. At the abbey of Saint-Denis outside Paris a seven-foot horn was kept for centuries in a chalice with holy water and used as a medicament, until it was destroyed at the French Revolution. San Marco in Venice possessed three, which were partly used as batons by the admirals of the city, and partly worn shiny by medicinal use. St Paul's Cathedral and Westminster Abbey in London, and Milan Cathedral, also had examples, for it was thought quite natural that the horn should be in the care of the Church. Dust was scraped from it and mixed with herbs or liquid, which was given to the patient. When Martin Luther fell ill the Margrave Albrecht of Mansfeldt mixed two spoonfuls of Unicorn powder for him to save his life, although God refused once again to cooperate.

The powers of the horn made it sought after by the upper classes, who were par-ticularly liable to poisoning. Gifts were exchanged of pieces or of whole horns, pro-cured at great expense, and people followed the old custom of setting them in goblets or mounts of gold. Inventories teem with horns: the Duke of Mantua, the Medicis of Florence, the French kings and the dukes of Berry and Burgundy – all had them. The well known Windsor horn, found by Sir Martin Frobisher, was pre-sented to Queen Elizabeth I as a suitable token of esteem from the great explorer.

In 1553 Pope Clement VIII held a competition for the gold setting of a horn to be presented to the French king François I. We know this from the autobiography of the goldsmith Benvenuto Cellini, in which he tells of himself and his rival Tobbia. Tobbia made the setting as a candleholder with four small Unicorn heads at its foot, and the horn was to be placed in this exactly like a candle. Cellini made a Unicorn head, in which the horn could naturally be fitted, and his design was combined of both a horse and a stag, furnished with a magnificent mane. "The horn itself had cost 17,000 ducats," writes Cellini, "and with the gold setting such a gift represented a small fortune."[4]

So if we could look into Renaissance palaces we should find whole or half narwhal tusks among other objects that were bought with princely sums and highly prized. The horn was hung with snakes' tongues over the table and was kept in princes' cabinets of curiosities in company with bezoar stones ("serpent stones"), red clay from Lemnos, "toadstones" (fossilized whale teeth), buffalo and rhinoceros-horn goblets, ostrich heads and vulture claws, which could extinguish fire.

Naturally, learned scholars were also interested in the horn, not merely doctors but also theologians and alchemists, because in their minds the Unicorn was still associated with Christ. Their preoccupation with the horn gives us excellent opportunities for studying the scientific mind of the Renaissance. During the sixteenth century, when discussion really speeded up, there is a sense of a changed paradigm, when the medieval and the new age collide and a different way of thinking slowly gains ground. After a long theological period, which had dominated the whole continent from late antiquity to the Renaissance, Europe passed through a period that some have called "metaphysical", to reach the practical-positivistic stance that still, to a certain extent, obtains today, and which promoted the development of modern technology and science.

Alchemy is such a metaphysical and transitional phenomenon. In many ways it is still attached to medieval thought; but behind its numerous allegories are a series of deep psychological perceptions which are far from outworn. The art of alchemy is at once a religious grassroots movement in a time of Church crisis, and an emergent study that sometimes stumbled on new chemical connections by a stroke of luck – and without doubt, in its experiments, caused many mercury poisonings.

It is almost impossible to follow the complicated cogitations of alchemy, particularly because the masters – like the freemasons – sought to veil their doctrine out of all recognition. But it is important to understand that the movement in its pure stage was of a genuine philosophical kind and completely different from the cheap "search for gold" which it probably became in its decadence. One of its principles was a parallelism between the *vita activa* and the *vita contemplativa* – the active and contemplative life – according to which an exterior material process, the chemical one in the alchemist's alembic, was the image of a spiritual transformation in the soul, attained through meditation. When seven phases were successfully completed, the Philosopher's Stone was left in the alembic as a material symbol of the success of the process, in which the soul experienced a corresponding metamorphosis leading to a rebirth, a union with the self and with God.

A complicated system of symbols taken from various cultures evolved and was written down and illustrated in long textbooks. It is a recondite world, but the symbols are taken to a great extent from the ancient and the Christian – particularly Neoplatonic – systems, so that we can identify a number of them. Among the three animal symbols that dominate alchemy are the Green Lion and the Unicorn. Both are royal animals and both are Christ symbols. The lion can devour, the Unicorn can thrust its horn through the tree. As the swallowing up (female) and penetrating (male) power they are an expression of the inner contrast in the androgynous planetary god Mercury or Hermes, who, with wings and serpent staff was the soul's guide through the "hermetic art", to which he gave his name. In chemistry they stand for quicksilver or mercury, the fixed catalyst in the alchemical process.

The counterpart to the Unicorn was the *cervus fugitiva*, or Fleeing Deer, which represents the female element or *anima*, hunted by the Unicorn or *spiritus*. Together they form the human entity or "substance", also manifested in the bisected landscape (see fig. on p.74). The two white animals, which approach each other in Lambsprinck's drawing, indicate a union of *anima* and *spiritus*, a sublimated marriage which will bring the Philosophers' Stone to life and recreate the entity that according to Plato was shattered by a Fall: in this way the Virgin myth can be included in alchemy, for the deer can be replaced by Mary. Deer/woman stands – like water – for the passive element contrasting with the active Unicorn's horn. In the Gyrstinge frontal we can sense the alchemistic spirit in the picture, as in so many other sixteenth-century works of art (see fig. on p.75).

The Unicorn is not often featured in the books on alchemy, in which lions, snakes and dragons take precedence. When it does appear it usually stands in front of the deer in the landscape, stirs the water with its horn or lies in the Virgin's lap. The final phase of alchemy is sometimes shown by a Unicorn lying under a Tree of Life as the *spiritus vitae* – the spirit of resurrection or Christ in his kingdom. Compare this with the last picture in the Verteuil tapestries, where the white Unicorn lies under the pomegranate tree.

The alchemical symbols help us to understand the tapestries, just as the tapestries and altarpieces shed light on the alchemical images. Everywhere we meet the same fertility mysticism and ideas of rebirth. The "hot" male element constantly meets water, woman or tree, both piercing but also vulnerable, since it must be torn apart, sacrificed and then put together again in order to give growth and salvation. It is a repetition of the Osiris myth, the Crucifixion and the slain Unicorn. In the same way the substances in the alchemist's alembic must be dissolved, conjoined, parted again and finally combined in a refined synthesis like the Stone, which can turn everything to gold, corresponding to the soul's unity with the self.

Gradually, as the horn became less rare and cheaper, it was stocked by regular apothecaries and sold with other remedies, which went on for about three hundred years. This is why many apothecaries show a Unicorn on their sign, for the powder stood high on their list of wares. They had to battle with fakes, however. People concocted powders of chalk or ordinary bones and sold them as genuine alicorn powder, or foisted off parts of fossils, elephant tooth or walrus teeth boiled and straightened out, on gullible customers. Naturally the next development was the invention of "alicornus tests". These could be drastic. For instance, a condemned criminal – or on occasion a servant or peasant – might be given a poison followed by the powder on offer to test it. If the guinea pig died, which usually happened, it was too bad. It was more usual, however, to experiment with doves and cats, or to apply the old nostrum: that the horn would give off bubbles in water or sweat in the proximity of poison. A circle could also be drawn with an alicorn or the powder, and a spider put inside it. If the material were genuine, the spider would not be able to escape and would die miserably. This is a form of magic we know from the pentagram, which could bind the Devil himself.

The zoologist Conrad Gesner discussed the problem of authenticity in his great *Historia Animalium* (1551–63). The book was a modern development of the old bestiaries, but with more criticism and less Christian moralizing. He makes much of the horn: its healing power is more powerful near the point than in the middle, and one should buy the whole or as large pieces as possible in order to avoid being cheated. The apothecaries say that the best pieces are the whiter and soft pieces of marrow. The outward parts are coarser and pale yellow-white. The sham can easily by discovered from the colour and other signs:

"It is also untrue to say that if poison is in the vicinity of the horn it will sweat; it may well be that it does sometimes sweat like other solid bodies such as stone and glass, on which vapour and damp can 'freeze' [that is, condense] and then vanish again without poison having had anything to do with it. For the same thing occurs with the stone known as 'Serpentine', which shows, they say, where poison is; but this is not true."[5]

Here the author has made an independent observation, which he follows up with reasoning. On the other hand, he does not doubt the horn's medicinal properties and advises purchasers to carry out the arsenic test on a couple of doves. He cites experts who have seen poisoned people make a good recovery by taking a little horn marrow in wine. The horn is effective for epilepsy, attacks of plague, rabies and infections from other animals, and for worms in the body which cause weakness in children.

With regard to epilepsy Gesner himself had seen good results in a patient given the following prescription: he took Unicorn horn, a little scraped ivory, amber, a little gold dust and coral, which he pounded coarsely, put into a bag of silk and boiled in water with redcurrants, cinnamon and other spices. Unfortunately:

"In Venice there are various wicked villains and vagabonds who mix pulverised flint, chalk or other stones with soap and make a paste of them which they sell as Unicorn horn, for when they take a pinch of it and pour it into wine it starts to bubble."

Others too were preoccupied with the forgeries. A Hebrew doctor and philosopher, David de Pomis, published a *Dittionario Novo Hebraico* (a Hebrew–Latin–Italian dictionary) in Venice in 1587:

"The Unicorn is an animal which has one horn in its head, and this horn is effective against poison and pestilential attacks."[6]

It should be noted, he says, that very little of the true horn is to be found, as most of what is sold is either hartshorn or elephant tusk. The usual test, which consists of placing the object in water to see if bubbles arise, is completely unreliable, and if one desires to exert good for the world and expose those wicked people who sell worthless things at high prices, one should take the opportunity to describe an accurate test whereby one can distinguish the genuine horn from the false:

"Place the horn in a vessel of whatever material you deem good, together with three or four living and large scorpions, and keep the vessel covered. If you find, four hours later, that the scorpions are dead or almost lifeless, it is a good horn, and no price in the world is too high to pay for it. Otherwise it is a fake."

Throughout the century doctors and philosophers argued bravely about the value of the horn, and at one point began even to discuss the more sensitive question of whether this animal, so seldom seen, really existed. We shall now follow the discussion between the learned Venetian Andrea Marini and the Pope's physician Andrea

Maiden and Unicorn
Illustration in an alchemical
textbook, the Codex Vossianus
Chymicus Tractatus qui
dicitur Thoma Aquinatis
de Alchimia, 1520, MS. 29,
fol. 87, Bibliotheek der
Rijksuniversiteit, Leiden

Note the disposition of the
landscape details and compare
with the Gyrstinge altar
frontal on p.75

Bacci, who was later employed by Grand Duke Francesco de' Medici in Florence. In 1566 Andrea Marini wrote a *Discorso . . . contra la falsa Opinione dell'Alicorno* (Discourse against the false opinion of the Unicorn horn), which was published by the famous Aldus Press in Venice.[7] He attacked the Arabs for passing off the horn as medicine and the swindlers for making fake horn. We have no idea, he said, whether the animal exists at all. The alleged horns come without any doubt from many different animals – not least from marine animals – so any possible effect must be true of *all* horns. Besides this, there are many different poisons, and the horns cannot affect them all. Moreover, horns definitely cannot "sweat". The ancients were often in error, for harpies and sirens certainly do not exist, although they spoke of them. Here for the first time a real sceptic raised his voice; but he did not go unanswered.

Andrea Bacci wrote a defence of belief in Unicorns and their power, *L'Alicorno*, published in Florence in 1582, possibly on the instigation of Duke Francesco and dedicated to him. He had been entrusted with the duke's library for his research. Bacci considered that an animal that had preoccupied so many great spirits could not be dismissed merely because it was rare. The shy animal lives within the great forests, so it is not remarkable that it is hardly ever seen. When it dies, the horn is carried down rivers to be washed up on the shore, which is why it is found there. He concludes:

"Whether the Alicornus sweats or no, whether it makes water boil or not – the belief that it does so causes no harm to the truth and will be of benefit to the state. No person with common sense should try to refute these things through reasoning, but ought to allow them and discreetly admit them, anyhow for the sake of those princes they wish to please with such a favourable opinion. Thus we are duty bound for the sake of the common good to write and to persuade the ignorant that what is said of the Alicorn is true, because such a belief makes wicked men powerless to cause evil by making them believe that the virtues of this horn will easily discover their failings and bring down ruin on their heads."[8]

The learned gentleman sits in a room where he has access to pieces of horn of various sizes. He discusses the "circle test" and other experiments; but not once does he stretch out his hand for a piece of horn and make a circle on the table to see with his own eyes what happens to the spider. Instead he gets the folios off the shelves and looks up Aristotle and Pliny, and then he repeats all the words he finds in them. For it was still felt that, as one writer has observed: "Wonderful things were precisely what one expected of nature."[9]

Ironically, a year or two later the duke and his wife, Bianca Capella, were poisoned by the duke's brother, Cardinal Ferdinand. Let us end this scientific journey with a shining example. The French Queen Catherine de' Medici had received an alicorn as a wedding gift from Pope Clement VII, which she made available to her unusually progressive personal physician, Ambroise Paré, the "Father of French Surgery". He experimented – and came to his own conclusions. He tried doves and arsenic, toads in water and spiders in circles, and saw through these tests. Unfortunately he seems also to have experimented on King Charles IX's chef, who had been condemned for some crime, and – predictably – died. His *Discourses* on mummies, Unicorns, poisons and plague were published in Paris in 1582, a hundred years before the works of Ole Worm and Thomas Bartholin in Denmark (see chapter 19).

Paré still believes – reluctantly – that Unicorns exist, for the Bible says so, but their medicinal value and the poison tests are nonsense, in his opinion. The horn sweats no more than glass, marble or other cold surfaces, and there is nothing very remarkable about that. Paré had his opponents, but when they said "It is better to be mistaken with the wise than to entertain ideas contrary to theirs", he replied: "I say, on the contrary, that I would rather do well on my own than be mistaken with not only the wise, but the whole world"; and concludes that the truth surpasses all human wisdom.[10] Here speaks a worthy contemporary of Galileo!

CHAPTER 19
The One-toothed Monoceros

I f debate see-sawed during the sixteenth century, it gave way to more sceptical reflections in the following one. Science was developing and larger areas of the globe were constantly being discovered, although there was no sign as yet of herds of grazing Unicorns.

Denmark made a distinguished contribution to the debate, particularly during the reigns of three kings, Christian IV, Frederik III and Christian V. At least Scandinavians knew where the narwhal tusk came from. As early as 1555 Olaus Magnus in Uppsala, Sweden, had written of the narwhal:

"The Monoceros is a sea monster which has a very large horn in its forehead, with which it can pierce through and destroy ships and kill many men."[1]

No doubt he had heard mariners tell of their meetings with whales, of the long tusk of the narwhal and of boats capsized after collision with the colossi of the sea.

The widely travelled polymath Caspar Bartholin (1585–1629) returned home after training as a medical doctor at Basle in 1610 and was appointed professor at Copenhagen University, at first in medicine and later in Latin and theology as well. He wrote numerous teaching books, including in 1628 a special study, forty-eight pages long, *De unicornu ejusque affinibus et succedaneis opusculum* (On the Unicorn and similar subjects), which dealt, as it were, with the Monocerine Idea.[2] It looks as if he was one of the first to sense that there is a psychological factor which makes "one-hornedness" attractive, but he is still a child of the compilatory method, believing in the infallibility of the Vulgate. He limits himself to describing the eight "species" in the world possessing one horn, including the Unicorn. They are the oryx (according to Aristotle), Garcia of Horto's African amphibium (a product of travel descriptions of 1567), the rhinoceros, the Indian bull, horse and ass (according to Ctesias), the Unicorn itself and the *Monodon Monoceros*, the narwhal. The evidence is taken from the Septuagint, the classics and finally the horn itself. He believes in the physical existence of the animals because he saw the horns owned by apothecaries in Montpellier when he was studying there.

"Only foolish people deny this; people who will believe nothing they have not seen for themselves, who completely overrule what so many reliable and distinguished authors in both profane and sacred literature have said about the Unicorn as a real animal.

"Nay, an intelligent man thinks quite otherwise. Before every corner of the world has been thoroughly investigated there is hope that one fine day a whole Unicorn may be brought back from some distant land."[3]

The book still cites many well known sources: the Bible, Pliny, Marco Polo and Vartoman; but he thinks that the magic is nonsense because experiments demonstrate the opposite and he takes Bacci to task, arguing that the authority of a prince must not alter our opinion, for it is never as important as the truth.

Caspar's son Thomas (1616–1680) followed in his father's footsteps as a doctor and scholar, likewise going to Basle, one of the greatest cultural cities of Europe. Here were the publishing houses and great printing presses that had published the works of Erasmus, and the famous university. At this, Thomas became a doctor of medicine in 1645. Later he became a professor in Copenhagen, in mathematics and anatomy, as well as personal physician to Christian V and a university librarian. Thomas was an even greater scientist than his father; he further developed Harvey's researches into blood circulation, and he too was obsessed by the "horn idea". In 1645 he published in Padua a "horn encyclopedia", fashionable at the time, *De Unicornu Observationes Novae*. It was reissued by his son Caspar in Amsterdam in 1678, and it is from this edition that we have a famous frontispiece.

Every possible horn is represented. Nature is personified in the centre with the horn of plenty; supporting herself against the noblest species, the Unicorn itself, as big as a horse and apparently with *hoofs*. Behind them stands a warrior with an oryx horn, horned birds fly in the air and on the earth crawl horned beetles. Another pair of quadrupeds is behind and, on the left, Moses pushes into the picture. Right in the foreground are mermen with armfuls of narwhal teeth; so three elements at least are present. The lady herself has a little curved horn on her brow exactly like the Persian demon. The horn of the animal just in front of the warrior sticks up in a strategically interesting place. We may wonder if this is by chance!

There are thirty-seven chapters on horns in the book. In one it is discussed whether human beings can have horns, or whether Moses' famous head gear is perhaps the result of an erroneous translation. Tertullian's statement that "the horn of the cross shall gore the nations" receives commentary, and there are descriptions of insects, birds and deer with horns, and of the Unicorn itself, which Bartholin does not dare to exclude, for here he follows Caspar's line.

Both books are still partly committed to traditional ideas, but are agreed in rejecting magic as nonsense. Only the idea of capture with the aid of a tree is accepted. Both clearly believe that what is sold on the market is narwhal tusk, and that the Virgin method of capture is a fable. So a distinction is developing between the possible – for example, the capture of the animal in a tree – and the fabulous, which is increasingly labelled as "old wives' tales". Science and folklore are about to go their separate ways in earnest.

It is not hard to understand why the animal itself took so long to follow suit. Behind it lay a thousand years of data, assurances of its existence by gifted writers and travellers, and not least the high moral and religious value that had been invested in it. Nor had the existence of the animal ever been disproved. It might perfectly well have lived, just like the narwhal and all the other animals on the frontispiece; its

Narwhall Hunt in Greenland
Illustration to Olaus Magnus,
*Historia de gentibus
Septentrionalibus*, Rome, 1555

Frontispiece to Thomas
Bartholin's book, *De Unicornu
Observationes Novae*, Amsterdam,
1678

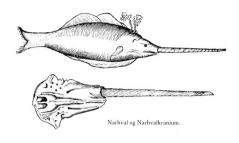

Narhval og Narhvalkranium.

The Narwhal, *Monodon Monoceros*
Ole Worm's drawing of the narwhal skull, 1655

appearance was reasonable enough. Why should it not have been found at the sources of the Nile? David Livingstone still believed that it might in the middle of the nineteenth century.

Nevertheless the frontispiece is a symptom of the new time: the Unicorn still stands in the middle of the picture, but quite definitely balanced by the pile of narwhal tusks in the foreground. Bartholin says of them, after describing the *Monodon Monoceros* of Iceland and Greenland with its strangely large tusk:

"However this tooth is the one which so many have sold as Unicornus and which is kept in the cabinets of various rulers on account of its reputation as genuine Unicorn horn. Renown like this could easily arise in earlier times because of the rarity of the tooth, for it only reached a foreign shore when the fish was stranded. Nowadays increasing trade with Greenland and in particular with Spitzbergen has revealed the nature of the tooth and the reason for its frequency. Our merchants have on every occasion filled whole ships' cargoes with the horn in question in recent years and would have imported them to Europe as genuine Unicorn horn if experts had not ripped off the mask and recognized the tooth as coming from the ocean."[4]

Here are two comments that it would be hard to find in a medieval treatise. One is that experts tear off the mask of falsehood through knowledge and observation, and the other is the use of the expression "nowadays", in relation to "earlier times". Little by little people start to think lineally and distinguish between the ignorance of dark centuries and the demonstrated proof of the new age.

The question of the Unicorn's existence came to a head in 1652, seven years after the book was finished, when an envoy from Africa during a tour of a cabinet of curiosities saw a "horn" recently brought back from Greenland. He maintained that he had often seen four-footed Unicorns in his homeland, where the animal was called "tore bina" – a horned animal that was swift and wild, big as a horse, living in the desert and impossible to capture alive. A horn protruded from a tuft of hair in the middle of its forehead, with which it cleaned the water before starting to drink. The horn, which was different from the Scandinavian kind, was used as an antidote. He told Thomas Bartholin about it and promised to send an example of horn and skin to Denmark after returning home. He must have forgotten, for no horn or skin ever arrived. His story, which otherwise seems rather glib, helped to preserve faith in a Unicorn in distant lands, still so mysterious to ordinary people.

The greatest Danish scientist of the century was Bartholin's contemporary Ole Worm (1588–1654). After attending Aarhus cathedral school in Jutland he travelled and studied all over Europe before starting a career in Copenhagen in 1615. His interest in the Unicorn was probably aroused when he was presented with a narwhal skull by Chancellor Christian Friis of Kragerup. Friis gave him the skull complete with tusk and so provided him with proof that had been difficult to obtain: the alicornus was indisputably attached to a whale. From that moment on Worm was never in doubt as to whether the numerous rumours were true: the "horn" was a tusk! We note that this occurred ten years before Thomas Bartholin wrote his book.

Worm had a sketch made of the skull and used it as an illustration for a thesis in 1638.[5] But there was still the question of whether the tooth might possess the same magical qualities attributed to hartshorn and other natural objects. He therefore undertook an experiment in the same year, following the good advice of the Italian scientist Julius Caesar Scaliger (1484–1558):

THE UNICORN

"It is very dangerous to draw conclusions from published books. The true knowledge of objects must derive from these objects themselves."[6]

This was a conclusion that Worm never tired of applying in his writings. On 3 October 1636 Worm and his friends, Doctors Fincke and Scheel, met to undertake an experiment in the house of Woldenberg the apothecary. They gave poison to two doves and two kittens and administered the "antidote" of grated horn to one of each species. One of the cats stayed alive for some hours, so that Worm was later rather equivocal about the result; but it appears that they had given the antidote in milk, which partly neutralized the poison. It was a common fault in scientists of this age that they forgot "concomitant circumstances" in their experiments. The horn was credited with cures without a thought for the herbs, wine or other medicaments taken by the patient at the same time.

Worm's considerations left their mark in a work published a year after his death in 1655, *Museum Wormianum seu Historia Rerum Rariorum* (The Worm Museum or History of Rare Objects).[7] It is a detailed catalogue of his famous collections, and includes three long chapters on whales and other marine mammals, with the drawings already mentioned. These offer the first scientifically constructed proof of the real origin of the Unicorn horn. Narwhal and Unicorn are compared and discussed, the story of the "tore bina" is referred to, as is the meeting with Christian Friis and the experiment with the poison. But in the final analysis Worm does not deny that the Unicorn may exist in some country or other, as François Marquis Ethiops Africanus, the Congolese king's envoy, had described it to the Danish king in 1652. Worm also mentions the numerous fossils that were in fashion at the time, which seemed to prove the existence of the animal. They already played a role in medicine. He could not, however, have knowledge of the German fossils that would shortly be famed throughout Europe!

In 1663, nine years after Worm's death a large find of fossils was made in a limestone cave at Quedlinburg. The nearby monastery had a number of them dug up and these were described, partially reconstructed and drawn by Doctor Otto von Guericke. In addition to other things, he reconstructed a Unicorn skeleton which stood upright on its hind legs, with a powerful tail like a kangaroo. It must have been the oddest Unicorn that ever hopped on earth. Later Leibnitz included this drawing of *Hercynian Unicornus* in his work *Protagaea* (1749), which dealt with the fossils of the province. In this way a "scientific" Unicorn lived on, and even provided support for the belief that the beast had perished in the Flood, that being the reason why it was no longer to be found.

It was many years before Worm's sane words put an end to the more fanciful beliefs in the magic horn. King Frederik III had a magnificent throne designed with columns made of narwhal teeth. Various other objects made of the same material are kept in Danish museums. The goldsmith responsible for the smaller ornamentations on the throne had a son who became an apothecary. In 1707 he established the first Unicorn apothecary shop at Christianshavn, in Copenhagen, with the animal's head on the signboard. Today the interior of this shop is in the Old Town in Aarhus, Jutland, but the horned head is still in place above the building on the square in Copenhagen.

Reconstruction of a "fossil Unicorn" by Otto von Guericke, illustration to Leibnitz, *Protogaea*, 1749

In other parts of Europe, Unicorn apothecary shops were common. There were over a hundred in Germany, and we have noticed the apothecaries' coat of arms in London. The animal was to be found on jars, bags and invoice headings until the mid-eighteenth century, as a reminder of the time when horn-powder was held in high esteem among pharmacists. The phrase *Venena pello* (I drive out poison) was hard to forget. In the second half of the eighteenth century, however, the Unicorn's prestige flagged. Prices sank and the narwhal tusk became more of a curiosity at the quack doctor's than a medicament to be taken seriously; the tooth was unsaleable. In William Hogarth's series of paintings and prints *Marriage à la Mode*, of 1743, we see in the third picture a reckless roué visiting a quack doctor with his ailing mistress. Here "the horn" hangs on the wall among other outdated medical wares. In these degrading surroundings we leave it to await better times, while the age of Enlightenment passes it by.

Throne of Christian V of Denmark
1670, Rosenborg Castle, Copenhagen

CHAPTER 20

The Modern Problem

Friedrich Schiller, the German Romantic poet, has the Unicorn both on his shield and as a crest, with a quotation from the ode "An die Freunde", which runs:

"All is repeated in this life,
eternal youth is but a dream.
Only what has never been
can alone never age."

There is no mention here of Christ or pharmacy. There is mention of a creature that may not exist, but which is alive in the imagination and precisely for this reason is immortal. Schiller's poem points to a reserve where the animal could live in peace. As a product of human creativity it continued to exist, even if one no longer expected to find it in the nearest forest.

Seen in that perspective, the Unicorn is more capable of survival than the rhinoceros or many other real animals that man is doing his best to exterminate. The salvation of the Unicorn is its non-existence.

Once Reason had reduced the animal to almost nothing in the eighteenth century, it survived unobtrusively in poetry and literature. This was nothing new; the Unicorn had been a theme for poetry since the Middle Ages, which had linked it with the Virgin and described it in the bestiaries. We have met it already in the spring-like grace of the songs to Mary, in the Arthurian legends, in fables and chivalrous romances, when the heraldic animals were brought to active life. It was always depicted in keeping with the meaning invested in it by tradition: in part a Christ symbol, in part an expression of knightly conduct – and sometimes demonic.

We shall now retrace our steps to the Renaissance. We have seen that ideas and painting changed character, and literature did the same. The Virgin hunt went out of fashion. The monasteries and their world of ideas lost their interest, and the Virgin hunt was replaced by more reasonable methods of capture, in which the bold hunter's ingenuity outwits the Unicorn. When animals play roles they are at the same time allegories of human passions. And to an increasing extent authors use the Unicorn individually, often playing on the animal's erotic overtones, now no longer kept in check by the solemnity of religion.

Friedrich Schiller's coat of arms

In the mid-sixteenth century we see how it can be done by François Rabelais. Pantagruel, who roams around in many strange lands, arrives in the "land of Satin", where he sees numerous animals taken from the bestiaries. He sees elephants fighting rhinoceros, and recounts:

"I saw there two and thirty Unicorns; they are a curst sort of Creatures, much resembling a fine Horse, unless it be that their Heads are like a Stag's, their Feet like an Elephant's, their Tails like a wild Boar's, and out of each of their Foreheads sprouts out a short black Horn, some six or seven foot long; commonly it dangles down like a Turkey Cock's Comb. When an Unicorn has a mind to fight, or put it to any other use, what does it do but make it stand, and then 'tis as straight as an Arrow.

"I saw one of them, which was attended with a throng of other wild Beasts, purifie a Fountain with its Horn. With that Panurge told me, that his Prancer, alias his Nimble-Wimble, was like the Unicorn, not altogether in length indeed, but in Vertue and Propriety: for as the Unicorn purifi'd Pools and Fountains from Filth and Venom, so that other animals came and drank securely there afterwards; in the like manner, others might were their Nags, and dabble after him without fear of Shankers, Carnosities, Gonorrhaea's, Buboes, Crinckum's and such other Plagues caught by those who venture to quench their Amorous Thirst in a common Puddle; for with his Nervous Horn he remov'd all the Infection that might be lurking in some blind Cranny of the Mephitic sweet-scented Hole."[1]

As a learned writer Rabelais starts as usual with descriptions from the classics. Again Pliny and Megasthenes oblige. But then he takes over the animal for his own use and creates a wholly original horn. The cleansing by water is mentioned only to be used by Panurge in a manner that dismisses any memory of Christ and directs attention to the animal's true sexual nature, showing us that we no longer live in the time of Gregory the Great.

Edmund Spenser and William Shakespeare are both exponents of the half scientific, half allegorical-mythical thinking of their age, full of doubt and unrest, and with a bent towards the psychological. In Spenser's poem *The Faerie Queene*, 1590, the hero Guyon, himself a psychological figure, meets his mortal enemy in single combat, and is likened to the proud lion who outwits the savagery of blind nature:

"Like as a lyon, whose imperiall powre/ a prowd, rebellious Unicorne defies,/ T'avoide the rash assault and wrathfull stowre/ of his fiers foe, him to a tree applies.

And when him running in full course he spies/ he slips aside: The whiles that furious beast/ his precious horne, sought of his enemies/ strikes in the stocke, he thence can be releast/ but to the mighty victor yilds a bounteous feast."[2]

Shakespeare uses the Unicorn in several places as poetic ornament, but always to reflect Elizabethan thinking. One instance is in *The Tempest*, 1611 (Act III, Scene 3). Under an enchantment on the bewitched isle Sebastian says:

". . . Now I will believe,/ That there are living unicorns; that, in Arabia/ There is one tree, the phoenix's throne."

Shakespeare borrows two creatures from the Physiologus, a four-legged one and a bird – both traditional Christ-symbols, but ones whose reality has begun to be doubted, to be acknowledged only in moments when imagination and enchantment hold sway. No one would have spoken like this in the age of the Grail Legend.

In the same manner Shakespeare uses an assemblage of generally familiar features from the tall stories in the Physiologus about hunting wild animals, but as images of the weakness of the human mind. In Act II of *Julius Caesar*, *c.* 1599, he has the conspirators preparing to murder Caesar. They are afraid he will not come to the meeting; but Decius reassures them:

"Never fear that: if he be so resolv'd
I can o'ersway him; for he loves to hear
That unicorns may be betray'd with trees,
And bears with glasses, elephants with holes,
Lions with toils, and men with flatterers:
But when I tell him he hates flatterers,
He says he does, – being then most flatter'd."

Caesar thinks he is far above human weakness and the possibility of being deceived; but he is merely a proud Unicorn. And the capture by means of the tree is such a commonplace that all would understand the reference.

In *Timon of Athens*, *c.* 1607 (Act IV, Scene 3) the misanthropic Timon expounds on nature's cruel world to the still more bitter hermit Apemantus, who wants to be an animal among animals. Here we are involved in the battle of all against all, in which one eats or is eaten:

"If thou wert the lion, the fox would beguile thee . . . if thou wert the wolf, thy greediness would afflict thee . . . wert thou the unicorn, pride and wrath would confound thee, and make thine own self the conquest of thy fury . . ."

This seems to refer once more to the capture by means of the tree; for the Unicorn belongs to a more dangerous species than the other animals. As in Spenser, it is self-destructive and easily becomes "a prey to itself". More than any other animal it is an image of man, who is at loggerheads with his own subterranean forces.

Finally, in *The Rape of Lucrece*, 1594, there is a monologue on the dream of the time of achieving the impossible – and what a series of deeds this is! "Time's glory is . . . to tame the Unicorn and lion wild" and this is not child's play, for as Christian Elling, the Danish writer, says, continuing the monologue from *Lucrece*: "To tame the Unicorn is momentous – like wearing holes in huge stones with drops and tearing feathers from the wings of ancient ravens."[3] Apart from the reference to the two proud animals, known to everyone from coats of arms, there is also a clear reference to alchemy. To "tame the Unicorn and lion" and to "take the feathers from the black raven" are allegories from the alchemist's workshop, where the black bird represents the first part, the "Black Phase" or "Nigredo". One is confronted with fearful powers here, and on the deepest level these forces are in one's own soul. In the truest sense the animals are "mental images". We note that Shakespeare uses the Unicorn above all as an expression of the wild and untameable.

Elling also points out the passage in *Hamlet* where the prince wants to lay his head in Ophelia's – the maiden's – lap and like a real troubadour play the part of a shy, vulnerable, infatuated Unicorn, homeless in the world. The age is so attuned to the Unicorn's behaviour that Shakespeare can refer without hesitation to all sides of its nature. Its universe is known to all. But in the poet's ambivalent words it comes to stand in a field of tension between the medievally literal and modern psychology.

Silence surrounds the Unicorn in the period between 1600 and 1800. It is occasionally used in pictorial art as a symbol of chastity, or the opposite, and mentioned now and again in literature, but casually in reference to the superstition about its horn. We can find it in Voltaire's *The Princess of Babylon.*

Strangely enough, early Romanticism, before 1800, does not make use of the Unicorn, even Goethe mentions it only sporadically. Its complicated nature, weighted with centuries of allegory, did not suit the Romantics. The Paris tapestries were rediscovered and described enthusiastically, but specifically because this gift from the Middle Ages contained everything the Romantics set store by: glowing colours, chivalrous atmosphere and beautiful young maidenliness. It is not until the second half of the nineteenth century – particularly in the Symbolist movement – that the Unicorn appears again in earnest. Then it does not resume its Christian career but plays a part in a process engendered in the Renaissance and now continuing on its inexorable course: the "Divine", projected in the Middle Ages outward into theology, was drawn by western man into his own mind and called "the unconscious". In the depths there he met the Unicorn. Not as Christ but as irrationality and poetry. It was agreed with St Augustine that it was of no consequence whether the Unicorn could be found at the sources of the Nile or not. In fact, the preferred attitude was rather in agreement with Rilke: the Unicorn is the animal that is not . . .

In England the Victorians nourished a particular fondness for the Unicorn, which becomes a touch diabolical in its painting and literature. Lewis Carroll uses the Unicorn in both *Alice's Adventures in Wonderland* and *Through the Looking-Glass.*[4] In both books it is an expression of what takes place below the threshold of consciousness. The animal does not appear in the light but roams around the nebulous wonderland among wicked queens, griffins and other heraldic animals, and if you wish to meet it you must follow the rabbit into the hole, just like the old alchemists, or break through the shining surface of the mirror.

In Symbolism the Unicorn remained beneath the surface of the mirror and again became sexualized – or rather, it returned to its original nature, liberated from religious duties. This is evident in both literature and painting. Aubrey Beardsley's novella *Under the Hill* of 1904 offended readers in its time and Gustave Moreau's pictures offended the eye. In the pictures in his museum in Paris naked women recline in landscapes shining with precious stones, playing with the Unicorn's provocative horn.

The Unicorn still survives in our technical and rational century, and we may feel some surprise at this. But it is in this age that we find some of the most fascinating descriptions of it – imbued with a deep understanding of its beauty and singular nature – and of medieval ideology. Among several fine Danish examples are Karen Blixen's stories. Blixen maintains medieval laws with great subtlety when she includes the Unicorn in her story "The Monkey". The hero – or antihero – is young Boris, who drives through a lovely autumn landscape to the castle of Hopballehus to propose to Athene, a girl chosen for him by his aunt:

"Boris was able now to believe what the old gardener at the convent had told him when he was a child: that he had once seen, about this time of the year and the day, a herd of unicorns come out of the woods to graze upon the sunny slopes, the white and dappled mares, rosy in the sun, treading daintily and looking around for their young, the old stallion, darker roan, sniffing and pawing the ground."[5]

Ladies and Unicorns
Gustave Moreau, *c.* 1890,
Musée Gustave Moreau, Paris

THE UNICORN

The Unicorn
Gustave Moreau, *c.* 1890,
Musée Gustave Moreau, Paris

THE UNICORN

The vision is in sharp contrast to the hero's struggle to tame Athene and to the monkey's behaviour at Seven Convent. Here the two animals are polarized, as in the Utrecht Bible or the Paris tapestries. As we know, the Unicorn seldom appears in a herd and never with females and foals, so this specific manifestation must mean that it is in the service of the family, as a sign of positive sexuality; and so rays of sunlight fall on its skin. By comparison, the monkey is the creature of night, solitary and associated with storm and disorder, the dark side of the goddess of love and the abbess's pet. But the Unicorns belong to Athene, we are told, and are a part of her deep, fertile underground. As this, she is, in Elling's words: ". . . proud, wild and noble and possessed of a frenzied desire for independence." The sight of her domestic animals signals a happy ending. The author has not for a moment betrayed the medieval Unicorn and shows her knowledge of its ideology and symbolism.

A more modern Danish author, Frank Jaeger, also uses the animal in a positive sense in his short story "The Unicorn".[6] A young woodcutter is out walking with his sweetheart in the forest. It is icy winter weather and although the month is April the cold will not relent. Then they meet a Unicorn with a horn larger than the elk's, as long and beautifully twisted as the tower of the Copenhagen Stock Exchange. The young man, who has not touched his girl, gets her to sit down and hide herself behind a tree, and the animal comes and lays its head in the right place. It gets her to scratch it between the eyes, so that the tears flow and begin to melt the snow. The animal asks the girl to unscrew the horn from its head and when she does this she becomes for a moment a goddess of spring with the horn of plenty, like the one on the cover of Bartholin's book, for spring itself wells from the horn, in birds, foliage and flowers. The woodcutter strolls home with the horn on his neck like Aladdin with his lamp. For the Unicorn is the reproductive power of nature, the spring itself, which is given to human beings if they will receive the animal with innocence. Jaeger follows this parable with another story in which the horn is misused and so does not bring happiness. If it is not respected but used for personal advantage, or for black magic that seeks to force nature with violence, it will act as a curse.

Alexander Calder (1898–1976) is one of America's great artists, known as the inventor of "the mobile" among other things, but also a humorous and clever draughtsman. He illustrated Æsop's Fables and a bestiary in the medieval style, including collected poems dealing with animals in interplay with human beings. With his wonderfully angular but dynamic strokes, as if they were woven out of steel thread, he draws horses, lions, pelicans and centaurs from the old bestiaries – and the Unicorn. The Unicorn accompanies a poem by George Chapman, contemporary of Shakespeare, which plays on the idea of the tree that can save the person from the horn.

> I once did see
> In my young travels through Armenia
> An angrie Unicorne in his full carier
> Charge with too swift a foot a Jeweller,
> Who sought him for th Treasure of his browe;
> And ere he could get shelter of a tree,
> Naile him with his rich Antler to the Earth.

La Licorne
Alexander Calder, drawing
from *Bestiaire*, published by
Maeght Editeur, Paris

The drawing shows the beast piercing a naked man who has tried to make use of its horn – a theme which can be seen elsewhere, in Gothic drôleries. As we recall, it appears also in Duvet's series from *c.* 1550. If I am not much mistaken, Calder may well have cast a glance at the scene in this series. In Duvet's series the action is part of an allegory about the good king and civilization, as opposed to barbarism. Calder is a modern artist and includes other overtones. He shows how animals react against ruthless human exploitation or actually take revenge: the horse bites its tormentor in the rear, and the Unicorn defends its horn by piercing the man. Weight is laid on new aspects, and here Calder reminds us of Frank Jæger, who also shows that abuse and greed carry punishment in themselves. Calder's picture and Jæger's story are endowed with the same spirit.

T. H. White, who published the medieval bestiary and had a deep knowledge of the medieval symbols, retains the imagery but applies it to modern psychology. In a chapter of his famous book on the life of King Arthur he describes a Unicorn hunt, the elements of which are taken from the bestiary, but with overtones that make it unforgettable and terrible.[7] The huntsmen are four boys, sons of Queen Morgause of the wild country, Dunlothian. Morgause is a witch in every sense of the word: a wicked mother who neglects her children, so that they cannot catch her attention. She asks some English knights to visit her, intending to seduce them, and at this point she is so remote from her children that they are in despair. They hear she has gone out with the knights to hunt the Unicorn, and that she is to play the part of the Virgin. It is not surprising that the hunters have no success.

Then the unhappy children hit on the idea of bringing her a sacrifice. Naturally the sacrificial animal will be the Unicorn she desires, and they kidnap an innocent kitchenmaid at the castle to be their virgin. Their heads, as the author says, are full of "wells, witches, unicorns and the behaviour of mothers". They drag the weeping girl into the forest and tie her to a tree by her plaits, then hide in the thicket to wait for the animal. It comes. The girl is innocent and the animal appears like a revelation of beauty and holiness. It does what is expected of it and lays its head in her lap, and she becomes queen of this moment, stretching out her hand to the animal, thrilled by its beauty.

Then the wildest boy comes up and thrusts his spear into the hindquarters of the animal, so that for a moment we see the picture we know from the sacred hunt of the manuscripts – the *Pietà*. The others follow, confused and uncertain of what they really want. The murderer is wild with rage: "The girl is my mother", he roars, "it laid its head in her lap. It had to die. I should have killed myself as well." This is patricide and divine sacrifice.

As it is impossible for them to carry the dead creature home in one piece, they try to dismember it and tear it to pieces like frantic wolves, until every remnant of beauty has been destroyed. The furious bloodbath is self-destruction, where hate, love and shame feed off each other in a bloody sacrificial ritual. Finally they cut off the head with the silvery horn and haul it behind them to the castle garden. There they place the sacrifice on a garden seat, as on an altar, and await the arrival of their mother.

The queen passes by in conversation with one of her guests and the four boys, standing guard before the altar, step aside: the Unicorn's head lies before her.

THE UNICORN

"She walks past.
She does not see it.
The sacrifice was in vain. They had chosen the wrong goddess!"

In the ballet by Jean Cocteau, *La Dame à la licorne,* we find a very poetic – and very personal – fantasy on the Unicorn. Jean Cocteau (1889–1963) was a versatile artist who included ballet in his œuvre. He worked for years with the renowned corps brought to Paris in 1910 by Sergei Diaghilev, for which he created various scenarios. *La Dame* was inspired by the Cluny tapestries and performed in Munich in 1953 to seventeenth-century music and with décor derived from the embroideries. It is about losing innocence – becoming adult – being disappointed and left only with death in one's loneliness. The lady lives in a blue tent in the forest with a little flock of Unicorns. She studies her face in her mirror – that is to say, she rests in her own identity – and

La Dame à la licorne
Scene from Jean Cocteau's ballet with Claude Bessy, Lyane Dayde and Michel Renault, at the Opéra de Paris in 1959

the white Unicorn eats from her hand. Then comes the sound of a hunting horn, and the smallest animals are alarmed, they leap away into the forest while she goes into the tent with her favourite. A knight appears, riding on a heraldic lion. He dismounts and lifts the flap of the tent, and the white Unicorn flees. Now the knight and the lady dance a *pas-de-deux*, he takes her mirror and in it his own face replaces hers. Her innocence has gone and together they go into the forest.

Now the Unicorn returns. The tent is empty, and in the mirror only the knight's face is seen. This vision is trebled and three identical knights dance with three identical ladies. The Unicorn pierces the mirror with its horn, breaking its virginity, and stirs up the water so that the knight's face vanishes. The lady comes back alone; but the Unicorn cannot – or will not – eat out of her hand any longer and it dies. The lady grieves over her white animal. Cocteau writes: "The knight enters; but she does not see him any more, and he disappears into the wings."

Later he returns on his lion, but only to cross the Unicorn's funeral procession, with the small Unicorns carrying the dead animal on their shoulders, while the lady grieves. Without knight or unicorn she sees the procession vanish among the trees. She goes to the front of the stage and points to a scroll descending towards her, with the inscription: "Mon seul désir." The light falls only on her hand and the scroll.

The lady stands between chastity and love. She meets – as she naturally must – love, which makes her into a woman, but also disturbs her identity. When it fails, and she loses her white animal because of it, all that remains for the wounded soul is death, in Cocteau's melancholy universe.

The ballet is ambiguous, however. It is not merely a dramatic copy of a medieval world. Cocteau reflects his own mind in the theme, and the white Unicorn stands also for poetry, so that he depicts the rift between the artist's fidelity to himself and his vocation, and earthly love, a conflict Cocteau knew only too well and which he never resolved. In the maiden's case it means that chastity is her identity. It is here that she must be faithful to herself. Chastity is the maiden's poetry. But this conflict is of course an absurdity.

What is interesting about this ballet, which has been called the first romantic ballet since *Swan Lake*, is, first, that it sheds light on the tapestries once again. It plays faithfully on the same symbols: the forest as the unconscious, the mirror, the lion and the white animal. But it also makes free play with them: we notice that Cocteau does not use the words from the tent to their full extent "A mon seul désir", but only has use for the ambiguous: "Mon seul désir". In the tapestry the lady does not wish for death.

Moreover, Cocteau's use of the tapestry shows how the Unicorn has moved from expressing accepted theological ideas and symbols via the Renaissance use of the animal to illustrate moral concepts, to the individualism of the modern world, in which each artist can make use of it to interpret their own conflicts and development. It becomes a device for the individual person and illustrates the wish and longing for death, subjecting itself to the needs of the individual. This is true of Rilke, of Gustave Moreau, as well as Picasso, Dalí and Cocteau. Here the animal probably shares the destiny of many other religious symbols which have made the journey from theology to depth psychology.

Let us conclude with Cocteau's own words from the libretto:

Surrealist Unicorn
Salvador Dalí, lithograph

THE UNICORN

"Cette masse attentive voit une licorne blanche mourir parce qu'elle ne peut manger que de la main d'une vierge. Elle voit une vierge aimer un homme et devenir une dame. Elle voit cette dame perdre sa licorne qui meurt et l'homme qui part.

Elle voit la dame seule. Elle voit descendre vers la dame la banderole des tapisseries rouges: 'Mon seul désir.' Elle voit le miroir dévirginsé par la corne de la licorne et cette solitude où le seul désir est la mort."

"This attentive crowd sees a white Unicorn die because it can eat only from the hand of a virgin. It sees a virgin love a man and become a woman.

It sees this woman love her Unicorn, which dies, and the man, who leaves. It sees the woman alone. It sees the inscription in the red tapestries descend towards the woman: 'My only desire'. It sees the mirror deflowered by the Unicorn's horn and that solitude in which the only desire is death."

In each of these examples the writer has laid weight on a different aspect of the Unicorn, but remained faithful to it; for the symbolism of the Middle Ages is elastic and can be extended without breaking. In our time, however, when individualism has dispersed so many collective symbols, the Unicorn runs a great risk of sharing the same fate. Anyone can take possession of the animal and banality lies in wait. When the Unicorn is used as a symbol for women's solitude, that is disingenuous, just as a one-sided emphasis on the sexual aspect is vulgar. Capriciousness and commercial triviality lurk once context and wider meaning are forgotten. The Unicorn is thrown into every image that seems good, in every story that calls for a dash of mystery. Snatched up in haste, it is made the logo of a bank or sold for Christmas, in pale blue plastic for small boys and pale pink for girls, with saddle and bridle as accessories. And so farewell to every myth and every value the Unicorn has stood for.

Finally, we can see Umberto Eco defining the Unicorn in his own way, according to his own special semiotic premises. In *The Name of the Rose* there is a conversation between William and the young Adso about the existence of the animal. They are walking in a garden, where on the previous evening the monk Venantius had been killed and dragged through the snow. It is the remaining traces of this that provoke the discussion. Adso sorrowfully asks his teacher if the beautiful creature is only a fable or a fabrication. William replies that the animal may well exist – one must never underestimate God – but that if it does it must be very different from the familiar presentations of it, for many varying descriptions have confused us. Adso, who loves the white hart, complains that one cannot then rely on books, because they distort things. William replies:

"'Books are not made to be believed, but to be subjected to inquiry . . . We mustn't ask ourselves what it says, but what it means, a precept that the commentators of the holy books had very clearly in mind. The Unicorn embodies a moral truth, or allegorical, but one that remains true, as the idea that chastity is a noble virtue remains true . . .'

'But what use is the Unicorn to you if your intellect doesn't believe in it?'

'It is of use to us as Venantius' prints in the snow were of use after he was dragged away. The Unicorn of the books is like a print. If the print exists, *there must have existed something, whose print it is*.'

'But different from the print, you say.'

'Of course. The print does not always have the same shape as the body that impressed it, and it doesn't always derive from the pressure of a body. At times it reproduces the impression a body has left in our mind: it is the print of an idea. The idea is signs of things, and the image is a sign of the idea – sign of a sign. But from the image I reconstruct – if not the body, the idea, the other had of it.'"[8]

We must regard the Unicorn in the same way: it is a track in the snow of the ideas of ancient cultures about the horned power. Naturally, behind the ideas lie physical impressions of large horned animals. The idea should not be seen as the result of a naive confusion, however, but rather in the light of a deep reverence for the power of the horn.

It is clear that literature can still make use of the Unicorn, but it is more difficult for the visual arts in our modern world. Like angels or dragons and other beings of the kind it has difficulty in manifesting itself. The problem can be evidenced very clearly: a year or two ago a group of young artists attempted to mount an exhibition with the Unicorn as the central theme. They were all to contribute works dealing with the animal. The exhibition was held in a "forest" installation of trees, moss and earth, which created a green stage-set in the centre of the gallery, in which about fifty works were gathered together. There were ceramics, glass pieces, sculptures and paintings, emerging from the "forest" or hung on the wall. The result was not convincing. There were numerous delightful glass animals with twisted horns, many pictures of the creature grazing in the forest and splashing in the stream. In other words: there was a large collection of illustrations.

Anyone can design a pleasant Christmas card with a Unicorn or two. Strictly speaking, it is no more than a stag or goat with a twisted horn on its forehead. But an empty form, torn from its context and from the age which created it to meet an inner necessity, loses its power. It is like a strong mixture that has been conserved in the wrong way and therefore loses its aroma. The same thing happened to angels, which in the urban milieu of the nineteenth century degenerated into the friendly servants of the bourgeoisie; sexless creatures in white nightgowns that walked around winged and on bare feet, saving small boys from falling into streams. They had never battled with dragons like the formidable Michael, or carried trembling souls to receive the judgement of God! Like scentless trodden-down plants in a herbarium, they ended up in the shiny picture books of our childhood.

The young artists in the exhibition made no attempt whatsoever to research the animal or explain its nature and function. They merely described what they had read. And therefore the Unicorn can become a part of the Barbie doll's world or the logo of a bank, which knows still less about it than the apothecaries who two hundred years before were yet convinced of the pharmaceutical power of its horn. It cannot be otherwise. When we neither believe in nor fear angels and dragons we cannot restore them to life on demand. Myths do not permit themselves to be fabricated; as mentioned earlier, they think in us, not the opposite, and they can never be "willed".

There is one Danish artist who knows what he is confronting. This is the sculptor Jørn Rønnau (b. 1944). With a strong feeling for nature he has specialized in a "forest art", in which he works with trees – frequently dead trunks and stumps. Under his hands and saw these turn into fabulous creatures that always grow out of the tree itself. In Denmark he transformed two barked trees into Unicorn horns that rise straight up in the air about twelve metres. One stands in a glade on the estate of Tranekaer on the island of Lolland. It is in luxuriant surroundings, among meadow flowers and small ponds, in a place where one can easily imagine a maiden settling down to pick flowers. It is still slightly wavy, as if it is not yet perfectly twisted. Rønnau has himself described how long it took him to find exactly the right back-

ground, and the right leaning tree to suit the image he had in mind. The other horn – from 1993 – called *The Tooth*, stands on the beach south of Aarhus; it faces the sea, as if defending the wind-blown trees and bushes forming its hinterland. The sea will gradually undermine it, until it falls and lies on the shore, reminding us of the stranded narwhal tusks that people in the Middle Ages devoutly collected and took to be the horn of the Unicorn. It is closely twisted and stiff, the natural colour of barked trees, with soft fibres below. Like bowsprits or sharp-pointed weapons they soar upwards with powerful mystery. And this mystery exists because we cannot see the animal itself. The artist has not dared to bring it into being. Like the narwhal, it comes from the deep and we cannot know its size, its form or its colour. Only the horn suggests its existence in those deep-rooted regions, where it lives behind the mirror (like Alice) in company with griffin and dragon. As Rønnau says: "On rare occasions though, you might seem to sense its presence."

Rønnau has also worked in England. In 1996 he carved – or rather, he released – another horn at the edge of Windsor Great Park (see fig. p.180). Here he found a gigantic ancient oak that had produced a horn itself, which rose high up among the dead branches. With other natural symbols offered by the tree, it demands our attention and reminds us that Unicorn and tree belong together. The horn also has

The Tooth
"The Unicorn's horn growing up from the hidden world"
Jørn Rønnau, 1993,
oak, 12 metres, Marselisborg Forest, Arhus, Denmark

a natural affinity with the place, and Rønnau has studied its history diligently. The great horn belonging to Sir Martin Frobisher, which he presented to Queen Elizabeth after his long voyage in 1577, was preserved as a jewel in her dressing-room and is still kept at Windsor. It may have been at about this time that the acorn was planted which today has become the "Poetree", as Rønnau calls it. With its serpent, its royal crown, the sword and the horn it has wondrously in our imagination become a part of the English environment, as well as the historical one. One feels that the Unicorn has come home. Rønnau tells us more about the animal today than the exhibition described earlier. He thinks medievally – that is to say, mythically – but remains well aware of the time he is living in.

Perhaps the modern Unicorn succeeds best in poetry. It is certainly striking how many young poets allow glimpses of it in their verse, when they want to break into the grey light of every day with a golden touch of hope, stillness or mystery. Since Rilke used the Unicorn as an expression of poetry itself, at the turn of the century, it comes and goes in many poems, usually without any clear indication of its genesis, but often as something positive: as in the last verse of Ib Michael's "Hymn", in which Unicorn and lady melt together in a remarkable way,[9] or in Pia Tafdrup's "Echo", where tranquillity begins with the grazing of a Unicorn in a monastery garden.[10] So it is natural to end the book with a poem by the Finnish-Swedish poet Solveig von Schoultz, which depicts one of the high points of the Unicorn story, in the Paris tapestries, a medieval dream seen through the imagination of a modern writer.

Poetree
Jørn Rønnau, oak, 1995–6,
Windsor Great Park

THE UNICORN

The Lady with the Unicorn
(Musée Cluny):

The lady's footstool, a little island
dark as the Middle Ages, strewn with flowers
small violets, sign of humility
anemones for sorrow
and the sweet lilies of annunciation.

Between the palm, protector of faith
and the oak with the acorn of life

she is in the midst of folksong.
The sky is red as blood
and in the heavenly meadow
small joyful hares are at play
a fox slinks through the long grasses
the wily skunk runs.

On guard, with a blue-white standard
stands the ancestral heraldic lion.

In pale brown brocade, pearls in her hair
a heron's feather over her lofty brow
the lady holds up a golden mirror
while she pensively strokes
the stranger's back.

He the most timorous creature
he who is hunted in vain
he has known the scent of chastity

he lies with the lady
his body that of a horse
beard of a goat
he rests on his hind legs, hoofs heavy
on the lady's knee, her mantle falls open

his fiery sapphire blue eyes
look into the mirror
his horn is upraised
the brave spiralling horn.

Why is the lady sad? Does she know
that only here, in a maiden's lap
can such a quarry be taken?[11]

Postscript

The most important thing is certainly not to inquire into whether the Unicorn issued from deer, narwhal, rhinoceros, oryx or a misinterpreted picture of a bull. Rather, it is important to realize that there was a need for the animal, that is to say, for the one-horn idea. It affected many cultures, which independently of each other sought for its ingredients wherever they might be found in the environment. From the concept of the horn's power a four-legged creature was built, which could serve as bearer and guardian of the power, supplied with fitting qualities: strength, pride and beauty.

Centuries passed while the animal was being created with the aid of words and pictures, feature by feature, until it was as clear in the consciousness as if it had been seen in the forest. It was never finished; but was constantly transformed and lived with its time, while keeping enough basic features to maintain an identity. By about 1400 it had become a little white horse-goat with a forelock, hoofs and narwhal tusk in the middle of its forehead, as the artist might have seen it one day, grazing in a clearing with the sun's rays slanting down upon it. Perhaps he had even seen the animal leap up to a girl and lay its head in her lap – or had he merely heard about it and believed he had seen it? However it may have been, he was in no doubt about its appearance and reproduced it as exactly as he might draw a horse or a stag – and far more accurately than an elephant! Why should one doubt the Unicorn? Seen in company with other animals from the bestiary, it is one of the more convincing beasts, among basilisks, griffins, camels and absurd giraffes. It *ought* to exist. It seems to fill a place in nature that Our Lord in his haste forgot.

The Unicorn is a male animal. This is due to the horn power which is its *raison d'être*, and which is inherent in its name. Yet there is also mention of a breeding season when this male grazes peacefully with the females. So there must also be Unicorn fillies or mares that walk around twitching their ears while they graze and look after their offspring. Amongst the flock are the kids/foals, small and white, some with little horn-buds, still soft, between their ears, while their indomitable fathers are already out in foreign hunting grounds fulfilling their great mission and being unfaithful to their mothers. A kid like this appears in the Paris tapestry, and Karen Blixen speaks of a flock. But the females are seldom seen. It is as if they exist only to produce new, vigorous males.

During more recent centuries scientists have been in the habit of treating the Unicorn with a patronizing condescension, which is insulting both to the animal and to its creators. They have been quick to demonstrate the faulty vision and errors perpetrated in the past, and to make observations such as: "The habit of primitive minds is . . ." or "Very simple men think . . ." The medical profession has never ceased quoting the term "placebo-effect" accompanied by a silent headshake. Odell Shepard implies that when great minds like Bartholin write about the Unicorn it is no more than a relaxing hobby, which he could not have taken seriously. Naturally there has been extreme caution concerning the animal's sexual character. Either there is complete silence or else disquiet over the disgraceful connotations with which gross minds have endowed this Christian symbol: "This . . . which we will swiftly pass over." As a result the cultural-historical meaning and mythical origin of the animal have been totally ignored.

To write about the Unicorn, one must be loyal to it and to its time. One must love and respect it as a distinguished manifestation of our forefathers' dreams and their attempts to explain the obscure challenges of existence. Let us not speak too loudly of "simple minds" when considering the imagery of the manuscripts or the tapestries. The apothecaries were certainly wise to include its head on their sign. For all the roles allotted to the Unicorn through the ages, it emerges again and again in its original guise: as a fertility animal from the forest with the horn of vital power in the middle of its forehead, desiring the tree, water and maiden. It was turned into a constellation and lived in the heavens among other great mythic animals. Not without reason.

Notes

LCL = Loeb Classical Library (parallel Greek or Latin text and English translation), Cambridge, Mass., and London.

Chapter 1
THE UNICORN FROM THE ORIENT

1. *Mahabharata*: Indian national heroic epic about the Bharata people and their wars, set *c.* 3000 BC, but first written down around the time of Christ. Recently, the French dramatist Jean-Claude Carrière has composed a mammoth version of the myth, which has been a worldwide success in Peter Brook's production. See A. Holzmann, *Indische Sagen*, Jena, 1921; W. Haug, *Studien zur Geschichte und Vorgeschichte des europäischen Mittelalters*, Munich, 1964. There is an English translation, *The Mahabharata*, by Narashinham Chakravarti, University of California Press, 1997.

2. On the prophecy of Ch'i-Lin, see C. G. Jung, *Psychologie und Alchemie*, Zurich, 1952, pp.624–5.

3. *Enuma Elish* ("Once, when the above . . . ", the opening line of the poem): Accadian-Sumerian Creation story and life of the hero Marduk, and the Flood, from possibly *c.* 3000 BC, later adopted and written down by the Babylonians.

4. *Gilgamesh*: Sumerian heroic epic, *c.* 1700 BC. Gilgamesh was prince of Uruk *c.* 2600 BC and the myths of his deeds and of Enkidu were adopted by the Babylonians. See W. Haug, op. cit.; A. Scott, *Das Gilgamesh-Epos*, Stuttgart, 1958; David Ferry, *Gilgamesh*, Newcastle upon Tyne, 1993.

5. *Avesta*: Persian legend of the Creation and Flood, recorded by Ardashir I (AD 309–379), in the Sassanid period. The cited text of the Great Ass is reproduced in C. G. Jung, op. cit., p.613.

Chapter 2
THE CLASSICAL INHERITANCE

1. See Ctesias, *La Perse, l'Inde: Les Sommaires de Photius*, ed. René Henry, Brussels, 1959, 1, pp.143–4.

2. Aristotle, *Historia Animalium*, 2, 1 and *De Partibus Animalium*, 3, 2, ed. J. A. Smith and W. D. Ross, Oxford, 1967. English translation of both works by A. L. Peck, in LCL.

3. Megasthenes, *Indica*, ed. H. E. Bahr, 1847.

4. Julius Caesar, *De Bello Gallico*, Lib. 6, cap. 26. English translation, H. J. Edwards, LCL, 1917, pp.351–3.

5. Pliny, *Naturalis Historia*, Lib. 8, cap. 31. English translation, H. Rackham et al., LCL, 10 vols, 1938–62, III, p.57.

6. *The Excellent and pleasant works: Collectanea Rerum Memorabilium of Caius Julius Solinus, translated from the Latin 1587 by Arthur Golding*, facsimile with introduction by George Kish, Gainesville, 1955. Solinus, *Polyhistoria*, Lib. 1, cap. 57, ed. Weidmann, 1958.

7. Aelian (Claudius Aelianus), *On the Nature of Animals*, Lib. 16, cap. 20. English translation, A. L. Scholfield, LCL, 3 vols, 1958–9, III, pp. 288–90. The Greek word for rings or spirals is ambiguous, meaning either bands wound round the horn, or ornaments, or something like the horn with spiral coils of Persepolis.

8. Cosmas Indicopleustos, *Topographia Christiana*, Lib. XI, *Patrologia Graeca*, 88, 444.

9. T. H. White, *The Bestiary: A Book of Beasts*, New York, 1960, p.29.

Chapter 3
BIBLICAL TEXTS

1. Passages quoted from the King James Bible.

2. In the Vulgate Bible: Numbers 23, 22; Deuteronomy 33, 17.

3. Job 39, 9–12.

4. Psalm 22, 21 (Vulgate, Psalm 21, 22).

5. Psalm 29, 5–6 (Vulgate, Psalm 28, 6).

6. Psalm 92, 10 (Vulgate, Psalm 91, 11).

7. Isaiah 34, 7.

8. Daniel 8, 5–7. The Book of Daniel was written about 165 BC, but the author places himself in the reign of Nebuchadnezzar, *c.* 560 BC, before Alexander's time and the events with which the prophecy is concerned.

9. Luke 1, 68–9.

10. Talmud (Hebrew, meaning "instruction" or "study"). The original oral teachings and exegesis of the Torah were partly written down *c.* AD 200 and editing continued through the following two centuries, growing into twenty-two volumes of laws, exegesis and legend, divided into the *Mishna* and the *Gemara.*

Chapter 4
INDUSTRIOUS THEOLOGIANS

1. Tertullian, *Adversus Judaeos*, Lib. 3, cap. 10, *Patrologia Latina*, 2, col. 62; idem, *Adversus Marcionem*, Lib. 3, cap. 18, *Patrologia Latina*, 2, col. 346. Similar passages occur in Irenaeus and Justinus.

2. Eustacius (Basileus), *Homilia in Psalmum 28*, *Patrologia Graeca*, 29, col. 295.

3. Ambrosius, *Enarrationes in Psalmos Davidicos*, *Patrologia Latina*, 14, col. 1099.

4. Ibid.

5. Gregory, *Moralia in Job*, Lib. 31, cap. 15, *Patrologia Latina*, 76, col. 589.

6. Ibid., col. 590.

7. Isidore of Seville, *Liber Ethymologiae*, Lib. 12, cap. 2, *De Bestiis, Patrologia Latina*, 82, col. 435. Translated by John of Trevisa in Bartholomeus Anglicus, *De Proprietatibus Rerum*, Westminster (Wynkyn de Worde), 1494, xviii, 90, which follows Isidore exactly.

8. Honorius of Autun, *Speculum Ecclesiae, De Navitate Domini, Patrologia Latina*, 172, col. 819 B.

9. Albertus Magnus refers to *De Animalibus*, Lib. 26, 12, trad. 3, cap. 7; but the text of this is incomplete.

10. Hildegard of Bingen, *Physica*, Lib. 7, *De Animalibus*, cap. 5, *Patrologia Latina*, 197, col. 1317.

11. Hildegard of Bingen, op. cit, col. 1318.

Chapter 5
"PHYSIOLOGUS SAYS . . ."

1. For the Syrian version, see P. N. Land, *Anecdota Syriaca*, 4, Leiden, 1870.

2. Quoted by T. H. White, *The Bestiary: A Book of Beasts*, New York, 1960, p. 245.

3. Ibid., pp.20–21, 43–44.

4. For the cleansing by water, see Emil Peters, *Der Physiologus*, Munich, 1921, pp.34–35.

5. A famous example is an altarpiece by Hieronymus Bosch, *The Garden of Earthly Delights*, c. 1504 (Museo del Prado, Madrid). On the left-hand panel God creates Eve in the Garden of Eden; in the background is the Unicorn between a line of other animals stirring up the water with its horn, while black salamanders and snakes crawl up on to the bank and flee.

6. *Lucidarius*, ed. Johannes Knudsen, Copenhagen, 1909, pp.144–45.

Chapter 6
PICTORIAL ART IN THE MIDDLE AGES

1. Herrad of Landsberg, abbess of a nunnery in Alsace from 1176 to 1191, was one of the great female characters in the German church at that time. The *Hortus Deliciarum* (Garden of Paradise) is a product of her teachings, presenting the moral teaching and work of salvation of the Christian faith based on earlier theologians. There were 342 pictures in the book, including 136 full pages in colour. Unfortunately this treasure was burned during the Franco-Prussian War in 1870, but it has been reconstructed on the basis of earlier reproductions.

2. *Millstätter Genesis, Physiologus*, c. 1174, orig. Regensburg (Archiv für Geschichtsvereines für Kärnten, Klagenfurt); cf. F. W. Einhorn, *Spiritalis Unicornis*, Munich, 1976, p.112.

Chapter 7
THE UNICORN AND THE HUNTSMEN

1. It was at this time that one of the Three Kings began to be depicted as a Moor or negro, indicating that the group was regarded as representative of the three parts of the known world.

2. Richard de Fournival, *Li Bestiaires d'Amours di Maistre Richart de Fornival*, ed. Cesare Segre, Milan, 1957.

3. Odell Shepard, *The Lore of the Unicorn*, London, 1930, p. 58.

4. Per Raev Lille, also known as Frater Petruz, a Danish cleric and author, who wrote poems to the Virgin Mary, c. 1500, in the troubadour style. The poem appears in Ernst Frandsen, *The Songs to the Virgin Mary*, Copenhagen, 1926, pp.39–42.

Chapter 8
THE SACRED HUNT

1. Niedersachs. Staats- und Univ. Bibl., Göttingen, cod. theol. 291, text fol. 107–109. Reproduced F. W. Einhorn, *Spiritalis Unicornis*, Munich, 1976, pp.203–204.

2. *Litigatio-spil*, ed. W. Stammler, *Spätlese des Mittelalters*, 2. Religiös Schrifttum, Berlin, 1930, pp.48–52.

3. Bernard of Clairvaux, *In Annuntiatione*, Lib. I, cap. 6–14, *Patrologia Latina*, 183, col. 385.

4. Conrad of Megenberg, *Das Buch der Natur*, in Otto Keller ed., *Die antike Tierwelt*, 1, Leipzig, 1909, p.419.

5. The Berne Physiologus also considers the huntsmen to be wicked. So there are two interpretations of the pursuers: an earlier one, mentioning the Jews, and a later one better suited to the late medieval view of the Atonement. A thirteenth-century poem by Guillaume le Clerc expresses the first: Guillaume le Clerc, *Bestiary*, translated by G. C. Druce, 1936: "This wonderful beast/ Which has one horn on its head/ signifies our Lord./ Jesus Christ, our Saviour./ He is the spiritual Unicorn,/ Who took up in the Virgin His abode/ Who is so especially worthy/ In her he assumed his human form/ In which He appeared to the world./ His people of the Jews/ Believed Him not, but spied on Him/ And then took Him and bound Him/Before Pilate they led Him/ And there condemned Him to Death."

6. Augustine mentions Danaë as a suitable illustration for Gideon's Fleece, and thus a "type" for the Virgin.

7. Louise Lillie, "Images in the Instruction of the Laity. The Wall-Paintings in the Churches of Sondersø and Bellinge", *Religion, Idé og Debat* [Religion, Idea and Debate], I, Copenhagen, 1984, pp.15–31.

Chapter 9
THE GYRSTINGE ALTAR FRONTAL AND DANISH MURAL PAINTINGS

1. Pernille Bronee, "Jagten pa Enhjorningen. Antemensalet fra Gyrstinge Kirke. Ikonografi, Konservering or Restaurering" [The Hunt for the Unicorn: The altar frontal from Gyrstinge Church, Copenhagen – Iconography, conservation and restoration]. Activities of the National Museum. 1985, pp.207–21.

2. See Giorgione's *The Tempest*, c. 1505 (Accademia, Venice); Titian's *Sacred and Profane Love*, c. 1515 (Borghese Gallery, Rome), whose landscape is divided into an earthly and a heavenly zone; Perugino's *Lamentation*, 1495, (Pitti, Florence), where tower and tree meet in the background; and Botticelli's *Annunciation*, c. 1490 (Uffizi, Florence). Similar examples can be found in Netherlandish altarpieces.

3. Isak Dinesen (Karen Blixen), "The Roads around Pisa", in *Seven Gothic Tales*, London, 1934. Similar use is made of the landscape in "The Monkey", in the same volume.

4. Henry James, *The Turn of the Screw*, London, 1898.

5. It is badly damaged. Both animals can be used as symbols of the soul, though with somewhat different connotations.

Chapter 10
THE UNICORN OF THE TROUBADOURS

1. Thibaut IV of Champagne (1201–1253), King of Navarre, one of the greatest lyricists in the troubadour genre. About sixty of his songs are extant, thirty-six being love songs: *Poésies du roi de Navarre*, ed. A. Wallenskold, Paris, 1925.

2. *Le Romans de la Dame à la Lycorne et du Biau Chevalier au Lyon*, ed. F. Genrich, Gesellschaft für romanische Literatur, 18, Dresden, 1908, pp.166–73.

3. Richard de Fournival, *Li Bestiaires d'Amours di Maistre Richart de Fornival*, ed. Cesare Segre, Milan, 1957, pp.166–73.

Chapter 11
THE FLEMISH TAPESTRIES

1. See J. Huizinga, *The Waning of the Middle Ages*, London, 1924; Barbara W. Tuchmann, *A Distant Mirror: The Tempestuous 14th Century*, London, 1985.

2. *Le Livre des Faits du bon Chevalier Messire Jacques de Lalaing*, ed. J. Kervyn de Lettenhove, Brussels, 1863–66, pp. 1–8. This partly fictional biography was written by the biographer of the Burgundian dukes, Georges Chastellain.

3. *Le Romans de la Dame à la Lycorne*, op. cit. (Chap. 10, n. 2).

4. Olivier de la Marche, *Mémoires*, ed. H. Beaune and J. d'Arbaumont, Paris, Société de l'Histoire de France, 1, 4, 1883–88.

Chapter 12
THE LADY WITH THE UNICORN

1. Plato, *Timaeus*, ed. R. D. Archer-Hind, London, 1888.

2. Rainer Maria Rilke, *The Notebook of Malte Laurids Brigge*, 1923.

3. Gottfried Büttner, *Die Dame mit dem Einhorn*, Stuttgart, 1990.

Chapter 13
THE CHASE

1. See James J. Rorimer, *Metropolitan Museum Bulletin*, New York, 1942; Margaret Freeman, *The Unicorn Tapestries*, Metropolitan Museum, New York, 1983.

2. Henri Zerner, *The School of Fontainebleau: Etchings and Engravings*, London, 1969.

Chapter 14
MAN TAKES CENTRE STAGE –
THE RENAISSANCE

1. Petrarch, *Trionfi*, ed. B. Geiger, Darmstadt, 1958; ed. H. C. Nuscetta and D. Ponchirioli, Turin, 1958.

Chapter 15
KING OF THE WILDERNESS

1. *Fiori di Virtù*, Biblioteca Nazionale, ms. B. R. 47, fol. 25.

2. Leonardo da Vinci, *Bestiarius*, Biblioteca Ambrosiana, Milan, Codex Atlanticus, fol. 210.

3. Gustav René Hocke, *Die Welt als Labyrinth: Manier und Manie in der europäischen Kunst*, Hamburg, 1977.

4. *Le Chevalier du Papegau*, ed. F. Heuckenkamp, Halle, 1896, p. 83. See also Haug, op. cit. (Chap. 1, n. 1), p.123.

5. Jacobus de Voragine, *The Golden Legend: Readings on the Saints*, trans. W. G. Ryan, II, Princeton, 1993, pp. 355–66; Felix Liebrecht, "Die Quellen des Barlaam und Joasaph", *Jahrbuch für romanische und englische Literatur*, 1860, pp.314–34.

6. Ibid., p.360.

Chapter 16
SHIELD AND SEAL

1. Marc de Vulson de la Colombière, *La Science héroïque*, Paris, 1644, p.259.

2. Christian Elling, *Shakespeare, Indsyn i hans Verden og hans Poesi* [Shakespeare, Insight into his World and his Poetry], II, *The Zodiac*, Copenhagen, 1974, p.181.

3. On the ex-libris, see Helmer Kofod, *Nordisk Exlibris Tidsskrift* [Nordic ex-libris Magazine], 1988, 40, nos. 1–2. Pamphlet 169–70. Danish Ex-libris Society. Ross King, *Ex Libris*, London, 1996.

Chapter 17
"WHEN SOMEONE MAKES A JOURNEY…"

1. "When someone makes a journey – we should have something to hear."

2. On Prester John, see Friedrich Zarncke, *Der Priester Johannis*, Leipzig, 2 vols, 1879–83.

3. *Grimm's Fairy Tales*, Copenhagen, 1975, p.69.

4. Marco Polo, "Il Milione", in *The Book of Sir Marco Polo*, ed. Henry Yule, II, London, 1903, p.285. Marsden W. Wright, *The Travels of Marco Polo*, London, 1997.

5. Mandeville, *Itinerario*, ed. M. Lorenzen, Copenhagen, 1882. Mandeville's "Aethiopia" is also situated on the borders of India. C. W. R. D. Moseley, *The Travels of Sir John Mandeville*, Harmondsworth, 1983.

6. Joannis de Hese, *Itinerarium Joannis de Hese, presbyteri ad hierusalem*, in Zarncke, op. cit., *Priester Johannis*, II, 1883, p.162.

7. Felix Faber, *Evagatorium in Terrae Sanctae Arabiae et Egypti Perigrationum*, ed. C. D. Hassler, Stuttgart, 3 vols, 1843–49.

8. *The Navigation and Voyages of Lewes Vartomannus, translated out of Latin into Englyshe by Richard Eden*, London, 1576, cap. 19; reproduced as Chapter 2 in Samuel Purchas, *Purchas his Pilgrimes*, London, 1625, Part II, p.1489. For the original, see Ludovico Barthema (Lewis Vartoman), *Itinerario*, Lib. II, cap. 15, Venice, 1518.

Chapter 18
SCIENCE ON THE MARCH

1. Quoted by Shepard, op. cit. (Chap. 7, n. 3), p.147.

2. The cerastes is a small poisonous snake from the Sahara region, with two protrusions on its forehead, which were thought to be a preventative against poison. According to the Physiologus, it captured its prey by digging itself into the sand with the two horns sticking up.

3. Sophus Michaelis and C. Fledelius, *Parzival*, Ydun, 1980.

4. Benvenuto Cellini, *Autobiography*, translated by George Bull, Harmondsworth, 1966, p.113.

5. Conrad Gesner, *Historia Animalium*, Frankfurt, 1551–63.

6. David de Pomis, *Dittionario Novo Hebraico … dichiarato in tre linge*, Venice, 1587.

7. Andrea Marini, *Discorso de Andrea Marini medico contra la Falsa Opinione dell'Alicorno*, Venice, 1566.

8. Andrea Bacci, *L'Alicorno. Discorso dell'Eccell. Medico et Filosofo M. Andrea Bacci, dedic. al serenissimo Don Franco Medici, Gran. Princ. di Toscana*, Florence, 1573 (Latin edition, Venice, 1566).

9. Odell Shepard, *The Lore of the Unicorn*, London, 1930, p.165.

10. *Discours d'Ambroise Paré, Consilleur et premier Chirurgien du Roy, a Scavoir de la Mummie, e la Licorne, Des Venins, et de la Peste*, Paris, 1582.

Chapter 19
THE ONE-TOOTHED MONOCEROS

1. Olaus Magnus, *Historia de gentibus Septentrionalibus*, Rome, 1555; Stockholm, 1976, p.744.

2. Caspar Bartholin, *De Unicornu ejusque affinibus et succedaneis opusculum*, Copenhagen, 1628.

3. Ibid., p.1.

4. Thomas Bartholin, *De Unicornu Observationes Novae*, Basle, 1645, and Amsterdam, 1678.

5. Ole Worm, *Medicarum Institutionum Libri primi sectio secunda*, Copenhagen, 1638.

6. Julius Caesar Scaliger, *Exotericarum Exercitationum*, Paris, 1557.

7. Ole Worm, *Museum Wormianum seu Historia Rerum Rariorum*, Amsterdam, 1655, pp.279–90.

Chapter 20
THE MODERN PROBLEM

1. François Rabelais, *The Lives, Heroic Deeds and Sayings of Gargantua and his Son Pantagruel*, translated by Sir Thomas Urquhart and Peter le Motteux, London, 1921, Book 5, chap. XXX, pp.318–19 (translation originally published 1653–94).

2. Edmund Spenser, *The Faerie Queene*, (book 1–3 published 1590, books 4–6, 1596); ed. A. C. Hamilton, London, 1980, p. 209. In Book II, canto V we follow the knight Guyon in his struggle with the monsters of the vices, among them Pyrocles.

3. Elling, op. cit. (Chap. 16, n. 2), p.183.

4. Lewis Carroll, *Alice's Adventures in Wonderland*, London, 1865; *Through the Looking-Glass and What Alice Found There*, London, 1871.

5. Dinesen/Blixen, op. cit. (Chap. 9, n. 3), p.97.

6. Frank Jaeger, "The Unicorn", in *Hverdagshistorier* [Everyday Stories], Copenhagen, 1951.

7. T. H. White, *King Arthur at Camelot*, London, 1939.

8. Umberto Eco, *The Name of the Rose*, London, 1984. pp.315–17.

9. Ib Michael, "Hymn", in *Vinden i metroen* [The wind in the metro], Copenhagen, 1939.

10. Pia Tafdrup, "Echo", in *Sekundernes Bro* [The Bridge of Moments], Copenhagen, 1989.

11. Solveig von Schoultz, "The Lady with the Unicorn", in *Ett satt at rakna tiden* [A Way to Measure Time], Helsinki, 1990.

Bibliography

Beer, Rudiger R., *Einhorn: Fabelwelt und Wirklichkeit.* [Unicorn: Fabulous World and Reality]. Munich, 1972.

Bronee, Pernille, "Jagten pa Enhjorningen. Antemensalet fra Gyrstinge Kirke. Ikonografi, Konservering or Restaurering" [The Hunt for the Unicorn: The altar frontal from Gyrstinge Church, Copenhagen – Iconography, conservation and restoration], Activities of the National Museum, Copenhagen, 1985.

Butler, Johanna M., "The Lover and the Unicorn." *Studies in Medieval Culture* 11, 1977.

Cohn, Carl, *Zur literarischen Geschichte des Einhorns* [Literary history of the Unicorn], Berlin, 1896-97.

Edsmann, Carl-Martin, *Enhorningsjakten i kristologisk og mariologisk tolkning: Kvindebilleder* [The Hunting of the Unicorn in christological and mariological interpretation: Images of woman], Copenhagen, 1989.

Einhorn, Jurgen W., *Spiritalis Unicornis: Das Einhorn als Bedeutungstrager in Lit. und Kunst des Mittelalters* [Spiritalis Unicornis: The Unicorn as a bearer of significance in medieval literature and art], Munich, 1976.

Elling, Christian, *Shakespeare: Indsyn i hans Verden og hans Poesi. II* [Shakespeare: Insight into his world and poetry], Copenhagen 1974.

Ettinghausen, R. *The Unicorn. Studies in Muslim Iconography.* Washington. 1950.

Frandsen, Ernst, *Mariaviserne* [The Songs to Mary], Copenhagen 1926.

Freeman, Margaret B., *The Unicorn Tapestries.* Metropolitan Museum, New York, 1983.

Gad, Tue, *Legenden i dansk Middelalder* [The Legend in medieval Denmark], Copenhagen, 1961.

Garboe, Axel, *Enhjorningen, isaer i Natur–Laegevidenskabens Historie* [The Unicorn, with special reference to the history of natural and medical science]. Medical-historical pamphlets, Tryde, Copenhagen, 1915.

Graff, Hellmuth, *Die Darstellung der sakralen Einhorn-Jagd in der altdeutchen Kunst* [The portrayal of the sacred Unicorn Hunt in early German art], Munich, 1925.

Hocke, Gustav R., *Die Welt als Labyrinth* [The world as labyrinth], Hamburg, 1963.

Holbek B. and Iorn Pio, *Fabeldyr og Sagnfolk* [Fabulous animals and legendary people], Copenhagen, 1979.

Janson, Horst W., *Apes and Ape Lore in the Middle Ages and the Renaissance* (Studies of the Warburg Institute, vol. 20), London, 1952.

Jung, C. G., *Psychologie und Alchemie*, Zurich, 1944.

Klingender, Francis, *Animals in Art and Thought to the End of the Middle Ages,* London, 1971.

Kofoed, Helmer, *Narhvalen og Enhjorningen* [The Narwhal and the Unicorn]. Pharmaceutical High School of Denmark, 1983.

Kretzenbacher, L., *Mystische Einhornjagd: Deutsche und slawische Bild-und Wortzeugnisse zu einem geistlichen Sinnbildgefuge* [The Mystical Unicorn Hunt: German and Slav reference in image and word to a symbol of spiritual obedience], Sitzungsberichte der Bayerischen Akademie der Wissenschaften, Munich, 1978.

Lauchert, Friedrich, *Geschichte des Physiologus* [The Story of the Physiologus], Strasbourg, 1889.

Rorimer, James J., "The Unicorn Tapestries Were Made for Anne of Bretagne", *The Metropolitan Museum Bulletin*, New York, 1942.

Saxtorph, Niels, *Jeg ser pa Kalkmalerier* [I look at Chalk Paintings]. Copenhagen 1967.

Sbordone, Francesco, *La tradizione manoscritta del Physiologus latino* [The tradition of Latin Physiologus manuscripts], 1949.

Shepard, Odell, *The Lore of the Unicorn,* London, 1930.

Schepelern, H. D., *Museum Wormianum,* Copenhagen, 1971.

Sonet, Jean, *Le Roman de Barlaam et Josaphat* [The Romance of Barlaam and Joasaph], Louvain, 1949.

White, T .H., *The Bestiary: A Book of Beasts*, New York, 1960.

Photographic credits

Photograph © Lauros-Giraudon/Bridgeman Art Library, London (1a)

Photograph © The Bridgeman Art Library, London (1b, 8, 31, 32, 33, 34, 35, 41, 48a, 48b, 49, 52, 82, 89, 90, 95, 106, 108)

Photograph courtesy Werner Forman (back cover, 2, 4, 6, 7, 17, 18)

Photograph by Werner Forman, courtesy Spink & Son Ltd. (3)

Photograph courtesy Kunsthistorisches Museum (10)

Photograph © Bildarchiv Foto-Marburg (13)

Photograph © Institut Amatller d'Art Hispanic (14)

Photograph © Six Italia (15)

Photograph © British Library, London (19, 23, 26, 30, 37

Photograph courtesy Bodleian Library (20, 36, 54, 55

Photograph © Burgerbibliothek (24)

Photograph © Bibliothèque Royale Albert 1er (25)

Photograph courtesy Odense University Library (28)

Photograph © The Metropolitan Museum of Art, New York, Harris Brisbane Dick Fund, (29, 63–68)

Photograph © MAK-Österreichisches Museum für angewandte Kunst (38)

Photograph courtesy Niedersächsische Staats- und Universitätsbibliothek, Göttingen (39)

Photograph © AKG, London (40, 79, 81, 84, 87, 98)

Rights Reserved © Museo del Prado (42)

Courtesy Nationalmuseet, Copenhagen (43)

Cliché © Bibliothèque Nationale de France, Paris (45)

Photograph courtesy Jens Sørensen (50)

Photograph courtesy Bayerisches Nationalmuseum (53)

Photograph © RMN–R.G. Ojeda (56-62); © RMN-Jean (109)

Photographs © British Museum (69-73, 83, 100)

Photograph © Visual Arts Library, London (74)

Photograph © Nationalmuseum, Stockholm (75)

Photograph © Board of Trustees, National Gallery of Art (76a)

Photograph courtesy Biblioteca Estense, Modena (76)

Photograph courtesy Musei Civici d'Arte Antica, Ferrara (77)

Photograph courtesy Rijksmuseum (80)

Photograph courtesy Ashmolean Museum, Oxford (90)

Photograph © E. Lind (92)

Photograph courtesy Museum Plantin-Moretus (99)

Photograph courtesy Bibliotheek der Rijks Universiteit (101)

Photograph © Agence de Presse Bernard (110)

Copyright © ADAGP, Paris, DACS, London, 1998 (111)

Courtesy Jørn Rønnau (113, 114)

Index

Note: Illustrations are shown in *italics*